John J. O'Meara

Municipal Taxation at Home And Abroad

John J. O'Meara

Municipal Taxation at Home And Abroad

ISBN/EAN: 9783744732178

Printed in Europe, USA, Canada, Australia, Japan

Cover: Foto ©Suzi / pixelio.de

More available books at **www.hansebooks.com**

MUNICIPAL TAXATION

AT HOME AND ABROAD.

LOCAL GOVERNMENT—INDEBTEDNESS AND VALUATION.

With Statistics relating to the Principal Municipalities of the World.

BY

J. J. O'MEARA,

SOLICITOR.

CASSELL AND COMPANY, LIMITED:

LONDON, PARIS & MELBOURNE.

1894

PREFACE.

———•:•———

" No one ought to feel discouraged from endeavouring to show
if, after full consideration of the subject, he feels convinced that
many taxes might be reduced, and many repealed, without any
risk with respect to securing a sufficient revenue for all the
services of the State."—*Sir H. Parnell on Financial Reform.*

THE publication of this work is due to the
importance of the subject of which it treats, and
to which it earnestly invites attention. So many
interests are involved in the question of Municipal Taxation, that every attempt to promote discussion respecting it is entitled to indulgent
consideration. A local debt of over two hundred millions sterling, and the ever-increasing
demands of our municipal institutions, do not
warrant the citizens of the United Kingdom in
passing carelessly over our municipal budgets,

and neglecting to examine the sources from whence the supplies are levied. One of the peculiarities of our forms of local government is that those who should be, and ultimately are, most interested in them, fail in the inclination to study their "ways and means," although they have to meet the demands of the budgets, and the budgets are the summary of the conditions and possibilities of municipal life. Ratepayers should familiarise themselves with the machinery of government, rather than with the government of the machine.

With this object I shall first endeavour to put every man, who will fairly and earnestly enter into the inquiry, in possession of a general knowledge of those systems of levying local supplies which affect the United Kingdom, and to show the real cause of the discontent existing among those upon whom the incidence of the local rates is placed. I shall then point out the most favourable way in which, in my opinion, extended and permanent relief can be administered, and a more equitable system adopted. I shall also give a general view of the systems adopted in the various European countries, and in the United States of America, for the purpose of comparison, so that the result of the work of the world's economists may be more easily seen. As regards the statistics given in reference to these latter, while every care has been taken in obtaining the figures from the various foreign sources, perfect accuracy cannot be guaranteed; yet I consider them sufficiently reliable to effect the object for which they are intended.

I tender to Her Majesty's Consuls throughout Europe my grateful acknowledgments for their extreme courtesy and kindness in supplying me with the various items of information which I sought from them.

I would invite my readers to reflect dispassionately upon the injustice of our present system of taxation and its inequitable incidence, in the earnest hope that they will not remain wilfully blind to the crisis that must inevitably follow its continuance, but that they will see the expediency and justice of the remedies I propose, and have the honesty and courage to advocate them.

J. J. O'MEARA.

Lr. Mount Street, Dublin, 1891.

CONTENTS.

CHAPTER III.—VALUATION OF PROPERTY.

CHAPTER IX.—AUSTRIA.

CHAPTER X.—SWITZERLAND.

CONTENTS.

XV

PAGE

CHAPTER XIII.—SWEDEN AND NORWAY.

Taxation system—Division of real estate—Income tax—" Bevillning " tax—Mode of assessment—Church tax—Same *per capita*—Provincial liquor licensing tax—Its allocation—Exemption of personal property—Military burdens—Tenure—Norway—Political independence—Taxation—Tenure and property in buildings . . . 274

CHAPTER XIV.—RUSSIA, POLAND, SPAIN, TURKEY, AND GREECE.

Russia and Poland—Imperial Taxation—Communal system—Cantonal system—Taxation in Warsaw—Tax on immovable property—Hearth tax—Industry tax—Hackney coach tax—Excise tax—Miscellaneous taxes—Tenure of lands and buildings—Spain—Novel fiscal system—Mode of assessment—Consumers' tax—Turkey—Difficulties in connection with—Greece—Retrogression—Taxation of Piræus 283

APPENDIX I.

Taxation of land and buildings in British colonies . . . 297

APPENDIX II.

Table of the financial condition and resources of the principal municipalities of the world in 1891 compiled from answers to queries submitted by author 311

MUNICIPAL TAXATION.

— ·· —

CHAPTER I.

LOCAL GOVERNMENT AND INDEBTEDNESS.

ALL civilised countries have their systems of Local
Government. In all, the sovereign authority
confers upon minor grades of government the duty
of giving effect to its ordinances, and the power to
administer within certain limits the public affairs
of the community over which they preside. Such
minor grades of government are various. Wherever
civic liberty obtains, the form of such minor grade
is accommodated to the opinions of the community : whatever that community may prefer,
and such institutions so established as to facilitate
admission of alterations, as greater light and
knowledge become diffused.

The decentralising temper of the age is en-
croaching more and more upon the domain of the
supreme authority, yet the equilibrium which these
countries have constantly maintained between
local and central government is one of the chief
securities upon which our constitution rests.

The limit of legal right to exercise sovereign

B

powers is found in the special functions assigned
to each such minor grade of government. Should
any of them undertake duties outside those assigned to them, they are acting illegally; for, in so
doing, they encroach either upon the jurisdiction
of one of the other grades of government, or upon
the domain of activity which Parliament, the
supreme authority, by failure to enumerate in any
of its grants of power, have thereby declared shall
not be entered upon by such public authority.
The harmony of such institutions is, in consequence, found in the public law, which assigns
duties to those bodies which it creates, while at
the same time it limits their activity to the
performance of the duties assigned.

Towns have their Municipal Corporations, and
the inhabitants of rural districts have likewise
some measure of autonomy; and between all, relations necessarily exist which affect the persons
governed and their property. The nature of our
constitution, particularly of those parts which
relate to the municipal institution, cannot but be
a subject of interest at the present time, when
changes are every year effected.

By means of these institutions, towns and
boroughs are capable of being made the greatest
blessings to the country, as they are the necessary consequence of great masses of population

collected together in particular spots, for the good government of whom they afford the readiest means. The confirming, improving and simplifying these institutions according to the best and safest principles, should be the practical object of the statesman, patriot, and legislator.

Advocates of Local Government reform seek to establish a graduated system in which every citizen, with the slightest capacity for public affairs, and desire to employ it, should be able to take his share in local administration ; a system extending from the parish to the kingdom ; a system of orderly subordination of authority to authority ; a system free from intricacy, and such as to leave full scope for the development of the interests of each locality by the men best qualified to understand them ; a system of local independence, subject only to the control necessary to preserve imperial unity ; a system which would attract the energies of the best men in each district.

The ideal which obtains in the United Kingdom is thus summarised by Mr. Chamberlain, M.P. : " The leading idea of the English system may be said to be that of a joint-stock or co-operative enterprise in which every citizen is a shareholder, and of which the dividends are receivable in the improved health and the increase in the comfort and happiness of the community.

B 2

" The members of the council are the directors of this great business, and their fees consist in the confidence, the consideration, and the gratitude of those amongst whom they live. In no other undertaking, whether philanthropic or commercial, are the returns more speedy, more manifest, or more beneficial. In Birmingham, for example, the initiative of the unpaid members of the council, and their supervision of the loyal and assiduous labours of the paid officials, have been the means of saving the lives of more than 3,000 persons in a single year ; and, inasmuch as for a single death many cases of illness not actually fatal may be reckoned, it is easy to see what a mass of human suffering has been lightened, and how much misery has been prevented. Under these circumstances, the primary object of all concerned is not so much to lessen expenditure as to spend most wisely and to invest the money of the community in such a way as to secure continuously equally satisfactory results in the condition of the people.

" This is the ideal at the present time ; but of one thing we may be certain. If ever the principles of action should change—if the best men should be so occupied with their own fortunes that they should leave the care of the commonwealth to those who will see in this duty only an opportunity for plunder—if office is sought, not for the good which can be done, but for the political patronage it may afford—if paid officials lose their pride in their work and their loyalty to the public that employs them—if incapacity is overlooked and corruption is condoned—then, if those things happen—the dignity, the efficiency, and the economy of our public service will all disappear, and the institution of local government, so long our pride and our glory, will be discredited in the eyes of the people, and will become a by-word and a reproach."

To exist as a nation implies the being bound together in an association or league, or into a series of associations or leagues, for the promotion of some positive ends. The diffusion of intelligence, the development of health and whatever else contributes to the formation of manliness of character; the extension of trade and the happiness of the people ; the exaltation of the national name, honour, power, and greatness ; the maintenance and advancement, in a word, of the civilisation of the country—these are amongst the prime functions and purposes which belong to a proper political organisation.

The obligations resting upon a State are extensive and multifarious, as are the powers inherent in that assemblage of numbers to which it owes its origin ; and the functions with which it is

endowed, and which, from time to time, are delegated to its minor organisations, ought to be of the
same high order with the duties it is called upon
to perform. Its institutions should make provision
for the most effective training and application of
all the better tendencies of society, and they
should be invested with the means of concentrating
and calling up into exercise all the public spirit
and patriotism that exists in the community.

An indentity of interest exists between our
cities and the nation. In the distant past, individual liberty found its bulwark in the Greek
cities. In every age of the world, in every great
time, and among every great people, the hopes of
men and women who have looked forward into
the coming future of their country have gathered
round the idea of a great and beautiful city. It
was so in ancient Greece. In the glorious times of
Pericles the idea of a beautiful and ennobled
Athens was the living inspiration of the heroes of
Attica—Athens, honoured among men for its
healthy and prosperous people, and, above all, for
the idea of civic unity which animated the lives of
the whole population. It was not a man or two,
nor a leader here or there—it was the whole
population which itself constituted Athens, and
inspired every man of them with the dignity of
Athenian citizenship.

Throughout the world it has always been the cities that led in the rising struggle for individual freedom and happiness which have given modern history its character.

We may not have all the incentives which lead some to personify their cities ; but when we consider the importance of our own, the increasing drift of the rural population into them, the magnitude of the interests, material as well as political, which hang upon their development, and the possible influence which their failure could exert upon the future history of our country, we must believe that the field for the exercise of the duties of citizenship is wide, and that nothing is more desirable for our social development and political peace than the growth of an intelligent devotion of each citizen to his own city, and a personal active interest in its healthy and honourable development.

More implicitly does a man serve his country by looking upon such duties as his personal service, and by recognising the fact that all great ends are attained by means of individual exertion in the first place, and by union and co-operation in the next.

Whatever the form of the minor grade of government may be—municipal corporations, County Councils, Grand Juries, or Boards of

Guardians, or boards of greater or lesser degree —whether one or more bodies, within the same area, direct the various objects of public utility, all are the creatures of the State, and wholly under its control. They are created by law, general or special, or by charter, and find in such law or charter the limit of both their duties, privileges, and responsibilities. According to the accepted theory of law, a municipality performs nothing for itself, but in caring for local affairs it performs a gratuitous service to the State. This theory gives colour to all contracts of inferior governments, but the character of sovereignty cannot attach to its promises or obligations, as it is the creature of the Imperial Legislature, and acts as the agent of the State. Thus it is universally provided that municipalities may be sued and made defendants in civil suits.

The purposes for which local authorities have employed their public credit are peculiar to the position which they hold in the general structure of government, and the rules by which their treasuries should be managed are shaped by the peculiar duties imposed. These duties are various, and are of ever-increasing importance. The special functions of municipal authorities may be broadly summed up as follows :—The enactment of bye-laws, and appointment, payment, and dismissal of

all necessary public officers and servants ; making,
naming, maintaining, cleansing, lighting, watering,
and general regulation of roads and streets ; provision for an efficient system of drainage, and
removal and disposal of sewage and house refuse ;
the contribution towards the maintenance of lunatic
asylums, hospitals, prisons, industrial schools, and
court-houses ; the care of the public health, including the inspection and regulation of lodging-houses,
the removal of nuisances, the enforcement of the
adulteration acts, and the provision of special
hospitals for infectious cases, and of the means of
disinfecting unclean houses ; the provision of
means of cleanliness and recreation, such as baths,
wash-houses, parks, and pleasure-grounds ; the
supply of light and water ; maintenance and control of markets, fairs, abattoirs, and regulation of
weights and measures ; establishment and maintenance of free libraries, museums, and art and
technical schools, and of all public buildings
necessary to local administration ; the control
and management of the City estate, and the levy
and collection of rates when such property is not
sufficient to meet the public expenses ; the execution of sanitary and other powers under the
Public Health Acts ; the execution of schemes
under the Working-Classes' Dwellings Acts of
sanitary improvement for the purpose of benefiting

the condition of the poorer class of residents;
the appointment and supervision of police and fire
brigades; the superintendence and enforcement
of educational regulations; the provision for facilities in traffic, and enforcement of the regulations
in connection therewith; and generally in the
management of all those things which locally
affect the community. Within these limits local
administration is of much service to the community. It brings into play local knowledge of
its requirements. It stirs the inhabitants of the
locality into an interest in public matters; it gives
them training in practical business, in controlling
expenditure, and in exercising some measure of
responsibility for their collective acts. In all
these functions, also, its teaching is more effective
because they are under the review of the technical
officers of the central government, who keep them
within the strict fence of the power delegated to
them by the public or local statutes, but whose
supervision and control is entirely compatible
with local freedom.

To carry out those duties borrowing powers
are conferred upon local authorities, which they
may exercise in various ways should the revenue
from the property of the community be insufficient
to defray the expenses incurred. They may
borrow in the open market, either in the mode

prescribed by the Act conferring the powers, or under the provisions of the Local Loans Act, and either with or without the sanction of any Government department. They may also borrow from the Government itself through its Public Works department.

Most of the loans are raised on the security of the rates levied by the local authority; but under the Municipal Corporations and certain other Acts, loans may be borrowed on the security of land and other property belonging to such authority. Loans raised for gas, water, market, harbour, and the like undertakings, by a rating authority, are usually charged on the revenues of the undertaking, with the rates as a collateral security in case of deficiency. In municipalities, new borrowing powers secure money for new purposes, while existing taxes expunge old debts.

Most local debts are contracted for some definite purpose, and their proceeds are employed in such a manner as to establish in the community some particular form of public service; it is natural, therefore, that the expungement of a local debt should conform to the manner in which its funds were invested. For example: Suppose capital to be borrowed for the purpose of paving streets or providing a sewage scheme, the service thus rendered is common to all members of the community, but of such a nature that the debt must rest upon taxes. But, what is of more importance, the local council cannot proceed as though the City would never be called upon to repeat its expenditure, for pavement and sewerage are subject to wear, and must sooner or later be replaced by new systems. From this it must appear that the payment of a local debt is not to be determined by the general industrial conditions of the country, but that sound policy demands the repayment of existing obligations before the public authorities find it necessary to borrow fresh capital for new improvements. But should the investment be of a permanent nature, it obviates the necessity of clearing off accounts before a similar expenditure of fresh money is required. It is of importance that the rate of taxation should not be changed with unnecessary rapidity, either by the rapid rise in tax rates, or by the rapid fall after the repayment has been accomplished.

All loans must be applied strictly for the purposes for which they are raised, and as a check upon extravagant expenditure by the local authority, the power to mortgage the local rates for certain purposes is limited.

Local debts have now, however, assumed such dimensions that they cannot be left out of account in estimating the burdens which have been imposed on the property from which the local rates are derived. It is true that a portion of them— *e.g.*, the greater portions of the loans of harbour, pier, and dock authorities—are not wholly charged on the rates. A further portion, consisting of the loans raised for the purposes of water-works, gas works, electric light works, markets, etc., and other undertakings producing revenue, is secured, as before stated, in many cases primarily on the revenues of the undertakings in respect of which it has been raised, and constitutes a charge on the rates only to the extent to which those revenues may be found insufficient to meet the repayment of the principal and interest. But, after allowing for these loans, about half of the gross debt falls directly on the rates, which have not only to bear the interest, but also to provide for the repayment of the principal within a prescribed period. It represents, therefore, a liability which for many years to come will have to be met by the ratepayers of the future, and its continuous increase of recent years forbids the hope that the properties which bear the rates, mortgaged to secure its repayment, will, within any measurable distance of time, be relieved from the additional local taxation which it has imposed on them. These considerations point

to the necessity of ascertaining what proportions
of so much of the debt as is charged on the
rates will have to be repaid by urban and rural
ratepayers in the United Kingdom respectively.

ENGLAND.

Purely Urban Debt.	Partly Urban and Partly Rural.	Purely Rural.
£183,915,189 …	£13,393,410 …	£3,906,859

SCOTLAND.

In Scotland the rural debt is not separated
from the urban debt, in consequence of the areas
overlapping. In 1891 the debt of the several
burghs amounted to £11,575,644, and that of the
burghs under the Roads and Bridges Act £413,050,
making a total of £11,988,698 municipal liabilities.
If to this we add the other liabilities secured upon
the rates—viz.: Harbour Authorities, £9,229,842;
Parochial Boards, £362,481; and Ecclesiastical
Boards, £14,902—we have the grand total of
£21,595,923.

IRELAND.

In Ireland the various local Municipal Authorities owed at the end of the year 1890 the sum of
£3,887,326, to which, if we add the debt due by
the Harbour Authorities on the same date, the
Urban Municipal and Harbour debt will amount
to £6,352,516. No returns appear to be published

of the Rural indebtedness, or that of the Urban
Poor Law indebtedness. From the purely Urban
debt, the debt of Harbour and Dock Authorities,
amounting to £30,958,246 for England, £9,229,842
for Scotland, and £2,465,190 for Ireland, must be
deducted in order to arrive at the debt charged
directly or as collateral security on the rates. The
purely Urban debt, so charged, was therefore
£152,956,943 for England, £12,366,081 for the
Municipal, Parochial, and Ecclesiastical debt in
Scotland, and £3,887,326 for Urban Municipal
debt in Ireland.

The proportion which the debt bears to the
rateable values of the areas in respect of which
it has been incurred varies greatly in different
localities. When the rateable value and the debt
of a particular district has been ascertained, this
information of itself by no means shows the
amount of the burden falling on the ratepayers in
respect of such debt. To ascertain this, it is necessary to discover the extent to which the debt is
covered by revenues other than rates. At the
same time the proportion which the debt bears to
the rateable valuation is a very important element
in considering what is the local burden. In England the rateable valuation of purely urban districts is £98,837,721 ; of partly urban and partly
rural districts, £120,519,112 ; and of purely rural

districts, £53,278,287. In Scotland the rateable valuation of purely urban districts is £12,518,192, and of purely rural districts £11,406,690. In Ireland the rateable valuation of the municipal districts is £3,044,796. These figures, especially as regards England, indicate the extent to which the Local Debt presses on the urban as compared with the rural districts.

Can we distinguish the various purposes for which loans have been raised by local authorities, and show the amounts owing in respect of each purpose? For answer to this inquiry we are obliged to rely upon the data furnished by the Local Government reports. The facts desired were not given until 1883-4, but since then they have been published each year. The following are the purposes of the loans outstanding in 1891 by all local authorities in England and Wales, which will sufficiently indicate the purposes for which such loans are required in the United Kingdom :—

Poor Law purposes	...	...	£7,056,166
Lunatic asylums	...	...	3,686,662
Police stations, gaols, and lock-			
up houses ...	...	...	1,122,548
Schools (including reformatories			
and industrial schools	...		18,616,269

Carried forward   £30,481,645

Brought forward	£30,481,645
Highway and street improvements ...	28,275,890
Electric lighting	56,942
Gasworks	14,991,197
Public lighting	46,095
Waterworks	38,325,912
Sewerage and sewage disposal works	19,969,077
Markets	5,380,982
Cemeteries and burial grounds	2,492,185
Fire brigades	489,741
Public buildings, offices, etc., not included under other headings	4,315,707
Parks, pleasure grounds, commons, and open spaces ...	3,992,137
Public libraries, museums, and schools of science and art	489,693
Baths, wash-houses, and open bathing places ...	950,308
Bridges and ferries	4,053,596
Artisans' and labourers' dwellings improvements	3,814,035
Diseases (Cattle) Prevention Act (compensation)	76,239
Hospitals	669,234
Tramways	1,317,555
Slaughter-houses	121,631
Allotments	14,164
Carried forward	£160,323,965

C

Brought forward	£160,323,965
Land drainage, embankment, river conservancy, and sea defences	3,147,417
Private improvement works	940,969
Other purposes ...	...	5,336,645
	£169,748,996
Harbours, piers, docks, and quays	31,466,462
Total debt	£201,215,458

The debt for harbours, piers, etc., includes the sum of £508,216 owing by Town Councils and other urban sanitary authorities, and charged on the local rates.

There are many significant items in the foregoing table. From a survey of the items mentioned it seems that the debts resting upon the cities and minor civil divisions are capable of a threefold classification. In the first class are included those debts incurred for the purpose of rendering a direct though a general service to the public. The building of highways and streets; the maintenance of a fire department; the construction of sewerage works, and the like, are examples of such services. The second class includes those debts incurred for the purpose of rendering a direct service to the public, but of a particular rather than a general character. This

division comprises such services as the supply of
water, or gas, or heat, to the citizens of a municipal
corporation. The purchase of burial-grounds for
re-sale to individuals would also be included in
this class. The third kind of local indebtedness
arises when the governing body employs its public
credit for granting assistance to private Corporations, believing thereby to serve the public indirectly through the institutions established.

The contraction of local debts is entered upon
with foresight, and not under the stress of any
emergency, as the Imperial Government often does,
so that it follows from this that common business
and economic maxims may be more closely observed, and general political considerations less
strenuously regarded.

As has been before stated, a revenue law that
makes sudden and rapid changes in the rate of
taxation is the occasion of unnecessary incon-
venience and vexation, and notwithstanding the
rise of extraordinary demands, the evils attending
such arbitrary changes may be easily avoided by a
resort to credit. It is therefore of common advantage that the municipalities should be permitted to
distribute the payment of their liabilities over a
long period of time.

In estimating the number of years for the repayment of such loans, calculations are often made

C 2

upon the income that may arise from the manner
in which the proceeds of a loan may be expended,
although not always, and the municipality can rely
upon other sources of revenue besides the taxes
for support of the debt. We have seen that it
frequently occurs that local authorities undertake
productive industries and derive a steady income
from the investment of monies borrowed. Thus
the proceeds of a loan are said to be spent for
remunerative purposes when invested in such a
manner as to render direct personal service to the
citizens. The furnishing of gas and other illumi-
nants, or of water, are illustrations of such services.
In cases of this sort, the burden of the debt is
thrown upon the public industry which its proceeds
established, and its support and final payment are
assumed to rest with those who are benefited by
the service in proportion to the benefit received.
For example, it is the common practice for water-
works to be supported by water rates: public
water rates where the supply is for public purposes,
and special water rates where the supply is for
private or domestic or manufacturing purposes,
and it conforms fully to the requirements of finance
that these rates should be so adjusted as to pay for
the plant and its maintenance independently of
general taxation, except so far as the city or community is itself a consumer. Such a method of

management, which leads to the assignment of specific funds to specific services, is not common in National or Imperial finances. But in local affairs, the principle thus disclosed is one of wide application, being the subject of statutable enactments, and modifies in a marked degree the general rules of the administration of local debts.

In addition to the revenue from productive municipal works, the public creditor has an assured and easy method of securing payment of a city's obligations.

Municipalities are compelled to found a sinking fund at the time of issuing a loan for the redemption of the debt in a specific period. Public interest is opposed to the perpetuation of local debts, consequently local authorities are bound to make adequate provision for expunging a debt at the time it is created. An additional value is given to those obligations by so doing, and in consequence an additional advantage to the municipality in the launching of its loans. For example, in the year 1890 the Dublin Corporation consolidated its liabilities and converted them into stock. The Corporation was bound by its local Act to form and maintain a loans fund, and to pay into it every year the aggregate amount of all dividends payable in that year, and such further sums as should be sufficient, with accumulation of interest,

to redeem all issues of Corporation Stock at the
end of the prescribed period.

The following circular, prepared by Mr. Sexton,
M.P., at the time of the issue of the Dublin Corporation Stock, will indicate the advantages which
such stocks hold out to investors :—

" DUBLIN CORPORATION STOCK.

3¼ per cent.

Its Value.—The stock is offered at the minimum price of par, whilst other stocks are at high
premiums in the market. The rate of interest, 3¼
per cent., is more than double the usual rate for
Bank Deposits ; it is very much higher than the
return for money invested in Trustee or Post Office
Savings Banks, and it is considerably in excess of
the interest yielded by Government funds and
British Municipal Stocks at their present market
value. The rate of interest will remain unchanged
until the term of redemption expires in 1944.

Its Security.—The stock and the interest are
secured by unlimited rating power. The stock
and interest will be the first charge on all the property, revenues, and rates of the City. Exclusive
of rates, the City property is estimated to be of a
capital value much exceeding the whole amount of
the City debt. Exclusive of rates, the annual income from City property is much greater than the

annual charge for Interest and Sinking Fund will be when the whole of the City debt has been converted into Stock. The Corporation Loans Fund, prescribed by the Act of Parliament, will be subject to the supervision and direction of the Local Government Board of Ireland. Owing to these concurrent securities, the Stock will be free from those causes of fluctuation in value which affect commercial and speculative securities, not excepting the Government Funds.

Its Convenience.—Dividends will be payable at any office of the Munster and Leinster Bank, and Dividend Warrants will be sent by post, when so desired, and made payable at any office of the Union Bank of London, the National Provincial Bank of England, or the National Bank of Scotland. Stock may be converted, at any time, free of all charge, on application by the holder, into Stock Certificates to bearer (with interest coupons attached) for £10 each, or any multiple of £10, and these Stock Certificates to bearer may be disposed of simply by delivery to the purchaser, without any form of transfer. All transfers and certificates will be free of Stamp Duty, and no official fees will be charged on any transaction in the Stock. As the Stock will bear interest at 3½ per cent. for the term of 54 years, it is an exceptionally convenient and desirable medium of investment for trustees, executors and administrators, for custodians of reserve and sinking funds, and generally for all who desire a permanent and secure investment at a certain rate of interest."

Such Stocks are largely availed of by investors and now by the Trust Investment Act, 1889, trustees, unless forbidden to do so by the instrument creating the trust, may invest the trust funds in them.

The extent to which these Stocks are in demand is evidenced by the readiness with which they are taken up, and the buoyancy which they constantly maintain.

The subjoined table shows how greatly the value of Municipal Stocks has been increasing in recent years :—

Amount.	Name of Stock.	Rate per Cent.	Price of Issue.	Latest Price Jan. 1894.	Yield per Cent.			1893 Highest—Lowest.
£					£	s.	d.	
3,650,000	Birmingham Corp. Stock, 1946	3½	Var.	113½	3	0	0	116⅞—112¾
1,319,445	" " 1947	3	Var.	102	2	18	9	104½—100½
2,235,850	Bristol Corp. Stock (Deb.)	3½	Var.	115	3	1	3	115¾—111¾
1,222,500	Cardiff Corp. Stock, 1935	3½	Var.	112½	2	18	9	115½—111½
204,500	Cork Corp. Stock	3½	Var.	101½	3	8	9	102½—100
1,055,285	Dublin Corp. Stock, 1944	3¼	Par.	100¾	3	3	9	105½—100¼
2,302,950	Leeds Cons. Deb. Stock, 1927	4	Var.	116	3	5	0	120 —115
7,893,815	Liverpool Corp. Stock	3½	Var.	116½	3	0	0	119 —115¼
16,961,638	London, Metropolitan, 1929	3½	Var.	114½	2	17	6	115½—112
10,850,000	" " 1941	3	—	106	2	16	3	106½—102⅝
3,700,000	" " 1919—49	2½	88	91	2	15	0	92⅞—88¼
3,775,735	Manchester Corp. Cons. Stock	4	Var.	132	3	0	0	134¼—128⅝
3,128,599	" " 1941	3	94	102	2	18	9	102⅛—98⅝
3,050,000	Nottingham Corp. Stock	3	85	101	3	0	0	103¼—99⅞
800,000	Swansea Corp. Stock 1951	3½	Var.	113	3	0	0	115¾—111⅞
100,000	Belfast Corp. Stock, 1912	3½	—	100	3	7	6	103 —100
150,000	" " 1921	3½	—	100	3	10	0	— — —
200,000	" " 1928	3½	—	104½	3	5	0	106¾—103

Municipal borrowing seems to have spread with great rapidity, and a slight consideration of the centres from which these large debts have sprung will show that the larger portion of existing local obligations is chargeable to the cities and large towns.

	Municipality.	Population.	Indebtedness.	Indebtedness per head of population.		
			£	£	s.	d.
England	Birmingham	478,113	10,388,413	21	14	6
	Brighton	117,833	816,615	6	18	7
	Bradford	216,361	4,691,621	21	13	8
	Cardiff	143,346	1,343,192	9	7	4
	Carlisle	39,176	178,335	4	11	0
	Hull	200,041	1,074,644	5	7	5
	Liverpool	517,951	7,893,814	11	7	6
	London County Council	4,232,118	30,621,813	7	4	8
	Manchester	515,567	10,399,145	20	3	4
	Oldham	131,463	1,528,023	11	12	5
	Nottingham	215,000	3,247,032	15	2	0
	Plymouth	85,000	462,000	5	8	8
	Sheffield	324,243	3,394,873	10	9	4
	Walsall	72,000	250,497	3	9	6
Scotland	Aberdeen	129,513	777,977	6	0	1
	Edinburgh	261,225	446,355*	1	14	2
	Glasgow	656,185	6,718,516	10	4	7
	Lanark	4,579	15,932	3	9	6
Ireland	Belfast	275,000	1,014,675	3	13	9
	Dublin	245,001	1,233,139	5	0	7

* Exclusive of water and gas debts.

The above figures do not adequately present the tendency towards the employment of credit that comes with increasing density of population; as between the cities themselves greater looseness in fiscal methods may be observed as municipal

numbers extend. The average debt per head of
these twenty towns is £9 4s. 7d., and as between
the towns themselves twelve contain a population
of 200,000 and over, and of this number there are
but five that fall below the average, while the
obligations of many of them are far beyond that of
the average town.

Even abroad the same tendency towards the
employment of municipal credit appears to exist, as
the following figures as regards the chief European
and American cities will show :—

Country.	Municipality.	Population.	Indebtedness.	Indebtedness per head		
			£	£	s.	d.
France	Paris	2,447,957	76,490,920	31	4	11
,,	Ghent	150,157	1,538,630	10	4	3
Germany	Frankfort-on-Main	185,000	2,450,000	13	4	10
Belgium	Antwerp	232,723	7,241,500	31	2	3
Holland	Rotterdam	222,270	2,634,500	11	17	0
,,	The Hague	160,531	981,608	5	9	11
Austria	Vienna	1,364,548	5,532,603	4	1	1
,,	Buda Pest	526,263	2,146,970	4	1	7
Italy	Rome	440,596	8,902,377	20	4	1
,,	Milan	420,000	3,966,915	9	8	10
,,	Genoa	200,495	2,138,184	10	13	3
,,	Florence	184,321	1,704,269	9	4	11
,,	Venice	159,038	283,234	1	15	7
Switzerland	Zürich	27,641	1,287,698	46	11	7
Denmark	Copenhagan	312,859	1,671,149	5	6	9
Sweden	Christiania	156,535	683,334	4	7	3
Russia	St. Petersburg	954,400	1,500,000	1	11	5
Poland	Warsaw	490,417	1,619,865	3	6	0
Portugal	Lisbon	450,000	2,334,684	5	3	9
U.S. America	Boston	448,477	11,713,639	26	2	4
,,	Chicago	1,500,000	2,783,297	1	17	7
,,	Denver	120,000	308,218	2	12	1
,,	New Orleans	265,000	3,350,639	12	16	4
,,	New York	1,801,739	20,341,544	11	10	7

In many cities municipal debts have grown more rapidly than taxable property or population. Instances of this fact can be multiplied without limit, but they are so often brought to public notice that they are no longer regarded with surprise.

The reason of this is not far to seek. The various Imperial Governments having ceased to largely employ their public credit, the cities and minor civil divisions have come forward as the chief borrowers of money. New duties have been imposed upon those who administer local affairs. Many of those cities are of ancient date, and required the application of the best modern scientific methods for the physical welfare of their inhabitants; the spread of the democratic spirit and the growing demand for the ameliora- tion of the condition of the poorer citizens have entailed obligations upon the various local authori- ties from which their predecessors were entirely free.

It is not our purpose to detail these new duties. It is apparent to all that a developing society must of necessity make continually large demands upon civic government, for the principles of common property under public management ex- tends to new objects, and embraces new purposes as a community grows in numbers, in education, and in riches.

People who rail at our growing expenditure forget that it is the nature of well-governed countries to improve ; and that improvement in a government, like improvement in an estate, is almost always a costly process. It is possible to govern cheaply by the simple expedient of governing badly, but efficient government implies efficient machinery, and this must be paid for. We cannot, therefore, share in the anticipation of those who look for any material reduction in the cost of civil government, whether imperial or local. If it were to take place, we should regard it as a morbid rather than a healthy sign. It would prove that the country was stationary, and had ceased to improve, or that the government had ceased to be equal to its needs. As the United Kingdom increases in population and activity, it can no more safely forego an increased expenditure upon government than a railway can increase in traffic without a rise in its working expenses.

CHAPTER II.

TAXATION AND ITS INCIDENCE.

THE political sub-divisions of the nation, made for the purpose of more efficiently administering the affairs of the country, have no inherent power to levy taxation. In the nation alone inheres such power, and the minor grades of government have only such power as is delegated to them. The charter of a municipal corporation—the statute defining its powers—is the source of its power to tax. It has such power on the subject as the statute or charter gives, and no more. The purpose of the local tax is local benefit. The Local Government can administer the affairs of its locality more advantageously than can be done by the imperial or supreme authority, and therefore the power to tax is given for the purpose of such local government.

This power must be plain and express; it cannot be gained by prescription; no length of time justifies it; it originates in the legislative will, declared by express statute, and it must appear in the statute by express words or necessary implication.

The power to exempt from taxation, like the power to tax, must be also specially conferred, and in statutes conferring the power to tax, the rate of taxation is often limited, which limit cannot be exceeded. However, the charters and statutes under which local authorities are created, and their powers and limits defined, may be changed, modified, enlarged, or repealed as the exigencies of the public service may demand.

The development of the Municipal Government and the magnitude of the debt already incurred needs a large periodical revenue. This revenue must, just as much as and even more than a large empire, be derived from the most legitimate sources. The burden of debt ought to be so adjusted that it will not gall the back that has to bear it.

Municipal revenue may be divided into two classes, (1) original revenue and (2) derivative revenue.

Original municipal revenue is that which the municipality derive directly from their own property. This source of income in many municipalities is of considerable extent, and, as we shall see when treating of Germany, does not necessitate, in a few instances, the levy of any auxiliary supplies.

Derivative revenue is the income derived by the municipality from the obligatory contributions produced by taxation, or those sums which the local authority levies on the wealth of private individuals in return for the services rendered to them by the administrative institutions of the municipality.

Those obligatory contributions may be again divided into two classes, (1) special and (2) general, and these are the main source of our local income. In other words, municipal revenue is mainly derived from special and general taxes and rates. Special taxes differ from the general taxes in that they refer to special services that have been voluntarily sought, whereas general taxes refer to general services that are compulsorily offered. Special taxes are such as special fees, costs, charges, or a special rate, or a tax for extraordinary services.

It is, however, with the income derived from the general taxation that we have to deal. The reason of such is evident. In order to satisfy certain collective wants, where it is quite impossible to decide what are the expenses caused by individual citizens, and where the direct performance of personal services, which would prove to be uncertain, inconsiderable, and badly distributed, would be of no use, there is required a common fund, to establish which voluntary contributions would not be adequate.

Taxes and rates are the necessary condition of municipal administration. When men are gathered together, it is found best to divide certain necessary work for the sake of economy and efficiency.

General taxation is, again, either direct or indirect.

Direct taxes are those which affect the citizen's more or less permanent condition, such as his existence, property, profession, or residence ; they are those imposts that are founded on essential and permanent relations between the citizens and the Treasury, which provides for their collection at fixed times. Indirect taxes are applicable to, we might say, acts such as the importation of a commodity, or the consumption of an article ; they are founded on relations merely accidental and temporary, and which, therefore, are usually collected by means of a tariff.

Carey, in his "Principles of Social Science," thus sums up the relative merits of each system :—

"Taxation tends to become direct as men become free. The strength of the State grows with growth in the value of land and labour, and with increase in the proportion borne by fixed to movable capital."

D

Adam Smith was the first to attempt to formulate the truths upon which a tax system should be based. His canons may be described as those of equality, certainty, convenience, and economy ; and Mill says that an examination of the leading authorities shows that, so far as they go, Smith's maxims have " been generally concurred in by subsequent writers," and that their application has been no less generally neglected.

These maxims are as follows :—

" 1. The subjects of every State ought to contribute towards the support of the Government, as nearly as possible in proportion to their respective abilities—that is, in proportion to the revenue which they respectively enjoy under the State.

" 2. The tax which each individual is bound to pay ought to be certain and not arbitrary. The time of payment, the manner of payment, the quantity to be paid, ought all to be clear and plain to the contributor and to every other person.

" 3. Every tax ought to be levied at the time and in the manner in which it is most likely to be convenient for the contributors to pay it.

" 4. Every tax ought to be so contrived as both to take out and keep out of the pockets of the people as little as possible over and above what it brings into the public treasury of the State."

To these maxims no fair objection can be made, but it is one of those true propositions which are so abstract and general that, notwithstanding their truth, they are of little use, from the difficulty of applying them rightly to any particular case. We learn very little when we are told that the best tax is that which is most conducive to the public interest, but we do learn something very useful when our attention is directed to any particular merit or demerit which ought to be sought for or avoided in any system of taxation. When it is necessary to raise a large sum by taxation, it becomes nearly impossible to avoid some objectionable taxes.

In the class of direct taxation a great subdivision is also in general held to exist, for direct taxation is looked upon as being divided into "Imperial taxation" and "Local taxation." The term imperial taxation is generally intended to include those taxes which are founded on the annual budget of the Chancellor of the Exchequer, and are levied by the direction of Parliament throughout the country, and in most instances by Imperial officers; while the term "local taxation" applies to those taxes (or, as they are more commonly called, rates) which are not sanctioned annually by Parliament, and which are levied within certain prescribed areas by the properly

D 2

constituted authority having jurisdiction for some special purposes within those areas.

Is there really that wide, almost generic distinction which is generally held to exist between the so-called "imperial" and "local taxation"? It is true that the taxes collected by local authorities are not looked upon as imperial taxes, but is that a right view to take of the matter? The answer surely must be No! for it cannot be held that these rates, not being collected for the benefit of any private individual, but to meet expenditure incurred for the good of the public at large, are as much imperial as those collected for the immediate use of the State for the same purpose.

The question of our local imposts ought not, therefore, in any discussion of the equitable readjustment of the taxation of the United Kingdom, to be ignored. Obviously the money expended for the relief of the poor, for the formation and repair of the public highways, for the prevention or for the punishment of crime, for the sewerage and sanitary regulations of towns, and for the other various objects of public utility for which local taxes are raised, is as necessary to the maintenance of the country in its political, social, and economical integrity as the imperial expenditure for the army, the navy, or the civil service.

The source from whence direct taxation should

be derived has long formed the subject of con-
troversies in every country that have not been
completely nor anywhere settled. The reason for
this is obvious. Property is of so varied a character
that an impost levied upon any one kind will
compel its proprietor to proclaim that such impost
is unjust because it confiscates a certain amount of
his capital corresponding to the impost, and leaves
untouched the capital of the proprietors of the
other kinds of property. It is a question that
comes home to each one, and is consequently a
subject in which all are interested.

Local taxes or rates are personal obligations of
certain individuals for, as we have said, the construction and use of roads, sewers, light, water,
protection of public health, and other parochial or
municipal provisions for the common benefit of the
residents in each locality.

They are not, as is generally supposed, taxes
on property, but on individuals, the rating of a
certain class of each man's property, as a house,
being merely a criterion of his general expenditure,
and of his potential use of the local works; and
the individual failing, the premises are not liable.
A man with a large house is supposed to have a
large income, a large establishment, and many
servants, while a cottager is taken to be limited in
these affairs. In the old times when a man built

a house he sunk his own well and his own cess-pool ; nowadays the county or town authority brings water to his door and carries off his sewage in the common sewer.

With few exceptions rates are struck periodically, and the demands and payments, allotted according to the rating or valuation, are an annual grant for an annual expenditure out of the annual income of the community. No doubt part of the expenditure is more of a temporary kind, but such expenditure is generally spread over a number of years in the manner we have stated, so that there is a fairly constant average rate from year to year. True it is that sometimes exceptional demands are made from the ratepayers, but even when it is so, the return is made in necessary or exceptional improvement and benefit, and a great proportion of the exceptional expenditure is thrown upon succeeding generations.

A characteristic of our local taxation, which is of a direct nature, is the narrow groove which it has kept, and the limited source from whence it is derived. The debt, as we have seen, and the expenditure to meet it and current outlay, have been advancing, but without any similar expansion of the source of supply, or the provision of any auxiliary help for its liquidation.

The fixed and permanent quality of the land

pointed it out as most peculiarly fitted to bear the
weight of necessary taxation. Next to the land,
houses assumed a character of permanency more
than any other description of property, and for this
reason became objects of taxation. In our fiscal
system, therefore, real property suffers an exceptional liability to taxation.

The amount of local taxation incident upon
real property is now known with great fulness, as
the following will show :—

ENGLAND.

Local income from rates
and taxes (including
water and gas rents)
levied in 1891 ... £34,654,591 or 67·37 per cent.
Local income from
other sources in 1891,
but excluding receipts
from loans ... ... £16,782,824 ,, 32·6 ,, ,,

SCOTLAND.

Local income from rates
and taxes levied in
1891 ... ... £3,020,908 or 80·03 per cent.
Local income from
other sources in 1891,
but excluding receipts
from loans ... ... £753,794 ,, 19·96 ,, ,,

IRELAND.

Local income from rates and taxes levied in 1891	£2,776,021 or 79·24 per cent.	
Local income from other sources in 1891, but excluding receipts from loans	£727,498 ,, 20·76 ,, ,,	

The receipts in Scotland do not include those by the fishery or harbour authorities.

We thus see that in England real property has to provide 67·37 per cent. of the total local income; 80·03 per cent. in Scotland; and 79·24 per cent. in Ireland.

This annual burden is raised upon an assessment of the property rated according to the valuation put upon it. This valuation is made in the United Kingdom in the manner explained in the next chapter.

These imposts upon real property are exceptionally severe. No doubt there has been a very considerable increase in the value of real property since it was made the object of legitimate taxation. Houses, mills, factories, railways, etc., may, and do, increase indefinitely; arable land cannot.

The total amount of the local rates raised in England in the year 1881 was £23,904,860 as compared with a total amount of £27,818,642 (excluding rates from water works and gas works) in 1891, being an increase of 16·37 per cent. in the latter year.

On the other hand, the Poor Law Valuation in 1881 was £139,636,307, as compared with a valuation of £152,116,008 in 1891, being an increase of only 8·93 per cent. Thus the local rates and taxes increased within these ten years 16·37 per cent. per annum, whilst the property out of which they are derived only increased 8·93 per cent. per annum.

It should be observed that in 1881 the total amount received by local authorities in relief of the rates from Treasury subventions and payments excluding contributions in lieu of rates, but including payment derived from the Local Taxation account, was £2,888,772, whilst similar receipts in 1891 amounted to £7,185,603. If the considerable relief thus afforded to local rates had not been provided, probably the deficiency would have been met by additional local taxation.

In 1881 in England the rate of local taxation in the £, calculated on the rateable value, was 3s. 5·1d., whilst in 1891 it was 3s. 7·9d., notwithstanding the large additional relief provided in that year, which represents an additional 11·33d. in the £.

Again, the local debt has increased more rapidly than the property which has to bear its burden.

In 1871 the local debt in England was
£92,810,100, which increased to £201,215,458 in
1891, showing an increase of 116·80 per cent.

In 1871 the valuation was £115,646,631, which
increased to £152,116,008 in 1891, showing an
increase of 31·53 per cent.

Thus, during a short period of twenty years,
the local burden increased 116·80 per cent., and the
property out of which it has to be repaid only
developed at the rate of 31·53 per cent.

But while certain kinds of real property have
made even this progress, notwithstanding the
burden upon them, it is certain that trade, manufactures, and professions have enormously dis-
tanced, in proportion, agricultural industry and
house property in the race for wealth. A comparison of the Income Tax Assessments under
Schedule A and Schedule D (the former being
in respect of the annual value of lands and houses,
and the latter in respect of the annual profits or
gains on property, business, and professions, trades,
etc.) will prove this.

SCHEDULE A.

Assessment in 1871.	Assessment in 1891.
£142,736,057.	£177,725,959.

SCHEDULE D.

Assessment in 1871.	Assessment in 1891.
£189,305,247.	£306,538,198.

Thus, during these twenty years, lands and houses only increased 24·5 per cent. per annum, according to the Income Tax Commissioners, whilst profits from property, businesses, professions, and trades, etc., increased 61·9 per cent. per annum.

It is well to remark that to 1875-6 the tax was charged on £100 and upwards, and since 1876-7 no assessment under Schedule D is made on profits less than £150 a year. Needless to say but for this the total assessment would be far larger. Owing, however, to the fluctuating and volatile character of personal property it was always deemed difficult to grasp with certainty, and therefore escaped being assessed for local taxes ; where personal property is so assessed, the assessors form some general idea of its value by reference to the position in life and manner of living of the owners.

However, when reality was originally fixed upon as the property to bear the incidence of taxation, the fact that it was of a permanent and visible character was not the only condition in its favour, but also that it was then considered the best measure of the ability of each to pay according to his means. It was more just then than under present circumstances, because the great bulk of income was derived from land, very little from trade or foreign commerce.

Real property is thus the special fund which

forms the source of local taxation. It consists of local property which is, no doubt, increased in value by expenditure out of local rates. It is a fund which in urban districts cannot increase in extent, but may in value, and therefore, perhaps, be more able to bear taxation. It is the property which local authorities always assess, and which they are, therefore, competent to tax ; but from time to time we hear statements of the injustice of real property alone paying rates, and personal property not being liable to pay any contribution to the local exchequer. There is a large amount of income derivable from property which can never be represented by the rental or valuation of lands and houses. Many millions of capital are, for instance, sunk in the funds, in foreign securities, debentures of all kinds, and in those trading concerns which have built up the nation's wealth. To the extent which that capital and the income from such escape from the poor and other local rates, the capital invested in lands and houses is unduly burdened.

Speaking on the subject at Exeter in 1892, the Marquis of Salisbury said : " We should be quite certain, then, that this question of rates will be thoroughly overhauled. There is no such crying injustice in this country as the system which places upon the owners of lands and houses the support of the poor, and, where there are school boards, the education of the poor. These are matters to which all the wealth of the country should equally contribute. There is no reason whatever why the holders of the 750 millions of Consols should go absolutely free and leave to their poorer neighbours who occupy or own lands or houses the duty of maintaining the poor and of providing education. I know that this question is full of difficulty. I know that it has baffled statesman after statesman; but I have a strong belief that there is not sufficient moving force behind, and that if I had the number of yeomen whom I should like to create in this country, we should very soon see the system of rates put upon an equitable footing."

As immense profits are now made from trade, these profits should contribute their just share of local taxation, along with all kinds of land, house, and other property, as in the case of the imperial income tax. That the demand for the taxation of personality is reasonable, will be acknowledged from a case in point. " A " is a merchant carrying on business in a city in an office rated at say £20, and " B " a workman, residing in a cottage of a similar valuation. Each bears a like proportion of the local taxation, although the former may realise an income of £2,000 per annum out of the business carried on in his office, whilst the workman may barely obtain a livelihood. The result of the local expenditure may be of more benefit to the merchant than to the workman, by carrying trade to his door and giving him greater opportunities and facilities for increasing his annual income without requiring from him any proportionate increase in his local rates and taxes.

This complaint of the freedom of personal property from taxation is natural. Why should the workman in the example given pay a proportion of the local rates equal to that paid by the merchant for the support of our public libraries, washhouses, streets, lighting, and other public municipal undertakings? or why should a man with £2,000 a year income pay only on the house he lives in, whilst another man deriving a similar income from house property pays the whole of the local rates? Income and household furniture bring nothing into the revenue, and all the vast accumulations of works of art that adorn the homes of the wealthy and well-to-do, and other creations for luxury, are untouched by the local tax collector, although the outlay by the local authority is beneficial to all alike, as every material improvement is projected for the convenience of all the people of the city; and by convenience is meant not mere comfort, but facility of passage tending to the benefit of trade.

Merchants and men of business who thus have the benefit of the improvements are infinitely more interested in the success and progress of municipal government towards the resources of which probably they may not contribute. Their assets, it is true, may not be sufficiently localised, nor obvious to the world, and are, besides, so multifarious, that they do not class under a special name. But if these people had retired from business and invested their capital in lands and houses at possibly a fifth of the annual return that they received from trade, then, if local improvements of any magnitude are promoted, they have to pay large annual outlays in the shape of local rates from which they had been previously free, although in receipt of a much larger income.

It is expanding commerce which necessitates good, wide and long roads, brings into existence quite an army of police to protect its products, which are generally of a movable character, requires hundreds of thousands of hands to work it ; and surely some portion of the income derived from commerce should be contributed towards the support of the local government. Not only the profits of commerce, but all kinds of personality, should contribute. Good roads are greatly for the convenience of the individual, as well as of commerce ; were roads narrow and in bad repair,

transit might not be safe, neither would wealth
accumulate so rapidly. Property or commercial
products would not be safe in banks and warehouses if streets were badly lighted or policed,
neither would public safety be secured.

In Scotland, under the old law, all the inhabitants of purely burghal parishes were assessed
for the relief of the poor " according to the estima-
tion of their means and substance " in terms of the
Statute of 1579, but in landward parishes " half the
burden was laid on the owners of lands and
heritages within the parish, and the other half on
the whole inhabitants according to their means
and substance." By the Poor Law Act of 1845
three modes of assessment were provided, and it
was left to each parochial board to adopt whichever of the three might be considered best suited
to the circumstances of the parish. Half the
assessment could be imposed upon the owners, and
half upon the occupiers ; or one-half upon the
owners, and the other half upon the whole inhabitants according to their means and substance ;
or the whole could be imposed as an equal percentage on the annual income derived from both
sources indifferently.

Whenever the first mode was adopted, the
parochial board was empowered to distinguish
lands and heritages into two or more classes,

according to the purposes for which they were used or occupied, and to fix such different rates of assessment on the tenants and occupants of each class as might seem just and equitable. In all these modes it was remarked " that which may be regarded as the national principle, that each man shall be assessed in proportion to his means, has in effect been preserved." ·

In determining the mode in which a parish should be assessed, the parochial board had not, therefore, to consider the principle as to whether each man should be assessed according to his means, but whether the assessment should be imposed directly upon his estimated means and substance, or indirectly by assuming that the house or lands occupied by him represented his means and substance proportionally with the other ratepayers.

The assessment upon means and substance, other than lands and heritages, was not generally directly enforced, as it was found too inquisitorial ; but gradually an indirect mode of estimating means and substance, by taking annual value or rent as a criterion, was adopted, until finally, by an Act in 1861, the assessment on means and substance was abolished.

Public opinion in Scotland now says that those wise and equitable provisions, designed to secure

E

that every one should contribute in proportion to
his ability, have been departed from, and that the
departure has led to inequality and injustice.
Upon this subject, Mr. Lamond, in his " History of
the Scottish Poor Laws," says : " They who bring
the complaint consist almost exclusively of those
who desire a return to the abandoned system of
levying the tax upon means and substance in
preference to rental. . . .

" Assessment according to means and substance was productive of wranglings and bicker-
ings of the bitterest kind—charges of conceal-
ment and dishonesty, actions for defamation, and
every unpleasant thing which should be absent
from any system of taxation. The supporters of
the old mode of levying the assessment were at
one time strong and zealous, and the system did
not fall without a struggle. The battle was waged
long and keenly in almost every parish where the
system was in operation. But as public discussion
exposed its inquisitorial nature and the evils
following from it, opinion latterly decided against
it, with the ultimate result of legislative prohibition. . . .

" Amid the mass of irrelevancies which have
since been written and spoken in favour of assessment on means and substances, the following may
be gathered and stated as reasons in support of

a return to the systems :—(1) Because it is more
equitable than the present method, and, as there
are difficulties attending any system, it is unjusti-
fiable to pursue one which is less equitable because
of difficulties standing in the way of carrying out
the more equitable ; (2) because it is no more inquisitorial than the collection of the income tax,
and no honest community should object to inqui-
sition into their private affairs if it is to produce
equality among contributors ; (3) because it would
catch a great deal of men's " substance " not now
subject to the tax ; and (4) because the poor have
a moral right to all the monastic and Church
property which was seized at the Reformation, and
the present system makes no attempt to get these
ancient hereditary rights back for the benefit of the
poor.

" It is obvious that the third of these reasons is
the only one which can be seriously listened to, as
having any pretensions to validity. The first argu-
ment has already been disposed of by the verdict
of public opinion. The second is not true. For
parochial assessment on means and substance is
more inquisitorial than the income tax ; and besides, even if it were not, two blacks do not make a
white. The income tax is both inquisitorial and
objectionable, but in a less degree than the parochial
assessment on means and substance was. For in

E 2

the collection of the income tax any private dis-
closures are made to sworn officers and to a board
small in number.   Further, anyone desirous of
preventing his fellow-townsmen from gaining a
knowledge of his affairs, has the option of passing
over the local commissioners, and making his return
direct to Somerset House.   But in the other case
the board is thirty at the least, and neither the
board nor the officers are sworn to secrecy.   On
the contrary, one of the complaints against the
system while it lasted was that it put a knowledge
of a man's profits and of his most private affairs at
the mercy of his rivals in trade, and that incom-
petent men frequently sought office as managers,
not from a sense of public duty, nor from a con-
sciousness of peculiar aptitude for the work of a
Poor Law manager, but from the base motive of
acquiring an insight into other people's affairs
which might be useful to themselves in the conduct
of their own.   The moral proposition contained in
the second reason it is needless to discuss.   We
fear it is utopian to expect people to submit to
disagreeableness, especially when they touch so
tender a subject as their profit and loss, for the
sake of any abstract idea or principle, however
just in itself.   It is a misfortune, of course, if communities are not honest.   But, so long as the
business of the world is regulated as it is, it will

be hopeless to expect the self-sacrifices to be made which would be involved in a parochial income tax."

We do not come to the same conclusions as Mr. Lamond. To be just, aids of money requisite to carry on the government of a State, or of a community to provide for its well-being, should be impartially levied upon all property, speaking in the widest acceptation of the term. Such are the legitimate objects of taxation when by taxation trade and commerce are not handicapped in their development. The science of government is wisely and practically shown, when the taxes are so ordered that each person pays in proportion to the value of his property, and not a certain class only, in proportion to the value of the expenditure.

Are the inhabitants of these countries so taxed? So far as our municipal expenditure is concerned, we have seen that they are not. The local taxes press intolerably upon one class of society, and no reduction that may take place, nor any retrenchment that our municipal expenditure is capable of, can reduce the pressure or attain the ends which all good men desire.

The duty of granting supplies is imperative. There can be no station in any community whatever that does not owe something to the State and to the municipality for protection, good order, and other essentials to civic liberty and happiness. This mutual obligation is the very bond of society, and each should observe it. No man should have a claim to the benefit resulting from social combination unless he furnishes his quota to the general good.

Although the present system has been sanctioned by long experience, yet its antiquity affords no excuse for the evil that is in it. Where is the advantage of experience, and of increased wealth, if we are not to adopt improvements? All arts and sciences have adopted new rules, as new light has been shed upon them; and shall political science alone stand still, when all others are in motion around her? It cannot be. Mankind is becoming too wise to suffer such a thing to happen, and now we have obtained a position by which we can compel justice to be done impartially to all.

If we cannot lessen the load of taxation, we should adjust it so that it shall not gall the back that has to bear it. If we cannot relieve a certain class of the community from the taxes themselves, at least we are bound to relieve them to the utmost of our power from the bitterness and irritation which they are apt to bring in their train. We can prevent the evil from obtruding itself constantly on their eyes, and can direct a portion of its pressure on the tough and callous parts of the body politic, sparing those that are weakly or tender. This is what we have to do to mitigate a burden which we cannot take away.

CHAPTER III.

VALUATION OF PROPERTY.

BEFORE property can be assessed for the payment of rates and taxes, it must be valued according to certain prescribed rules, the observance of which makes the property immediately liable to assessment.

As the method of valuation of property differs in the United Kingdom, a comparison of the different systems may be useful.

The English and Scotch Acts dealing with the subject embody much that may be desired, yet it is apparently merely provisional. The preambles of the principal Acts are unquestionably sound and, if acted upon, are well calculated to effect the object in view, namely, a uniform valuation. But the details to be observed by valuators in attaining this object, when brought to practice have, to some extent, been found defective.

Poor rates are of so ancient an origin in England, and the parish vestry was found so convenient an organisation, that a number of other rates, for purposes wholly unconnected with the relief of the poor, are assessed and collected with the poor rate.

The valuation list for poor law purposes in England thus became conclusive for the great majority of local rates, *i.e.*, for the poor rate and all those levied on the basis of the poor rate, including borough and urban sanitary rates, and also highway rates. Besides the valuation for poor rate, there are (outside London) separate and independent valuations for county and other (*e.g.*, sewer) rates, and for property tax.

The County rate is assessed by the County Council, and the property tax is assessed by the Commissioners under the Income Tax Acts. By the Municipal Corporation Act, 1882, if the council of a borough think that the valuation list for poor rate is not a fair criterion of value, they may cause an independent valuation to be made. Similarly in other cases.

The ordinary mode of valuation in England is, however, under the Union Assessment Act, 1862 - 1880, which applies to all parishes in a union under the Poor Law Amendment Acts, and may also be applied by order of the Local Government Board to other parishes, whether under separate boards of guardians or in union under any local Act.

Under several local Acts there are a number of

places excepted from the operations of the Union
Assessment Committee Acts, such as Liverpool,
Manchester, and Birmingham. In separate parishes
not under the Union Assessment Acts, or a local
Act, there are no valuation lists properly so called,
but the assessment is made by the overseers, and
is subject to appeal to the Justices. In these cases,
however, a general survey and valuation of property
rateable in the parish may be made at any time on
application of the overseers by order of the Local
Government Board.

The valuation list of each parish is made by the
overseers, who are the principal officers of the
parish. They are appointed annually by the
justices. They number from two to four, but in
small places a single overseer only is appointed.
Anyone can be appointed, but they ought to be
good and substantial householders. The appointment of a labourer as overseer was held to be good
in the case of a rural parish ; but it was at the
same time stated that such an appointment might
be improper in a place where there were many
opulent farmers. Service of the office is com-
pulsory, subject to appeal and to various exemptions and disqualifications. The guardians of
every union annually appoint an Assessment Committee out of their own members. If the union is
conterminous with a municipal borough, the

council of the borough may, on the invitation of the guardians, appoint an equal or less number of councillors to be members of the committee.

The overseers in every parish prepare a list, which is ordinarily a copy of the last approved valuation list, with such alterations (if any) as the overseers think proper to make, and after publication it is transmitted to the assessment committee. The committee hear and determine objections made by any aggrieved person, and make such alterations as they think fit, or employ a person to value generally or in any special case. When satisfied, the committee approve of and sign the list, and upon delivery to the overseers it becomes the valuation list in force, and, as before stated, becomes the legal basis for the poor rate and the majority of the local rates which are levied upon the same basis.

The valuation list is a statement of the gross estimated rental and rateable value of all rateable property in the parish. By the Assessments Act of 1836 every poor rate must be made "upon an estimate of the net annual value of the several hereditaments rated thereunto ; that is to say, of the rent at which the same might reasonably be expected to let from year to year, free of all usual tenants' rates and taxes, and the tithe commutation rent charge (if any), and deducting therefrom

the probable average annual cost of the repairs
insurances, and other expenses (if any) necessary
to maintain them in a state to command such
rent," and under the Act of 1869 " rateable value "
means the gross value after deducting the probable
annual average cost of the repairs, insurances, and
other expenses as aforesaid.   By the Act of 1862
every valuation list must also show the " gross
estimated rental," which is defined to be " the rent
at which the hereditament might reasonably be
expected to let from year to year, " free of all
usual tenants' rates and taxes, and tithe commutation rent charge (if any)."   It will be observed
that when calculating the " gross estimated rental "
the deductions permitted when estimating the
" rateable value" are not applicable.

It would appear, therefore, that the amount to
be entered in the valuation list as the " gross
estimated rental " of a hereditament is the sum at
which the hereditament might reasonably be
expected to let from year to year, if the tenant
undertook to pay the usual tenants' rates and taxes,
and tithe commutation rent charges (if any), and
if the landlord undertook to pay the cost of repairs
and insurance, and the other expenses (if any)
necessary to maintain the hereditament in a state
to command such rent.   If the owner undertakes
to pay the usual tenants' rates and taxes, the

amount of those rates and taxes must be deducted from the rent in order to ascertain the gross estimated rental. On the other hand, if the occupier undertakes to execute the repairs, or to defray the cost of insurance, or other expenses necessary to maintain the property in a state to command the same rent, an addition in respect of these expenses should be made to the rent in order to arrive at the gross estimated rental.

In practice, overseers appear to act upon the fact that the rent actually paid is the best criterion of value. It is no doubt *prima facie* the estimate, but it is not conclusive. Take the case of houses let to weekly tenants. The rent charged to the tenant is often in consequence of the frequent changes in the occupation of this class of property, the loss of rent which those changes involve, and the trouble attending the collection of the rent, at a higher rate than the rent which the premises would command if let on an annual tenancy. When the weekly rent gives an amount for the year in excess of the rent at which the hereditament might reasonably be expected to let from year to year—that is to say, on an annual tenancy—it would appear that a proportionate reduction should be made to arrive at the gross estimated rental.

Similarly in Scotland. Section 6 of the Valuation Act, 1854, enacts that, " In estimating the yearly value of lands and heritages under this Act the same shall be taken to be the rent at which, one year with another, such lands and heritages might in their actual state be reasonably expected to let from year to year ; and, where such lands and heritages consist of woods, copse, or underwood, the yearly value of same shall be taken to be the rent at which such lands and heritages might in their actual state be reasonably expected to let from year to year as pasture or grazing lands ; and where such lands and heritages are *boná fide* let for a yearly rent, conditioned as the fair annual value thereof without grassum or consideration other than the rent, such rent shall be deemed and taken to be the yearly rent or value of such lands and heritages in terms of this Act. Provided always, that if such lands and heritages be let upon a lease the stipulated duration of which is more than twenty-one years from the date of entry under the same, or in the case of minerals more than thirty-one years from the date of such entry, the rent payable under such lease shall not necessarily be assessed as the yearly rent or value of such lands and heritages ; but such yearly rent or value shall be ascertained in terms of this Act irrespective of the amount of rent payable under such lease, and the lessee under such lease shall be deemed and taken to be also the proprietor of such lands and heritages in the sense of this Act, but shall be entitled to relief from the actual proprietor thereof, and to deduction from the rent payable by him to such actual proprietor of such proportion of all assessments laid on or upon the valuations of such lands and heritages made under this Act, and payable by such lessee, as proprietor in the sense of this Act, as shall correspond to the rent payable by such lessee to such actual proprietor as compared with the amount of such valuation."

Section 42 defines the property rateable. " Lands and heritages shall extend to and include all lands, houses, shootings, and deer forests, where such shootings or deer forests are actually let ; fishings, woods, copse, and underwood, from which revenue is actually derived ; ferries, piers, harbours, quays, wharves, docks, canals, railways, mines, minerals, quarries, coalworks, waterworks, lime-works, brickworks, ironworks, gasworks, factories, and all buildings and pertinents thereof, and all machinery fixed or attached to any lands or heritages."

By the Act of 1886 the condition that shootings and deer forests must be actually let before they become rateable was repealed, and the words " are actually let " in the Act of 1854 struck out.

Now if the rent-roll of the rateable property above described is to be taken for the actual valuation as here stated, why go through the form of a valuation at all? Lands of the same quality, and yielding the same amount of produce when similarly husbanded, may be let from year to year in adjoining estates or townlands on very different terms, as the valuators in such cases are guided only by terms agreed on by the landlord and tenant in returning the valuation of those lands—a valuation, be it remembered, that forms the basis of taxation.

It is true the Select Committee on Rating and Valuation in Scotland, which reported in 1890, stated that they saw no cause to recommend that any other basis should be adopted in place of the lettable value. They stated in their report that it seemed reasonable that the proprietor should be taxed upon what he receives in respect of his heritable property, as it might be assumed that he obtains as high a rent as he reasonably could, while the lessee endeavours to get the right of occupancy as cheaply as possible ; so that, where the subject is let, no better test of its value for rating purposes could be suggested than the actual rent.

However, such a system is defective, since it has been considered by those fully competent to judge of such matters that no valuation should be affected by any private contract made between landlord and tenant.

As regards the provision in the latter portion of

the sixth section of the Scottish Act, it was generally supposed that it was introduced with the view
of preventing the assessor from departing in his
valuation from the rent stipulated in the lease on
account of any rise or fall, from natural causes, in
the letting value of the lands and heritages during
its currency, or owing to voluntary outlay by the
tenant in improving a farm or other holding, in
which outlay he hoped to recoup himself before the
expiry of the lease. But the provision has received
a much wider application by the decisions of the
Courts.

It was mentioned before the Select Committee
that it had been held that where a tenant takes a
piece of ground or other holding on a lease for not
more than twenty-one years, and erects buildings
upon it, the annual value of the buildings, however
great, cannot be entered in the valuation roll
during the currency of the lease, if the letting,
when the lease was entered into, was a *bonâ fide* one,
and without grassum or consideration other than
rent ; and that it had further been decided that
where a lessee under such a lease sublets the
holding, the rent payable under the principal lease,
not the rent payable under the sub-lease, must be
entered in the valuation roll. It was proved—the
committee state—that many thousands of pounds
of rental or annual value, especially in great towns,

F

escape valuation and local taxation under this statutory provision, as it has been authoritatively interpreted. With a view to effect a remedy, the Committee suggested either that in such cases all structural erections, alterations or improvements during the term of the lease be taken into account in estimating the yearly value, and the landlord to have recourse to the tenant or occupier for the increase thus caused in the valuation, or that the tenant who had made the erections be assessed as proprietor in respect of the increase of value thereby caused, and thus avoid the difficulty of charging the true proprietor with the rates in the first instance, and giving him recourse against the tenant for his portion of the rates.

Valuators in England and Scotland being numerous, and acting simultaneously in different districts, the chances of having them skilful and impartial are diminished. Inequalities must also necessarily arise from the different judgments of so many individuals acting separately and independent of each other ; and being subject to yearly election it can hardly be expected that there is absent that certain degree of favour which most men who act in offices of this nature are found to exercise towards their connections, friends, or patrons. Extreme accuracy cannot be expected in valuations under such conditions.

In Scotland, again, under Section 36 of the Act
of 1845, power is given to the parochial boards to
classify lands. The section runs—"That where
the one half of any assessment is imposed on the
owners, and the other half on the tenants or occupants of lands and heritages, it shall be lawful
for the parochial board of supervision to determine
and direct that the lands and heritages may be
distinguished into two or more separate classes,
according to the purposes for which such lands are
used and occupied, and to fix such rate of assessment upon the tenants or occupants of each class
respectively as to such board may seem just and
equitable."

The power of classification is separate and
distinct from the "deductions" which are to be
allowed in estimating the annual value of the lands
and heritages. But the arrangements regarding
classification are defective, as they are only per-
missive, and there is no standard of uniformity.
The classification varies in nearly every country,
and the grouping of the different kinds of property,
Mr. Lamond writes, is often absurd—almost as
absurd if they had been drawn by chance out of a
hat.

It appears that only 186 parishes have classifications under this section, while 693 parishes have
no such classification. In many cases the character

F 2

of the properties in the parishes has greatly changed since the dates at which classifications were made, and in many cases these old classifications have become inapplicable to the present condition of the property in the parish. Thus it was stated before the Select Committee, that it appeared in a recent case that in 1846 a parochial board adopted a classification of lands and heritages for occupants' rates into (1) land let for farming ; (2) houses let as dwelling-houses and shops ; the former being assessed at one-sixth of their value, and the latter at their full value. At that date there were no railways in the parish, but a railway was constructed in 1850. It was assessed in Class 2 at its full value, but in 1886, on appeal, the Court held that the classification was invalid on the ground that it was not exhaustive of the lands and heritages in the parish, and that until a legal and valid classification had been adopted and approved, the company were entitled to interdict against the parochial board levying from them, as occupants, higher rates than were imposed on any other occupant of lands and heritages in the parish.

The great variety and arbitrary character of the existing classifications is well illustrated by a return obtained in 1886 (Sessional Paper No. 154 of 1886).

The Select Committee stated that the undoubted

evil thus existing should be remedied either (1) by giving an initiative in altering classifications to the board of supervision upon the representation of any ratepayer in a parish, or (2) by providing for a statutory classification such as is done in the Poor Law Assessment (Scotland) Act, 1861.

In Ireland a better system prevails. Under the Valuation of Ireland Act, 1852, a general valuation of Ireland was established. The valuation is controlled by a central authority in Dublin, with valuators and a staff acting upon the same principles and carrying out similar instructions for their guidance.

The valuation is general, for all other systems of valuation have been superseded by it; and it may be termed just, because it is based on such principles of justice and equity that the wealthy nobleman and struggling farmer are treated alike in the administration of the laws laid down for the guidance of those appointed to value their holdings.

The principle on which the valuation was made, as regards land, differs from that on which land is valued in England and Scotland, where, we have seen, the valuation is based on an estimate of the rental. The principle on which the valuation was made in Ireland is set out in the 11th Section of the Act, every tenement being valued in the actual

condition in which it was found. The section
runs as follows :—

" That in every valuation hereafter to be made,
or to be carried on or completed, under the provisions of this Act, the Commissioners of Valuation
shall cause every tenement or rateable hereditament hereinafter specified to be separately valued,
and such valuation, in regard to land, shall be
made upon an estimate of the net annual value
thereof, with reference to the average prices of the
several articles of agricultural produce hereinafter
specified ; all peculiar local circumstances, in each
case, being taken into consideration, and all rates,
taxes, and public charges, if any (except tithe rent
charge), being paid by the tenant. . . . And
such valuation, in regard to houses and buildings,
shall be made upon an estimate of the net annual
value thereof; that is to say, the rent for which,
one year with another, the same might, in its
actual state, be reasonably expected to let from
year to year, the probable average annual cost of
repairs, insurance, and other expenses (if any)
necessary to maintain the hereditament in its
actual state, and all rates, taxes, and public
charges, if any (except tithe rent charge), being
paid by the tenant."

Section 12 defines what are to be valued, as
follows :—

" For the purposes of this Act, the following
hereditaments shall be deemed to be rateable
hereditaments—viz. : all lands, buildings, and
open mines ; all commons and rights of common,
and all other profits to be had or received or taken
out of any land ; and in case of land or buildings
used exclusively for public, scientific, or charitable
purposes, as hereinafter specified, half the annual
rent derived by the owner or other person interested in the same, so far as the same can or
may be ascertained by the said Commissioners of
Valuation ; and all rights of fishery ; all canals,
navigations, and all rights of navigation ; all railways and tramroads ; all rights of way, and other
rights or easements over land, and tolls levied in
respect of such rights and easements, and all other
tolls ; provided always that no turf bog or turf
bank used for the exclusive purpose of cutting or
saving turf, or for making turf-mould therefrom, or
for fuel or manure, shall be deemed rateable under
this Act unless a rent or other valuable consideration shall be payable for the same ; and provided also that no mines hereinafter to be opened
shall be deemed rateable until seven years after
the same shall have been opened ; and mines
bonâ fide re-opened after the same shall have been
bonâ fide abandoned shall be deemed an opening
of mines within the meaning of this Act."

And by Section 7 of the Valuation Revision
Act, 1860, directions were given that "in making
the valuation of any mill or manufactory, or building erected or used for any such purpose, the
Commissioners of Valuation shall in each such
case value the water or other motive power thereof,
but shall not take into account the value of any
machinery therein, save only such as shall be
erected and used for the production of motive
power."

The difficulties that naturally present themselves to a valuator are manifold where acres of
land have to be valued, and a relative valuation
maintained throughout every townland and tenement in the country, and in such a manner that
the interest of all parties might be fairly consulted
and general satisfaction given. To do this, he
should be first acquainted with the chemical com-
position of the soil, the climate that influenced it,
the proximity of lands to the sea and market
towns, the annual produce it yielded, and the price
that that produce brought on an average for a
certain number of years. In fine, he should become acquainted with every circumstance by which
property was affected before he could submit to
the public a valuation list that was to become the
basis of taxation. To help towards the removal
of these difficulties, and to establish, so far as

practicable, a uniform system, a scale of prices
of agricultural produce was agreed upon by the
legislature as a standard according to which the
tenement valuation was made.

The following is the scale of prices per cwt.
of 112 lbs. in the Act of 1852 :—

					£	s.	d.
Wheat	...	...	...	...	0	7	6
Oats...		...	...	...	0	4	10
Barley		...			0	5	6
Flax ...		...			2	9	0
Butter	...	...	...		3	5	4
Beef...	...	...	...	...	1	15	6
Mutton	...	...	...	...	2	1	0
Pork...	...	...	...	...	1	12	0

The valuation of house property is based on a
principle equally just as that of lands, and as
regards the value of mills there are many conditions requiring due and careful consideration,
among which may be classed (1) the horse-power
and the circumstances affecting it, (2) the quality
of the machinery erected and used for the motive
power, (3) the nature and quantity of the work
done by the mill, and (4) the distance from town
or market. To determine the horse-power, the
following data was found : (1) the mean velocity
of the stream, (2) the section of water, and (3) the
fall. Formerly, under the Act of 1852, the water-

power was only to be valued according to the time
it was actually used, but the section of the Act of
1860 referred to before repealed this limitation.

In estimating the value of mines, lengthened
experience is required in the valuator. All expenses of working, and the proceeds of sales for
three or four years, are first ascertained previous to
any valuation being made ; and mines that have
not been worked for seven years previous are, as
the Act states, subject to no rate whatever.

In the case of railways, etc., the "rateable
hereditament," says Sir Richard Griffith, " is the
land which is to be valued in its existing state, as
part of a railway, etc., at the rent it would fetch
under the conditions stated in the Act. The
profits are not directly rateable themselves, but
they enter most materially into the question of the
amount of the rate upon the land, by affecting the
rent which it would fetch, or which a tenant would
give for the railway, etc., not simply as land, but
as a railway, etc., with its peculiar adaptation to the
production of profit, and that rent must be ascertained by reference to the use of it (with engines,
carriages, etc., the trading stock), in the same way
as the rent of a farm would be calculated by
reference to uses of it with cattle, crops, etc. (likewise trading stock). In neither case would the
rent be calculated on the dry possession of the

land without reference to the power of using it, and in both cases the profits are derived not only from the stock, but from the land so used and occupied. It will be necessary, therefore, to ascertain the gross receipts, for a year or two, taken at each station along the line, also the amount of receipts arising from the intermediate traffic between the several stations; from the total amount of such receipts the following deductions are to be made—viz.: (1) interest on capital, (2) tenants' profits, (3) depreciation of stock, (4) working expenses, (5) value of stations."

The values of railway-station houses are returned separately.

Though provision has been made for the annual revision of the valuation "of the rateable tenements and hereditaments, the limits whereof shall become altered, and also of those the net annual value of which is liable to frequent alteration"—such as fisheries, railways, canals, tolls of bridges, mines, gas and water works, and buildings —there is no power to disturb the general basis of the valuation as fixed under the Act of 1852, without a resort to the provision contained in Section 34.

This section enables the Lord Lieutenants, "at or after the termination of 14 years from the period of the final completion of the first general tenement valuation," if he shall think fit to do so, and, "on an application by the grand jury of the county," to cause a new valuation to be made, and so from time to time, after the expiration of every succeeding period of 14 years.

Up to the present time, however, no such application has been submitted, and, as a consequence, no such re-valuation has taken place in any county in Ireland, though, as a matter of fact, a considerably longer interval than 14 years has elapsed since the completion of the existing valuation, and which in a few places, having been made at a period of depression and general derangement, has ceased, it is alleged, to furnish a reliable criterion of the actual value there, such as by the Act of 1852 would appear to have been contemplated. Yet to a large extent its general accuracy has been prominently evidenced during the sittings of the courts on the fixing of judicial rents.

In the northern counties, where the valuation was brought to a close at a later date, and in the towns, especially in Belfast and the southern portion of Dublin, which has been of recent creation, there is, however, a much nearer approach to general accuracy to be met with.

Since the scale of prices in the Act of 1852 was fixed, considerable changes have taken place in connection with agricultural interests. The value of every kind of produce has altered, and

foreign competition has still further reduced the
value of land.

However, the equity of the principles upon
which the Irish valuation was directed to be made
must be acknowledged by all ; and that such have
been fully and impartially carried out, the owners
and occupiers of house property in the various parts
of Ireland have borne testimony, from time to time,
for the past forty years, by the comparatively few
appeals made against the valuation of tenements
or holdings, and by the fact that the right to
demand a re-valuation has never been exercised.

In Ireland it is held that the grand and funda-
mental principle that should pervade every system
of valuation purporting to be fair and impartial,
should be to effect in every district of a country
what has been effected in Ireland, namely, a relative scale, based upon the letting value of property
from year to year and not upon the rent that a
tenant may be obliged to pay.

The several rates and taxes made for public
purposes are an equal poundage rate, calculated on
the valuation made in manner described, with two
exceptions, however, viz. :—First, under the provisions of the Towns Improvement Act, 1854, in
which a distinction is made between different
classes of property in regard to their liability to
assessment for the purposes of that Act, Section 62

providing as to this as follows :—" For the purpose
of any rate to be made or levied under the provisions of this Act, or of any Act incorporated
herewith, all lands used as arable, meadow, or
pasture grounds only, or as woodlands or market
gardens, or nursery grounds, and all lands covered
with water, and used as a canal, and any towing
path to the same, and all lands used as a railway
constructed under the powers of any Act of Parliament for public conveyance, shall be assessed
and liable in the proportion of one-fourth part only
of the net annual value of such lands respectively."
And, secondly, under the Lighting and Cleansing
Act, 1828, by which a graduated scale of rating is
applied to tenements according to valuation—that is
to say, occupiers rated under £5 are exempt from
the improvement rate, and not only the occupiers,
but also the premises. Then from £5 to £10 the
rate is only 6d. in the £ ; from £10 to £20, not
exceeding 9d. ; and from £20 upwards, 1s. However, there are only three towns now under this
latter Act.

The result of the authorities upon the exemption
from rateability would seem to be, that premises
are exempted from rateability, first, upon the
ground that they are used or occupied " altogether "
for public purposes ; i.e., (1) Where they are occupied for the benefit of every member of the com-

munity ; for then the public are the occupiers, and
the public cannot be rated ; (2) When they are
used or occupied by the Sovereign, or by the official
servants of the Sovereign for and on her behalf;
secondly, upon the ground that they are used or
occupied "exclusively" for charitable purposes, i.e.,
when nothing is earned, directly or indirectly, by
such use and occupation, however small the amount
so earned may be, even though it produce no profit,
and though it be applied to the charitable purposes
of the particular institution ; thirdly, when they are
used and occupied by a society established exclusively for the purpose of science, literature, or the
fine arts, and the society has complied with the
requirements of the law relating to such institutions.

In England, upon the construction of the
statute of Elizabeth, railways are rateable as
"land," and canals as "land covered with water";
in Ireland and Scotland they are specially enumerated as rateable hereditaments. In England nothing is rateable but "land," so that incorporeal
hereditaments, if severed from the "land," are not
assessable to the poor rate ; while in Ireland "any
right over land" is rateable. A lessee or grantee,
therefore, of any incorporeal hereditament, such as
a right of shooting, fishing, tolls, etc., severed from
the soil, cannot in Ireland escape from rating, as he
may in England.

Manufacturers throughout England who use machinery for carrying on their industries have, for some years past, complained of the action taken by local authorities in trying to bring within their rating powers various classes of machinery which at one time were not thought to be rateable. A series of decisions of the courts of law have drawn the net closer and closer around the manufacturer, until, instead of it being exceptional for machinery to be rated, he sees before him no chance of any machinery escaping from rating. At one time it was considered that only machinery fixed to the freehold in such a manner as to pass in a demise with it was rateable. The criterion, in fact, was whether the machinery was in law realty or personalty. If the machinery was merely a tenant's fixture, which he could remove at his pleasure, it was considered to come within the terms of the Act of 1840, which did away altogether with the rating of personal chattels, and rendered it unlawful to tax any inhabitant in respect of his ability derived from profits of stock-in-trade or any other property. But it is represented that the law was, little by little, strained against the owners of machinery "attached" or "annexed" to the premises. Several cases have been decided wherein it was laid down that in estimating the rateable value of premises used as a manufactory, machinery and plant placed therein, for the purpose of making them fit as premises for such manufactory, are to be taken into account as enhancing the value of the hereditament, although such machinery and plant remain personal property, and are not physically attached to the premises. Manufacturers see in the cases already decided upon the subject the possibility of an enormous extension of the rateable value of all mills and factories which contain machinery of any class fitted for carrying on the business for which the premises are used. But apart from what they allege to be the want of equity in rating machinery placed by them on the premises for the purpose of their business, they are more concerned with the uncertainty which prevails as to how far the law, as determined by the judges, will be carried into effect by the assessment committees of particular unions. The Select Committee who reported on the Rating of Machinery Bill of 1887 were agreed that the practice with respect to the rating of machinery had widely differed in various parts of the country, and that without further legislation it would continue to do so. They strongly upheld the principle that uniformity should prevail throughout the country, and recommended the Government to deal comprehensively with the whole question of rating with the least possible delay.

G

No legislation has, however, taken place on the subject, although Bills have been introduced from time to time, and deputations have waited upon the Ministers in power both for and against the measures proposed.

Instances of the anomalous state of affairs which now prevails are numerous. Lace machinery, we are told, is not rated in Nottingham, but is in some other towns. It is not often rated at anything like its value, as a compromise is arrived at with the manufacturer; and if he shows any inclination to fight, he is likely enough to be let off altogether.

Those rating authorities who have taken advantage of the law, as expounded by the judges, to largely widen the area of rating are not likely to view with equanimity any measure so far as it is likely to curtail the rateable value from which they raise their revenue. From their point of view, the uncertainty which now prevails is not so great an evil as a material shifting of the incidence of local burdens. In one large manufacturing city it is alleged that such a measure would be to diminish the rateable value to the extent of £30,000, and about £8,000 now paid in rates by manufacturers would be levied on other contributors, chiefly consisting of the already overburdened small shopkeepers. However, uniformity throughout the country is desirable on every ground, as the present lack of uniformity necessarily leads to uncertainty, which is not satisfactory to those either for or against the rating of machinery. We have seen that under the Irish Valuation Act machinery is not to be taken into account unless it is erected and used as a motive power.

It is very significant that Parliament has not placed any reliance upon the valuation lists prepared under the Union Assessment Acts for imperial purposes, or under certain circumstances for the purposes of the county rates in England.

The Clerk of the Assessment Committees has, indeed, to send annually to the clerks of the County Councils copies of the totals of the valuation lists, but they do not bind the County Councils in preparing a basis for the county rates, as they can make an independent valuation of any parish, etc., in their county, which then forms the basis for the county rate. Even for borough rates the valuation lists are not necessarily conclusive. It is a matter of notoriety that there are many unions where the valuation lists are in a most unsatisfactory state, both from the point of view of comparing union with union, and from the point of view of individual assessments in the same parish. Systematic under-assessment widely prevails, as may be seen by comparing the totals sent by the clerks and the

G 2

actual figures which formerly the justices, and now the County Councils, find it necessary to adopt for the county rate.

The Inland Revenue officers proceed quite independently of the parochial authorities in making their assessment for the imperial taxes.

In 1890 the gross value in the income tax assessment under Schedule A was, for the whole of England and Wales, £164,541,187; but the rateable value by the assessment committees was only £150,485,974. In Ireland a nearer approach to accuracy is made, for in the same year the total poor law valuation was £13,994,254 and the income tax assessment under Schedule A was £13,600,828.

In England, even if those unions were deducted in which the valuation lists were well made, the figures would show a still more startling discrepancy for the remaining unions. In this respect the rural unions are the greatest offenders. It is evident, therefore, that the restricted purposes and machinery of the Assessment Committee Acts want extending, and strengthening into a system which shall furnish reliable values for the purposes not alone of local but also of imperial taxation.

A common measure of rateability or taxable value of property is a question which has excited some interest, and has engaged the attention of

the British Association for the Advancement of
Science. A committee of the Association have
issued a report upon the subject, which is worthy
of perusal and study.

Values are the object matters of taxation ; their
measurement and comparison are the necessary
condition of its equal incidence; and measurements
with unequal measures are like weighings with
unjust balances. Taxation, however pure its
intention, without a common measure of value is
what navigation is without sextant and chrono-
meter.

There are two methods of general valuation—
Capital value and Usable value. Measurements of
the value of things (employing this word "things"
as inclusive of land, houses, labour, stock, etc.) may
have reference to their absolute worth or their
temporary uses. They may have reference to
their property, capital, or absolute values, or to
their products, profits, or annual values. The one
measure is exemplified in contracts of sale and
purchase ; the other in contracts of letting and
hiring. Each has its special advantages and
special applications. Capital or absolute value
is applied to the assessment of probate and legacy
duty ; usable value in the assessments of local
taxation and in those of the imperial income tax.
The idea of capital value is tolerably well fixed,

but that of usable or lettable value is indefinite.
Usable value is, or is equivalent to, the consideration paid for the income received from the use of
things. This consideration, however, may be paid
under such totally different conditions of contract
that, unless these conditions are first assimilated,
the payments, regarded as measures either of the
values of things or of the abilities of their owners,
are worse than useless—they are misleading.

Things having a use, and hence capable of becoming sources of income, are all, by the very
nature of the process, liable to outgoings ; some
more, some less. Production involves productive
consumption. Efficiency implies cost- cost, for
the most part, of insurance against risk; of repairs ;
of necessary depreciation. But the user of a thing,
be it land, a house, labour or stock, may engage
for its use with or without liability to these outgoings ; their cost may be borne by the user or by
the owner, or they may be divided between the
two in any proportion that convenience may direct.
The user may bear repairs, and the owner natural
risk and depreciation, or the user may bear all and
the owner none, or the user none and the owner
all, the consideration given (the income received)
of course varying accordingly. Were the things
valued by absolute sale or capitalisation, all the
incidents, whether of efficiency or cost, plus or

minus, would be wholly and uniformly included, and the test would fix the things' relative positions. In valuations by uses, however, it is evident that these incidents are not as a matter of practice uniformly included, and the valuation founded upon unfixed conditions can fix nothing; its possibilities of variation are co-extensive with those of free contract itself.

As the inequalities of valuation arise from the different conditions in respect to outgoings under which the various incomes are calculated, the remedy must be the assimilation of these conditions ; and the case of principal and interest, which in one respect may be regarded as a common expression of sources and uses generally, may be employed as a precedent. Interest is the income from a thing free of outgoings. It leaves the thing or its capital value unimpaired. The extension of this idea to revenues or incomes in general is simply the universal deduction from them of their productive outgoings, equivalent to the general restoration of the capital values of their respective sources. Under such a *régime*, returnable and taxable income would not be land rent, house rent, mine royalties, labour wages, but land rent minus land outgoings, house rent minus house outgoings, mine royalties minus mine outgoings, labour wages minus labour outgoings ; and similarly with terminable annuities and profits of business, the outgoings, however, being in all cases only the necessary ones of the production. The result thus obtained would be what by analogy may be called the interest value of the various sources; and such interest value of land, of houses, of labour, of stock, etc., would be the common measure required, and would represent the returnable income for taxation.

The question now arises, Are such deductions of outgoings on the sources of income and the determination of the interest value practicable? As we are only concerned, at present, with one particular class of capital—real property—the different Valuation Acts hereinbefore referred to have, so far, practically solved the problem. A difference will, however, be found in the nature of the deductions permitted. Interest value is capital value for a year; but the capital out of which this interest value is derived may determine. It may be held only for a limited tenure, and its capital value may be less than that held permanently. Land is permanent in its nature, but houses are not. The latter depreciate in value and wear out, and this fact appears to have been carefully considered in the Irish Valuation Act. Under this Act, consideration is to be given to "other expenses (if any) necessary to maintain the hereditament in its actual state"—that is, to the expenses necessary to permanently maintain the source of income in its present condition. But such houses may only be held by the party assessed for a limited tenure, and its capital value may be much less than if it was of a fee-simple tenure. In such cases the interest value for taxation is disproportionate, as interest value presupposes permanency in tenure or in the existence of the capital.

CHAPTER IV.

OCCUPIER AND OWNER.

IN the second chapter, the incidence of our local taxation as it affected a certain kind of property was considered ; but there is a more material distinction still, and that is as the incidence affects the class of persons assessed in respect of such property.

The law with regard to the principles of rating in the United Kingdom is extremely intricate and technical, and as it is beyond our scope to treat of it in detail, we will describe only its general tendencies and provisions.

In reality, it is a somewhat rough way of taxing the land and buildings of the country through the occupier. It has been said that " the whole capacity of the parish is to be called in aid of the poor of the parish," but under every form of our local government the occupier is the person primarily liable for the payment of the rates, save in those excepted cases where, under both the Poor Law and Municipal Law, the owner is substituted as regards all tenements below a certain specific valuation.

We have seen that the poor rate is the principal rate in England, and that the majority of the local rates are assessed and collected with it. The incidence of all is therefore the same, and the unfortunate occupier is the individual whose back has to bear the burden which grows heavier and heavier each year according as the exigency of the public service requires new works to be executed and new duties to be performed. In Ireland the poor rate is separately collected, and the other local rates and taxes are assessed and collected by the authorities levying them. As against the practice in England, in Ireland, therefore, a distinct machinery is found for the assessment and collection of each separate rate and tax.

The cases in which the owner is rated and assessed for the local rates and taxes are not very numerous.

In England under the Poor Law Amendment Act, 1819, it is enacted that it shall be lawful " to resolve and direct that the owner or owners of all houses, apartments or dwellings, being the immediate lessor or lessors of the actual occupier or occupiers, which shall respectively be let to the occupiers thereof at any rent or rate not exceeding £20 nor less than £6 by the year for any less term than one year, or on any agreement by which the rents shall be reserved or made payable at any shorter period than three months, shall be assessed to the rates for the relief of the poor for or in respect of such houses, apartments, or dwellings, and the outhouses and curtilages thereof, instead of the actual occupiers."

In Ireland the occupation of a holding imposes on the occupier the immediate liability to the payment of the rate, and confers on him, in turn, a personal right to set off against his landlord a proportion of what he has, as such occupier, paid. The principle of occupation is departed from in cases of small holdings where the whole of the rateable hereditaments in the union occupied by any one person does not exceed £4, if the occupier has no greater estate therein than a tenancy from year to year, or holds by lease subsequent to 1843.

In such cases the poor rate is made on the "Immediate Lessor." In Dublin the owner is liable to the whole of the poor rate where the premises are valued under £8.

Again, where any house is let in separate apartments or lodgings, the occupier of such apartment or lodgings is not liable to the poor rate, but the rate in respect of the whole house is made upon the immediate lessor under whom such apartments or lodgings are held. In Dublin, when the premises are assessed at £8 or under, and elsewhere under £10, the municipal rates are levied off the owner, and likewise when the premises are let to weekly or monthly tenants. In all other cases, however, in Ireland the occupier is primarily liable for the rates. In certain boroughs in the United Kingdom exceptional, and a different, law may exist, but the foregoing is the general law, and sufficiently enunciates the partial way in which owners of property have been treated by the legislature.

The principle, however, seems to have been adopted in Scotland that a portion of the local taxation ought to be thrown upon the owner. This is, practically, the universal principle.

We have seen that under the Poor Law (Scotland) Act one half of the gross sum to be raised for poor rates is levied from the owners, and the other half from the occupiers, but it does not follow that the two portions are precisely the same in any particular case. This arises from the fact that, as regards the occupiers' half, the Act permits the classification which we have already explained. The classification arises from the nature of the occupation, the principle of which is that all residential occupancies shall be charged at a high rate, whilst an occupancy merely for the purpose of business or manufacture should be charged at a comparatively low rate. Farms, of course, are assessed, where the classification is made, at a low rate compared with dwelling-houses, and the classification only becomes necessary where the parish is of a mixed nature, because if a parish is composed entirely of land there is no use for the classification at all. If it is composed partly of land and partly of houses, the classification is deemed necessary in point of equity. As we have before stated, the classification is sanctioned by the Act, but it is not enjoined, and the greater number of parishes do not establish it. The county rates in Scotland are levied from the owners, but as regards the road maintenance assessment portion of the rate the owner can recover one half of such assessment from the occupier. This also applies to the cattle disease assessment when levied.

Like the county rate, the Scottish owner has to bear portion of the borough rates. Thus the police assessment, which includes watching, lighting, water, and certain criminal expenditure, is levied entirely upon the occupier ; the sewer rate is levied upon the owner ; the public health rate is charged upon the occupier, and the prisons and roads assessment upon the owner and occupier equally. Of these assessments a separate and distinct collection is made from the owner and

occupier, and the latter is not called upon to pay
the full amount and deduct it from the landlord.

In Glasgow, under the Police Act, 1866, occupiers of rateable hereditaments of the yearly rent
or value of over £4 are liable for the assessment,
and in Ireland, in the case of poor law rating, the
occupier is entitled to deduct from each pound of
rent paid by him one half of the poundage rate
(not exceeding in any case one-half of the entire
rate paid), while both the county and municipal
rates fall altogether upon the occupier exclusively,
the owners of property, except in the cases mentioned, being entirely relieved from any direct
contribution whatever to the taxation coming
under these heads.

The original Poor Law (Ireland) Act, 1837, not
only expressly provided for the foregoing division
of the rate between the owner and occupier, but
likewise insured that the arrangement should be
practically enforced by rendering all contracts on
the part of the tenant to forego such deductions
null and void—a restriction subsequently and
somewhat unaccountably removed by the Poor
Law (Ireland) Act, 1849.

Under the Land Act (Ireland), 1870, a provision
was for the first time introduced enabling occupiers
" under any tenancy whatever created after the
passing of this Act " to make in regard to county

cess a deduction from rent similar to that always allowed to poor rate, but this was not accompanied by any restriction similar to that which, it has been seen, accompanied the original Poor Law Act, and as the result of any person's experience who has made careful inquiries, and who has had opportunities of noting the contracts of tenants for nearly every class of real property, it may be confidently affirmed that, with few exceptions, the provision referred to has remained almost absolutely inoperative, tenants in some cases being found willing to forego this claim in preference to the alternative arrangement of submitting to a corresponding increase in the amount of rent, and in others having had to forego the claim whether they liked it or not, without any corresponding reduction in the rent.

Judicial rents were now fixed in Ireland on the assumption that the tenant of the holding to which the Land Acts apply is to pay the whole county cess as well as half the poor rate, except in cases of tenants of holdings rated below £4.

The county or grand jury cess in Ireland is applied to the purposes for which the county rate, hundred rate, and police rate, are applied in England. Unlike the system in England, in Ireland, as before stated, no other rates are included in and paid out of the poor rate, but a large number of assessments are put upon the county cess, which is the most important in rural districts.

In certain cases, again, the owner may become directly liable to the payment of the rates by compounding for them. Thus, if a person owns a number of cottages, and he undertakes to pay the rates thereon, whether they be all occupied or not, the local authorities are at liberty to "compound" with him, and to deduct one fourth from the amount he would otherwise have to pay, such deduction being in contemplation of the contingency of some of the buildings being from time to time without tenants.

Under the Poor Rate Assessment and Collection Act (England), 1869, it is provided, "In case the rateable value of any hereditament does not exceed £20, if the hereditament is situate in the metropolis; or £13, if situate in any parish wholly or partly within the borough of Liverpool; or £10, if situate in any parish wholly or partly within the city of Manchester or the borough of Birmingham; or £8, if situate elsewhere, and the owner of such hereditament is willing to enter into an agreement in writing with the overseers, to become liable to them for the poor rates assessed in respect of such hereditaments, for any term not being less than one year from the date of such

H

agreement, and to pay the poor rates whether the hereditaments be occupied or not, the overseers may, subject nevertheless to the control of the vestry, agree with the owner to receive the rates from him, and to allow him a commission not exceeding 25 per cent. on the amount thereof."

There does not appear to be any liberty to compound in the Irish Acts, but under the Dublin Corporation Act, 1890 (Section 75), where premises do not exceed the annual value of £8, and are suitable as dwellings for, and are occupied by, artisans or labourers, the local authority can compound with the owner for the municipal rates on a reduced estimate of the net annual value, but not less than two-thirds nor more than four-fifths of such net value. The whole year rates, however, on such reduced estimate must be paid on or before 1st March in each year. A landlord who compounds for the payment of rates is in a similar position to the landlord of tenements which are wholly let out in apartments, he being in both cases the person whom the authorities look to in the first instance for payment.

Both in cases of compounding, and where a landlord expressly undertakes to pay the rates (needless to say, a very rare arrangement), such owner is answerable to the tenant for any consequences of his failure to pay ; and he is bound to

submit to a deduction from rent of any amount
which the tenant may be called upon to pay. This
liberty to the tenant to deduct the amount paid by
him is necessary; for even though the owner may
compound with the authorities, he may fail to pay,
and should payment not be made from himself or
his property, the property of the tenant becomes
liable for the rates unpaid, to the amount of any
rent which may actually be due.

The power to compound appears to prevail
extensively in England. Before the committee on
town holdings, it was stated that rates were compounded for in Wolverhampton to the extent of
two-thirds of the residential assessment. In Birmingham nearly half a million sterling out of the
whole residential assessment is compounded for,
and that represents at least a half of the total of
such assessment.

Experience has, however, shown that where the
owner is made directly liable for the payment of
the local rates in the cases stated, or elects to
become so by compounding for them, he generally
recoups himself for the amount paid by an increase
in the rent. In such cases he had every opportunity to shift the burden off his own shoulders.
In the case of the small rating, he is aware of his
primary liability, and will consider this in any
contract with the tenant, the occupier, and require

II 2

such a rent as will recoup him for the amount expended.

In case of weekly tenants, and those holding under less than or under a yearly tenancy, an early opportunity is afforded him to readjust the terms of his contract. He has the power to do so, and has always been found disposed to use it.

In every case, therefore, it is the tenant or occupier who pays all the local rates ; either directly or indirectly, in the rent, he has to pay for the premises occupied.

Closely associated with the liability for rates and taxes lies the question of occupancy. The rate is a personal tax in the United Kingdom, although made in respect of real property—that is to say, the rate is not a charge on the land or other property ; but the person occupying it in cases mentioned is personally liable. The circumstances in which the property stands, or the uses to which it is put, may, however, prevent its being actually rated for the time being. Thus property that is unoccupied, e.g., an empty house, is not rateable while it continues empty. Again, property in the occupation of the Crown is not rateable, nor churches, nor museums, etc., under certain circumstances. It is almost impossible to define accurately what is the meaning of occupation; thus, an owner of land is in possession of the minerals underneath, but if he does not dig for them he is not in occupation of them. The owner of an empty house is in the same way, though in legal possession, not in occupation. On the other hand, without legal possession, a person may be in occupation; thus a mere squatter on a common is in occupation of the land he uses. Occupation may be said to involve the idea of control and employment.

We thus see that the person who idly or wantonly suffers his land or house to remain unoccupied and unproductive, as in the case of an owner who looks for a higher rent than a tenant is willing to give, is completely exempted from local burdens, whilst he who applies his capital and energies to the improvement of a neighbourhood, or the encouragement of industry, is hampered at every turn by the additional risk of having his contributions to the local rates augmented to an extent calculated to impair very seriously the advantage of his enterprise.

However, special powers are sometimes given in local Acts to rate the owner for unoccupied premises. Thus, under the Dublin Act, 1890, an owner of unoccupied premises is liable to such items or proportion of the municipal rates as the local authority may determine, but such items or proportion cannot exceed one-third of the municipal rates.

The question of the general rating and taxation of the owner's interest in lands and houses is fast becoming a burning question. The occupier is usually a tenant holding for a short tenure, and who, out of his industry, savings, or public spirit, is engaged in improving the owner's property, and not only bestowing on the owner all the outlay he makes, but, as time goes on, he is regularly paying a rent on the improvements which his rates and taxes have effected.

In other words, the occupiers are, at their own expense, to keep up the letting value of premises for the purpose of occupation. Enormous additional value has been given to the land, and especially to town plots, by the great sanitary and other public improvements. Many of the high rates paid for houses in our large cities and towns are due not to the excellence of a particular site, but to the ability of the occupier. A tradesman, by his energy and enterprise, builds up a valuable business. Immediately that his lease or contract of tenancy expires, the landlord or owner comes down upon him for increased rent before he will consent to grant a renewal, not because his house is worth more than before to other people, but because it is worth more to the tenant; for if he loses that house, he loses all the business connection he has created. The owner, in fact, has got him so that he can enforce the last penny from him. The struggling tradesman or householder is as much in need of protection as any of Her Majesty's subjects. Again, say a new bridge has to be erected. It is clear that the value of the land or houses in the vicinity will be raised in consequence. The occupier, if he has a lease, will get the immediate benefit. The owner will get it at once, by being able to raise the rent if there is no lease. Instances of this can be multiplied, and in any case he will get it in the end.

Considerations such as these have produced in many minds a strong conviction that our artisan population, and the occupiers of houses, daily suffer injustice at the hands of the owners of the soil and of the proprietary interests in houses.

Not alone have local bodies protested against the injustice of saddling occupiers with the entire cost of public improvements, but several committees of the House of Commons have also affirmed such protests.

Sir Thomas Farrer and Professor Rogers impressed upon the recent Town Holdings Committee that the state of public feeling on this subject was such that great danger might result if action were not taken to meet it. The former said that it seemed to him that "if there was one thing in which the voters in London were interested it was this question of rating, and of throwing some part of the incidence of the rates upon the owner. Feeling about it is so strong that, unless something is done to allay that feeling, it may become a very dangerous element."

Professor Rogers agreed that landowners do not bear their proper share of local burdens, and that public opinion was so inflamed on the subject that legislative action was called for, and suggested that the rates should be equally divided between owner and occupier.

The committee finally recommended the course suggested by Professor Rogers, but as regards future contracts only.

The question is not of recent investigation; neither was the Committee on Town Holdings the first to enquire into the subject. So far back as 1870, a Committee on Local Taxation was appointed by a Liberal Government, and, again, in 1878 another committee was appointed by a Conservative administration.

The committee of 1870 was under the presidency of the Right Hon. Mr. Goschen, and included the late Right Hon. W. H. Smith, and amongst other matters reported, "That the existing system of local taxation, under which the exclusive charge

of almost all rates leviable upon rateable property
for current expenditure, as well as for new objects
and permanent works, is placed by law upon
occupiers, while the owners are generally exempt
from any direct or intermediate contribution in
respect of such rates, is contrary to sound policy.

" That, subject to equitable arrangements as
regards existing contracts, the rates should be
collected, as at present, from the occupiers (except
in cases of small tenements), power being given to
the occupier to deduct from his rent the proportion
of the rates to which the owner may be made liable,
and provision being made to render persons having
superior or intermediate interests liable to proportionate deductions from the rents received by
them, as in the case of the income tax, with a like
prohibition against agreements in contravention
of the law."

The Committee of 1878 was under the presidency of the Right Hon. Sir Michael Hicks Beach,
and reported that the arguments urged in support
of a division of the rates were mainly :—

"That it was neither fair nor expedient that
the pressure of taxation when increased should fall
in the first instance solely on one, and that the
poorer, class of the community -viz., the occupiers ;
nor was it wise in the interests of owners of property
that they should not practically feel at the time

the rise and fall of rates, particularly when large expenditure is imminent, much of which was at first met by loans " ; and, further, " that the division of the taxation would be just in itself, and would justify the division of power, and the character of the governing bodies would be raised by the addition of a more educated and independent class of representatives."

This committee finally decided to recommend the proposed division of rates and representation. They did not attempt to define the word " owner," but would include under the name those so included under the Poor Law Acts, provided they resided within twenty miles of the town. The same subject, and the rating of the owner's interest in the land, was touched upon by Mr. Esslemont, M.P., and others, before the Select Committee on Scottish Rating and Valuation in 1888.

These authoritative declarations show that it is not just that occupiers should continue to bear the entire cost, whilst the several proprietary interests reap the maximum of benefit without rendering any assistance or pecuniary contribution towards the projects which lead to the enhancement in the value of their property. In the end the owner suffers for having this advantage, for it prevents him, as it was argued before the different committees, from discerning his interest in the proper administration of local affairs, and emboldens him to neglect his duty in the public service. It is to his interest that the rise and fall of rates should come home directly to him, for then he would be induced to concern himself with the progressive administration of matters in his own locality.

Although the Committee on Town Holdings recommended the division between the occupier and owner for adoption as regards future contracts only, yet, even as regards existing contracts of tenancy, many rates have been established or increased since those contracts were entered into, and circumstances have arisen which could not be anticipated by the tenant or occupier when the contract was made. Such additional rates defray the cost, probably, of works which permanently increase the value of the owner's interest, and from which he will derive a greater revenue at the termination of the existing contract. What with the growing needs of the community, and the development of science, we know that many of the improvements carried out in our towns are entirely new departures, which could not be foreseen when the pre-existing leases or contracts of tenancy were drawn up, and the cost of which ought to have been specially divided between occupiers and owners in the Acts sanctioning them. The occupier is rarely a free party to the contract contained in the lease of land for a house, and it is not, therefore, this contract which makes him liable to pay the whole local rate, but the general presumption of liability contained in the older Acts.

In a large number of the States in the American Union there is a provision by which, if an owner of land or houses is benefited by the improvements made by the public, he must contribute under the name of "betterment" to the expense of those operations which have enhanced the value of his property.

In our own Public Health Acts we have, in a small way, somewhat similar provisions for the direct and ascertained improvement of a district. For outlay incurred for private improvements—such as the making of new roads, etc.—the sanitary authority can levy a rate upon the occupier, who, in his turn, can deduct it from the rent payable to his landlord ; but even in this case there is no prohibition of contracts to release the owner from this ultimate liability ; and very often the occupiers, by the nature of their contracts of tenancy, are debarred from making the deduction which the Acts authorise, although the possibility of the levy of such a rate might not have been an element under consideration when arranging the terms of the contract.

Apart from the division of municipal taxation,

the question of poor rate and county rate lies deeper, and involves the question whether the moral and historical obligation to contribute, as evidenced by the Irish Poor Law and Land Act, 1870, lies in any special and peculiar degree upon the owners.

When advocating the division of local taxation between the occupier and owner of each proprietary interest, we must not be taken as suggesting the relief of the occupier from a portion of every rate. There are some rates and taxes which are imposed for his benefit, as for lighting, domestic water supply, and for police, etc., which should necessarily be borne by him alone ; but a portion of those rates for works which are essential to the beneficial ownership of property, or levied for the benefit of the community, should be borne by the owner, as the taxes imposed to defray the expenses necessary for the maintenance of public health, for maintenance of roads, for public water supply, etc., etc., and releases from this liability should be prohibited.

Difficulties must, of course, arise in the case of leases, and existing contracts must be met, so far as possible, by well-considered provisions. Upon this point, Dr. W. N. Hancock, in his evidence before the Irish Committee, 1877, suggested that the difficulty could be overcome by taking the

average of the rates for three, five, or seven years
back, whichever was thought to be right, and in all
past contracts to add that to the rent, and divide
the liability for the future.

However, the Scottish system has had its
administrative advantages, as the owner, being
directly called upon to pay a proportion of the
rates, takes an active interest in their administration. Similar beneficial results, it is anticipated, would follow the like assessment of each
proprietary interest in England and Ireland.

CHAPTER V.

SUGGESTED REFORMS.

IN the preceding chapters it has been shown that
no complaint is made of the amount of local taxation. It is not of the extent of the taxation ; it
is not the sum which passes into the local treasuries
—it is the manner in which it is raised which
hampers the development of one class of property,
and checks the energy and industry of particular
members of the community. It is the incidence of the taxation to which we have to
look. This is the only standard by which we can
measure the equity of the local taxation of any
country ; and this has been the concurring opinion
of all who have studied the subject.

We find it in the United Kingdom, and we
find it in other countries ; and, turning to the
leading authorities here and elsewhere, we find all
agreed upon the importance of the incidence of
taxation, whether imperial or local.

How are the local taxes raised in the United
Kingdom, in which it should be our special care to

make every individual contribute according to his ability, and proportionate to the benefits received by him from municipal outlay? It has been shown that in our local finance little attention has been paid to this maxim, and that whilst the species of property which has had to bear the entire burden has been handicapped in its development, the more favoured species has been enabled to augment to colossal dimensions. The one increases in magnitude at the expense of the other; and even the treatment of that latter has in it the elements of unfairness.

It is now proposed to state shortly the reforms which a consideration of the subject has suggested. The distinct advantages which real property derives from municipal institutions justify the existence of special imposts upon the property itself, therefore :—

1. The larger burden of local taxation should be assessed upon real property, not in its legal sense, but including therein the soil and all attached to it, as houses, buildings, and permanent fixtures, irrespective of the interest, term or tenure for which it is held.

2. That, as to all local taxes assessed upon such real property, the owner should bear a portion of such taxes and rates as are levied to defray the cost of permanent works, and of the performance

of those duties which partake more of a national than a local character, proportionate to their respective interests in such property.

3. That, in order to effect a partial relief in the amount necessary to be raised by local taxation, a percentage be added to the imperial death duties (on real as well as on personal property) payable on probates and administrations, for the benefit of the municipal authority having jurisdiction where such property is situated.

4. So that personal property shall bear a just proportion of the local expenditure, a percentage be added to the imperial income tax payable under Schedules C, D, and E.

Sufficient has been said upon the equity of the first and second proposals, and on the injustice of assessing the occupier of realty for the maximum local expenditure. It only now remains to explain the advantages of the third and fourth proposals.

The Imperial Government at present levies the following death duties upon probate, etc. :—

I. Probate duty upon probates of all wills and letters of administration ; on confirmation of testaments, testamentary and dative ; and on inventories to be exhibited in the Commissary Courts in Scotland.

The duty is payable upon the value at the time of proving the will or obtaining the letters of

I

administration, in respect of all the personal property of a deceased and not on the value at the
period of the death.

The personal property liable to the duty is as
follows :—

All Government, bank, or other stock, funds,
annuities, bills, etc. ; all stocks, shares, and securities of every kind which may be bought and
sold in these as well as in the foreign countries
where the undertakings were inaugurated or have
offices ; copyhold property which descends to the
executors or administrators ; leasehold property,
whatever may be the length of the term ; personal
estate, of any kind, over which the deceased had a
general or absolute power of appointment, or, in
other words, a right to dispose of in whatever way
he might have thought fit ; the purchase money of
freehold property which the deceased may have
during his lifetime entered into a written binding
contract to sell, although the time for completing
the purchase may not have arrived ; and the value
of any vested reversionary interest.

Property in several colonial banks is exempt
from probate duty, as likewise copyhold and freehold property which descends to the heir-at-law,
whether the latter is or is not subject to ground
rent or other charges ; also personal property of
any kind over which the deceased had a power of

appointment, but restricted by the instrument under which the power or trust was created; money agreed to be paid for the purchase of freehold property, although the time for the completion of the contract had not arrived; or on any contingent reversionary interest.

In the latter case, the duty must be paid when the property becomes vested.

The scale of duty is : under £100, no duty is payable; over £100 and under £300, not deducting debts, £1 10s. duty; on estates over £100 and not above £500, two per cent.; over £500 and not above £1,000, two and a quarter per cent.; over £1,000, three per cent.

II. Succession duty is payable upon every description of property by reason whereof any person has or shall become beneficially entitled to any property, or the income thereof, upon the death of any person either immediately or after any interval, either certainly or contingently, and either originally or by way of substitutive limitation, and every devolution by law of any beneficial interest in property, or the income thereof, upon the death of any person to any other person, in possession or expectancy.

III. Legacy duty is payable upon the value of all legacies, whether specific or general.

The scale of duty upon successions and legacies

I 2

is a percentage varying according to the degree of consanguinity of the successor or legatee of the deceased.

IV. Account ; V., Estate ; and VI., Corporation Duty.

We see that probate duty is only payable upon personalty, but if an additional schedule was added to the forms at present in use, to contain the description and capital value of all the realty, of whatever tenure, the deceased died possessed of, distinguishing the localities where it is situate, ample material would be provided for the assessment of the local death duty.

The local death duty could be assessed upon the aggregate of the personalty and capitalised value of the realty possessed by the deceased, and added to and collected with the existing imperial probate duty in a manner similar to the percentages and surtaxes levied by the local authorities in America, France, Germany, etc, and which will be referred to later on. Like the probate duty, the local duty should be payable by the executors or administrators of the deceased ; and when paid, the Inland Revenue authorities could allocate the amount realised by the assessment upon the realty (including leaseholds) among the local authorities having jurisdiction over the area in which it is situated, each such local authority receiving a sum proportionate to the value of such realty (including leaseholds) within its jurisdiction. The local duty upon the personalty (excluding leaseholds) to be added to and applied in the same manner as the amount received from the municipal percentage to the imperial income tax.

Such a local death duty would be reasonable and just. Every class of property benefits by communal life and communal enterprise. If a demand is made on property for local works, all property should then be subject to the claim. The owner cannot complain because the duty would not become payable until after his death, and as he is assumed to be the absolute owner, and to have complete control over the disposition of his property, his successors or legatees cannot complain. It would be a tax, therefore, only on those who have no vested interests in the property taxed. They may only exist in expectancy of a future benefit, and no one can allege that the intrinsic value of the property taxed will be lowered by the levy of the duty.

The practice, introduced by Mr. Goschen, M.P., of allocating one half of the imperial probate duty in relief of local taxation favours the adoption of the municipal percentage.

In 1891 probate and succession duty was paid upon the following sums:—

1891.	Gross value of property assessed to probate duty.	Net value of property (after allowing debts, etc.) upon which probate duty was charged.	Net value of property assessed to succession duty.	Total net value of property assessed to both probate and succession duty.
	£	£	£	£
England	157,871,000	144,418,000	40,620,000	185,047,000
Scotland	15,338,000	13,754,000	4,616,000	18,370,000
Ireland	8,360,000	7,157,000	4,805,000	11,962,000
United Kingdom	181,569,000	165,329,000	50,050,000	215,379,000

Now as regards the fourth proposal. The imperial income tax is levied from year to year, and under the authority of an Act of Parliament passed annually, which determines the amount of the tax for the current financial year—that is, for the year which begins on the 6th April and ends on the 5th April following. Speaking generally, we may say that everything in the nature of property which produces, or is capable of producing, or itself consists in, an annual income or revenue, is the subject of the taxation we are now considering, if either the property is situate, or the income enjoyed, in the United Kingdom.

For the purposes of classification and distinction, and for applying the provisions of the various Acts relating to the income tax, the several kinds of property in respect of which the duty is granted are arranged in five "Schedules," each schedule

being marked alphabetically, and each containing a
description of one kind, or class, of property.

Schedule A. Under this schedule the duty is
charged "for and in respect of the property in all
lands, tenements, hereditaments, and heritages in
the United Kingdom," for every twenty shillings
of the annual value thereof. The word property
is used to designate the interest in land of the
"owner," as distinguished from that of the "occupier." The duty is therefore imposed upon, and
has ultimately to be paid by, the owner, and not by
the occupier of land. True, it is generally paid in
the first instance by the occupier, who deducts
what he has so paid from the rent he pays to his
landlord. The general rule enacted for ascertaining
the annual value is "The annual value of lands,
tenements, hereditaments, or heritages, charged
under Schedule A, shall be understood to be the
rent by the year at which the same are let at rack
rent, if the amount of such rent shall have been
fixed by agreement commencing within the period
of seven years preceding the 5th April next before
the time of making the assessment; but if the same
are not so let at rack rent, then the rack rent at
which the same are worth to be let by the year."

Under Schedule B the duty is chargeable on
the occupation of lands, etc., as are comprised in
Schedule A, except dwelling-houses, with their

offices, not occupied with farms of land, or tithes, for farming purposes, and except warehouses, or other buildings, occupied for the purpose of carrying on a trade or profession, for every twenty shillings of the annual value thereof. The duty we thus see is imposed under this schedule on, and has to be paid by, the occupier, and not by the owner. In Ireland this tax is assessed upon the Government valuation, and the Commissioners allege that this assessment cannot be reduced even where the occupying farmer shows conclusively that his annual profits fall far short of the Government valuation. In England, where the rack rent is taken as the basis for assessment, this rule certainly does not apply.

It is now optional with farmers to elect to be assessed to the duties of income tax under Schedule D, in lieu of the assessment under Schedule B.

Schedule C deals with interest and dividends payable out of public funds, and is not of much general importance, as the tax upon such securities is deducted from the interest or dividend, and the balance alone paid. The duty extends to all public annuities wherever payable in Great Britain or elsewhere; and all dividends and shares of such annuities respectively. The exemptions from this schedule are the stock, etc., of friendly societies, savings banks, and charitable institutions.

We now come to the principal schedule, namely, Schedule D. Under it, duty is charged " for and in respect of the annual profits or gains arising or accruing to any person residing in the United Kingdom, from any kind of property whatever, whether situate in the United Kingdom or elsewhere ; and for and in respect of the annual profits or gains arising or accruing to any person residing in the United Kingdom from any profession, trades, employment, or vocation, whether the same shall be carried on in the United Kingdom or elsewhere ; and for and in respect of the annual profits or gains arising or accruing to any person whatever, whether a subject of Her Majesty or not, although not resident within the United Kingdom, from any property whatever in the United Kingdom, or any profession, trade, employment, or vocation exercised within the United Kingdom," for every twenty shillings of the annual amount of such profits and gains ; and " for and in respect of all interest of money, annuities, or other annual profits and gains not charged by virtue of any of the other schedules," for every twenty shillings of the annual amount thereof.

The sources from which annual profits or gains chargeable under this schedule arise are divided into six classes, and for the case of each of those six classes there are provided special rules for ascertaining the duties payable, some of the rules being common to more than one of the classes. The simple rule in arriving at the sum liable to duty is to include all moneys received or due (except bad debts), and to deduct from the sum-total nothing but the necessary and actual expenses of carrying on business.

No sum can be deducted for interest on capital employed, money expended in buildings or improvements, annuities payable out of profits (to a retired partner or otherwise), or moneys recoverable under insurances or indemnities. Voluntary payments, although often essential to the success of a business, cannot be deducted in estimating profits. A sum is allowed for ordinary repairs on a three years' average. Wear and tear and depreciation of machinery, etc., is also considered.

In calculating income, no personal expenditure is to be taken into consideration. A man's income is considered that which comes to him, not what he saves and puts by. Therefore the rent of a dwelling-house, the cost of supporting a family, etc., is not a deduction from income under the Acts, but rather an application and use of income actually received. One most reasonable exception is made to this rule. The tax-payer may deduct the premium on assurance of his life, or that of his wife, where the sum is payable either at death or on the attainment of a certain age, either in a bulk sum or as an annuity, and either for the benefit of the next-of-kin or of the widow or children of the assured. Although a married woman now retains full control and ownership of her property, and can prevent her husband touching a penny of it, yet husband and wife living together are still to be taxed as one person—that is to say, the husband must include in his return his wife's income as well as his own. Where one individual carries on two or more businesses, the losses of one may be set off against the profits of the others.

Under Schedule E the duty is charged " for and in respect of every public office or employment of profit, and upon every annuity, pension, or stipend payable by Her Majesty, or out of the public revenue of the United Kingdom," except annuities charged to the duties under Schedule C, for every twenty shillings of the annual amount thereof.

Where the total income from all sources is less than £150, no duty is payable by the individual ; but public companies paying dividends to him will deduct, in most cases, the tax. In such a case a refund can be obtained.

Where the total income is over £150, but less than £400, no duty is charged on the first £120 thereof.

Such are the properties and incomes liable to

the duty. We have given nothing more than a brief outline of the principles, as many subtile distinctions exist as to what is income and what is not. We have seen, however, that the regulations now in force make no distinction between a precarious and settled income, causing the tradesman or professional man, whose revenue dies with him to pay as heavily as his neighbour who has inherited or acquired property, of which those dependent upon him will not be deprived by his decease. Speaking upon the Budget of 1848, Cobden dwelt upon the inequalities of the income tax, which was then still talked of by Chancellors of the Exchequer as a temporary measure. " Make your tax just," he said, " in order that it may be permanent. It is ridiculous to deny the broad distinction that exists between incomes derived from trades and professions and those drawn from land. Take the case of a tradesman with £10,000 of capital; he gets £500 a year interest, and £500 more for his skill and industry. Is this man's £1,000 a year to be mulcted in the same amount with the £1,000 a year derived from a real property capital of £25,000 ? So with the cases of professional men, who literally live by the waste of their brains. The plain fair dealing of the country revolts at an equal levy on such different sorts of property. Professional men and men in business put in motion the wheels of the social system. It is their industry and enterprise that mainly give to realised property the value that it bears; to them, therefore, the State first owes sympathy and support."

Again, under the present system, when a man has passed the £400 limit, he has to pay as heavy a percentage on his income, precarious or permanent, as the wealthiest millionaire amongst us.

It is no wonder, therefore, that a demand should be growing for a graduated income tax.

Mr. Chamberlain, speaking in 1885, said : " Is it really certain that the precarious income of a struggling professional man ought to pay in the same proportion as the income of a man who derives it from invested securities? It is altogether such an unfair thing that we should, as in the United States, tax all incomes according to amount. . . . Prince Bismarck, some time ago, proposed to the Reichstag an income tax to be graduated according to the amount of the income, and to vary according to the character of the income. We already have done something in that direction in exempting the very smallest incomes from taxation; but I submit that it is well worthy of careful consideration whether the principle should not be carried a little further."

Within latter years the demand for a graduated

and progressive income tax has grown more rapidly.
The adherents of the progressive tax start from the
idea that taxation should, above all other considerations, perform a social function. Taxation, they
say, should prevent the accumulation of wealth in
few hands, or, at least, bring it about that the
burden should press equally upon the tax-payers ;
in other words, it should consider what is left to
the tax-payer, and not merely what is paid, and
should bear upon what is superfluous, rather than
upon what is necessary. The suggestion of a progressive tax is no new-fangled idea. We have seen
the principle regulating assessments under the
Lighting and Cleansing (Ireland) Act, 1828, and
the difference in the death duties, according to the
degree of relationship of the beneficiary, indicates
that the law recognises the reasonableness of
graduating the burden according to the shoulders
which have to bear it. Even in the present income
tax system itself we find incomes under £150
exempt, while those between that sum and £400
are subject to a reduction which lessens the percentage of the tax.

The progressive system in Germany and Switzerland holds good, and has not had apparently
the effect of driving capital away which the
opponents of the system alleged would be the
result of its introduction. From its working it

cannot be honestly argued that such a system is either immoral in design or impossible of execution.

Now, if personal property, or the income derived from it, whether graduated or not, is to bear a portion of the annual local burden, what better system of assessment for such purposes could be adopted than the addition of a municipal percentage to the imperial tax under Schedules C, D, and E, the produce added to that of the produce from the percentage on probates of personal property to be divided amongst the several local authorities, proportionate to the rateable valuation in each district. The percentage would be small, and as few grumble at an additional penny on the imperial levy, the municipal percentage would hardly be felt.

The collection would be easy and, as the existing machinery could be utilised, economical. Our familiarity with the income-tax has made us practically forget that the law under which it is enforced is only an annual one. But although its advent was strenuously opposed, yet no extraordinary hardships have followed in its train, and we have gradually understood that income is the only fair object for taxation, and that this is a truth so palpable that nothing short of stupidity can question it, and nothing but a dereliction of principle can raise a wish to impugn it.

Of course clamour may be loud against the idea of taxing the income of property in the funds, stocks, shares, etc., for the benefit of municipal improvements ; but elsewhere we have pointed out that such improvements are as necessary to the well-being of the community, to the security and happiness of the subjects of the State, as the expense incurred upon the army, navy, or Civil Service. It would be absurd to suppose that a person having property in stocks, shares, trade, or professions should receive income and enjoy the protection and fruits of well-considered schemes of improvement of the government, whether imperial or local, without contributing to its support. The labour of the country, and every species of the property of the country, are the sources from which all taxes must be paid ; and as Government —throughout its several grades or political divisions—is created for the purpose of protecting both labour and property, the expenses of government should fall upon both.

No real infringement on the rights of individuals would be committed by giving effect to these proposals. The magnitude of the local indebtedness is admitted—it was fairly contracted and it was increased within recent years for the benefit of all within the various districts. Those who now escape from contributing towards the repayment of this debt, but who would be compelled to do so by the proposals here made, cannot fancy that they have purchased the blessings they enjoy at too great a price. Let them briefly review the present condition of our municipalities, and recollect the miseries which the absence of efficient local administration entailed upon the inhabitants of these countries. Our cities, our villages, and our country districts have been improved, and good order and facilities for public and private employment prevail. Our comforts and conveniences have been augmented in a degree scarcely to be credited; and according as our social wants have multiplied, they have been supplied. All such works tend to increase the national capital; and who will cavil at the cost, or refuse to bear his just and equitable portion of its repayment? We must pay our lawful debts, and disown that conduct as a body which the least informed among us would scorn to be guilty of individually.

The plan proposed is politic; it is necessary, and pre-eminently so at the present time. Its accomplishment may for the moment be arduous, but that will be no bar to its success if its advocacy is heartily and steadily pursued.

J

Undertakings from which the boldest private speculators must shrink, works wonderful as the Pyramids of old, but, unlike those mighty structures, of palpable utility, might, by the aid of each contributing his just proportion of the expense, spring up in every quarter of the kingdom.

CHAPTER VI.

MUNICIPAL TAXATION ABROAD.

UNITED STATES OF AMERICA.

IT is noticeable that while in the United Kingdom and on the Continent, and indeed in most civilised countries, a land tax, or a tax upon land values, and an income-tax, are principally depended upon as the necessary contributions for the support of government, in the United States, apart from the indirect taxation of commodities by the government, the States, for both general and local purposes, depend almost entirely on direct taxation of land and personal property.

Franchise taxes, or corporations' inheritance tax, and some other methods of raising money of minor importance, have been employed of late years in some of the States. The main dependence, however, in nearly all the States of the Union for raising money for State, county, and municipal purposes, is a general tax levied upon land and upon the mass of the taxpayers' personal property.

J 2

Each State devises its own system of taxation, and the way in which taxes are levied is as follows :—The legislature of the State determines upon the probable amount of money required for State purposes from year to year, and it votes that amount.

This is apportioned upon the cities and towns according to their ability to pay, as shown by the returns of their taxable property. The County Commissioners of each county, whose duty it is to look after the public highways, bridges, and other county matters, determine about how much they will require, and it is apportioned in like manner among the cities and towns of each county. The cities and towns determine the amount required to meet their own local expenditure, and to this they add the quotas apportioned upon them by the Legislature and the County Commissioners, collecting the whole sum at the same time once a year.

Then the State quota is paid into the State treasury, and the county quota into the county treasury. This system seems to be quite simple and inexpensive. At all events, it is democratic.

The assessment is almost universally made a matter of record. This record is called the roll or list. This roll contains the names of the persons taxed, the description of the personal property owned by each person, the value of it, and the amount of the tax; a description of the land owned by each person, the number of acres, the situation and the value, with amount of tax and the total amount of tax assessed upon each person for all the property listed. In many of the States the roll enters minutely into detail, giving the various classes of personal property—as household furniture, money, bonds, stocks, etc., and as to real estate, giving the value of land and buildings in separate columns. The licence and probate taxes are not placed on the roll, but in some States where a poll-tax is levied it is so inserted. Generally the owner of property is required to deliver to the assessor a list containing a description of all his taxable property, and from this the assessment is made: but the assessor is not concluded by this statement of the owner as to the property included, if he has reason to believe the statement is not a true one; and in such case, or where the owner omits or refuses to deliver the list, he may proceed upon the best information he can obtain to make a correct assessment, adding property omitted by the owner. Nor where the statute enumerates certain sources of information for his guidance in ascertaining who is to be taxed for certain property and its value, is he bound by them. These are only to aid him in doing that which is essential to ascertain the amount of taxable property and the names of the persons taxable.

The estimate of the value is a judicial act. The assessors are chosen specially to perform this duty, and their decision is based upon all the information they possess, whether derived from the owner or otherwise.

In many of the States, in some by constitutional provision and in others by legislative enactment, the lands in the State are required to be valued at regular intervals of time varying from five to ten years, by persons specially appointed for the purpose. In others the valuation of lands, like that of personal property, is annual, made at the time of making the list ; and even in those States where there is a periodic valuation, the assessors in making their annual assessment add to the land theretofore valued the increased value by reason of improvements which have been placed on it since the last periodic valuation ; but in all other respects they follow such valuation.

Where a statute requires an increase in valuation, " if any building or addition is erected on any lot," such language does not apply to an addition to the height or depth of a building, or changing the interior structure thereof, but only to a lateral addition. The value of improvements on land is often placed in a separate column. In the States where mining is conducted, these improvements, where owned by a person other than the owner of the land, are sometimes assessed separately as personalty; otherwise, they are included in the value of the land.

The question, How is land to be valued, or upon what basis? has given rise to much discussion in the different legislative bodies. The difficulty is generally to obtain a uniform valuation throughout each State, so that each part of the State may bear its appropriate part of the burden. This difficulty arises whatever may be the standard of valuation, and an attempt has been made to obviate it by boards of equalisation, to be hereafter explained. In Michigan and California the standard is the cash value; in New York it is at "a sum which the majority of the assessors decide to be the true value thereof, and at which they would appraise the same in payment of a just debt due from a solvent debtor"; in Virginia, at the cash value, which is ascertained by fixing the value thereof upon the usual credits in the neighbourhood, and rebating interest when interest is not usually allowed on deferred payments.

The expression in most of the States is either "cash value," "fair cash value," "at its time value in money," or "in ready money." In Iowa it is at its time cash value, having regard to its quality, location, natural advantages, general improvements in its vicinity, and all other elements of value. In Arkansas, water privileges are specially designated as an element of value; and in Illinois the value of growing crops is expressly excepted as an element of value. The substance of this provision is the same in each State, the assessment being based on the value of the land, looking to all the circumstances of its surroundings, or what may be regarded as the cash market value. The income derived from land is not considered the proper criterion in ascertaining this value; and especially when contrasted with the price which the land brought at a recent public sale, the latter is always regarded as *prima facie* correct.

The result arrived at by comparing the authorities on the subject seems to be substantially that which is expressed in the Iowa statute—that all the elements of value are to be considered in assessing land, and an exemption of buildings in a town is invalid where the constitution requires property to be assessed *ad valorem*. A mortgage on land is not to be deducted from its value in assessing the tax, but in some of the States the mortgagee is allowed to deduct the mortgage debt, and other debts, from the amount of property which he returns for taxation.

As a general rule, the tax on land is a personal

charge against the owner. In the statutes of all
the States there is something to indicate this, and
almost universally the collector is required to make
the tax out of the goods and chattels of the person
assessed with the tax. The name of the owner of
the land, or of the occupant where the statute
directs it to be assessed to the occupant, is an
essential ingredient in the description of the land.
It is the right of every citizen to know for what
property he is assessed and is required to pay taxes,
and in those States where the law allows land to
be assessed as unknown, it is only on condition
that the name of the owner cannot be found.
There are exceptions to this proposition as to
certain classes of land in particular States. Thus,
in Pennsylvania, uncultivated lands are assessed
without particular reference to the ownership; in
Maine and in Massachusetts, "unimproved lands
of non-residents"; and in Illinois all lands are
assessed *as lands*, without any reference to the
person who may own them. The land, and not
the owner, is considered the debtor for the tax.
As to all such lands, the name of the owner is
not essential.

The person holding the legal title is the person
to be assessed with land, unless by special provision the statute directs otherwise. It is the fee-
simple in land that is assessed. The law does not

regard the different interests in the assessment. It looks to the person having the present right of enjoyment, whether tenant for life or years, for the tax on the fee-simple value of the land and the improvements—*i.e.*, buildings thereon—and such person is the one to be assessed with the land. By statute in Pennsylvania, where one party owns the coal and another the land, each party is assessed with his interest—one with the land and the other with the coal. So with rents issuing out of land, the owner of the rent is assessed with it as personalty, and the owner of the land with it as realty.

Irrespective of the name of the owner, there must be a description of the land on the roll, not only that each person may see that his land is properly assessed, but also because in case the land is sold for non-payment of taxes, as hereafter explained, the title of the purchaser depends on the accuracy of the description on the roll; he becomes the purchaser of the tract described on the roll, and it is important that it should be so described that it can be easily identified.

The sweeping character of the enactments of the several States on the subject of taxation of personal property can be best appreciated by a reference to the provisions of the laws of New York State defining personal property liable to taxation. The statute, after enacting that "all personal estate within the State, whether owned by individuals or by corporations, shall be liable to taxation," subject to the specified exemptions, provides as follows :—

"Section 3. The term personal estate and personal property, whenever they occur in this chapter, shall be construed to include all household furniture, money, goods, chattels, debts due from solvent debtors, whether on account, contract, note, bond, or mortgage, public stock, and stocks in moneyed corporations ; they shall also be construed to include such portion of the capital of incorporated companies liable to taxation on their capital as shall not be invested in real estate."

This definition of personal estate or personal property is intended to embrace everything that can be conceived of as included in these general terms, and it is reasonably successful in its purpose. In fact, personal property consists, under the laws of the State, of bonds, mortgages, and other forms of capital ; food, clothing, and the things necessary to satisfy human desires.

The statute is somewhat confusing in its reference to the stocks and capital of corporations. The practical effect of its provisions, taken with others bearing upon the same subject, is that substantially all corporations of the State, except

banks, life-insurance companies, and savings banks,
are liable to taxation upon all their personal property, except stocks in other companies. The
same rules apply to personal property as to real
estate. It is to be assessed at the true market
value in cash.

Two methods have been employed in the
United States for the purpose of ascertaining the
amount of taxable personal property owned by
individual citizens.

1. In several States, such as Massachusetts,
Connecticut, and Illinois, the taxpayer is required
to give each year to the assessor a detailed and
verified statement, carefully itemised, of all the
personal property owned by him or under his
control, and of every kind, sort, and description.
This method is generally known as "the listing
system." In several States the principle that a
State can tax only that which is within its terri-
torial jurisdiction is ignored, and even visible,
tangible property situated outside of the taxing
State is required to be returned for the purpose of
taxation.

2. The other and more general method of
ascertaining taxable personal estate is that with
which the citizens of the New York State are
familiar, by which the assessor guesses at the
personal property of the individual, and places him

upon the list at such a figure as either his information or imagination sustains him in considering to be that which justly represents the personal estate of the taxpayer.

It is obvious that in cases of special partnerships, trustees, and executors who may have recently accounted, persons who have taken estates upon the settlement of which inventories or accounts may have been filed, and, indeed, in all cases where a record of the transactions of personal property has been made, a vigilant assessor is reasonably successful in reaching all the personal property of the individual ; and also where the property is of a tangible and visible nature, such as stock, cattle, and horses—especially those in the hands of farmers, the details of whose affairs are well known to their neighbours. Beyond these the assessor cannot go with any certainty. He has absolutely no resource except to guess at the assessment from the place of business or residence of the taxpayer. If the tax in such a case is paid cheerfully for two or three years, the personal assessment is usually then increased periodically until the taxpayer cries out against it. When this happens, the assessor is generally sure that the limit of actual ownership of personal property has been reached, if not passed, by his efforts.

As might be expected, the operation of this

system in New York State results substantially in the collection of no tax on personal property except from three classes of taxpayers :—

(1) Corporations who are obliged to make sworn returns, not only to the assessors but also to other public officials.

(2) Executors, trustees, and in cases of partnerships.

(3) Those who are too conscientious, too careless, or too ignorant to arrange their affairs in such a manner as not to be liable for taxation on this class of property.

It is absolutely essential to the maintenance of the supremacy of the Federal Government within its own sphere that the taxing power of the States should not extend to the obligations of the general government. The sovereign power of the State of New York, therefore, cannot reach for purposes of taxation the instrumentalities of the United States Government. This law affords people who own personal property an opportunity of evading any assessment by converting such property into Government securities.

Another matter to be borne in mind in this connection is that the *situs* of an individual for purposes of taxation upon personal property in New York State is fixed by his place of residence and ownership of property upon a day certain,

when the assessors have completed their pre-
liminary inquiries, have arranged their assessment
rolls, and open them for correction.

Throughout the State of New York, generally,
that day is the 1st July. In the city of New York
it is the second Monday in January. What a man
owns in personal property in the city of New York
on the day specified, and the manner in which his
investments are made upon that day, determine
the question whether or not he is taxable for
personal property.

The different dates upon which assessment are
made in Brooklyn, Jersey City, and New York
City, furnish an additional facility for evasion of
personal property by transfers of ownership on
subjective sales.

Still another element in the combination is the
principle that in New York State the debt of the
taxpayer can be deducted from his assessment.

The extent to which taxation upon personal
property is evaded is evidenced by the official
returns.

In 1890 New York County was assessed on
$220,000,000 of personal property. A recent
writer stated that, as a matter of fact, about
$1,500,000,000 of taxable personal property was
mostly hidden. That the $1,500,000,000 repre-
sented an average of $1,000 to each man, woman,

and child, and the personal property in the shape
alone of food consumed was about equal every day
to the highest figure that has been set on the
valuations of all forms of personal property.

In the city of Baltimore the assessed value of
all property liable to taxation in 1891 was
$276,408,052, upon which was paid a State tax of
$17\frac{3}{4}$ cents, and a city tax of $1.55 per $100.00. The
State tax of $17\frac{3}{4}$ cents was made up of :—

(1) Levy for public school tax $10\frac{1}{2}$ cents per $100.
(2) Levy for defence redemption tax at $5\frac{1}{2}$ cents per
$100.
(3) Levy for treasury relief tax at $1\frac{1}{2}$ cents per $100.
(4) Levy for exchange loan of 1886 tax at $\frac{1}{4}$ cent per
$100.

In New York in 1886 the assessed valuation of
all taxable property was 1,371,117,003 dollars,
viz. :—

	Dollars.
Real estate	1,168,443,137
Personal estate	202,673,866
	1,371,117,003

and the tax rate was 2.40 dollars per cent.

In 1888 the assessed value was :—

	Dollars.
Real estate	3,122,588,084
Personal estate	346,611,861

The real estate paid 90·01 per cent. of the State

tax, and the personal 9·99 per cent. of the State tax.

In 1889 in the State of Illinois the percentage of taxation was 3·41 per 100 dollars of assessed value.

The amount levied

			Dollars.
For local purposes was	...	...	26,659,382.48
For State purposes	...	...	4,318,959.19
Total levied on real estate	...		30,978,341.67

and the percentage of the amounts raised by taxation on real and personal estate were as follows :—

			Dols.
Real estate	...	...	79.82 per cent.
Personal estate	...	...	20.18 per cent.

In Iowa in 1889 the equalised value for taxation was 522,567,477 dollars, the percentage being 2·8 per 100 dollars of assessed value.

The amount levied

			Dollars.
For local purposes was	...	...	13,484,185.57
For State purposes	...	...	1,248,100.77
Total amount levied		...	14,732,286.34

Real estate was taxed at above 40 per cent. of the total amount raised.

In some States poll and income taxes are levied.

In Ohio and Maryland, poll taxes are declared

K

oppressive and prohibited, but in some other States they can be levied as follows :—

    (1) Not to exceed 1 dollar a head, Rhode Island, Virginia, West Virginia, Tennessee, Arkansas, South Carolina, Georgia, and Florida.

    (2) Not to exceed 1.50 dollars a head, Alabama, Louisiana.

    (3) Not to exceed 2 dollars a head, North Carolina.

    (4) Not to exceed 4 dollars a head, Nevada.

    (5) Not less than 50 cents a head, Tennessee.

    (6) Not less than 1 dollar a head, Texas and Tennessee.

    (7) Not less than 2 dollars a head, California and Nevada.

In several States poll taxes are to be applied exclusively to the common-school fund.

In Virginia, North Carolina, Tennessee, Texas, and California, income tax may be imposed, but in Virginia it is limited to incomes of over 600 dollars a year, and in North Carolina and Tennessee it cannot be imposed on incomes derived from taxed property.

For the supply of water and light, special charges are made in different cities. In New York the average charge for water per dwelling is $6 ; in Chicago, $14 ; Philadelphia, $9 ; Brooklyn, $8 ; St. Louis, $14 ; Boston, $12 ; Baltimore, $7; San Francisco, $20 ; New Orleans, $25 ; and Washington, $4.50.

In addition to the general tax levy as before explained, cities derive revenue from licences, market rents, ferry and dock-rents, street railroad and elevated railroad franchises, bridge tolls, water and light rents, street vault rents, fines and penalties, fees, and a large number of other miscellaneous sources, amounting in New York City in the year 1886 to about nine million dollars. In the same year the general tax levy yielded over thirty-one million dollars, which included the city's proportion of the State tax of over four million dollars.

Quite a large revenue is derived in large cities from the licences granted to liquor dealers. These latter are obliged to pay to the city or town in which they are permitted to do business a considerable licence duty every year, in addition to £5 a year of special internal revenue tax. Licences are not granted to premises as in the United Kingdom, but to individual citizens.

Taxes are collected in advance. In Philadelphia the taxes for 1893 are payable from January in that year, and if payment is made before the 30th June, a discount of 1 per cent. is allowed on the city taxes, but no deduction is allowed on the State tax. If not paid before the 1st July, a penalty of one-half per cent. is imposed, and so on, the penalty increasing in amount at later periods

K 2

of the year. The taxes become delinquent after the end of December of the current year. The usual mode of collecting the tax is that the roll or list is placed in the hands of the collector, whose duty it is to collect the taxes and account for them to the proper officers designated by statute. When in the hands of the collector, it is not merely an account to be collected, but it has the force of an execution, which the collector may satisfy by levy or distress of the goods and chattels of the taxpayers. It has all the force of an execution issue from a court, upon a judgment regularly obtained.

The personal estate of the taxpayer is the primary fund for the payment of the taxes. This is the general rule, but it may be, and often is, changed either by express provision of statute or by implication, as in those cases where the tax is imposed on the property as such without reference to the ownership, and the proceeding to enforce payment is a proceeding *in rem*. Such is the case in Massachusetts and New York, as to lands owned by non-residents, which have a distinct legal character.

In some States the collector is authorised, if the taxpayer refuses or neglects to pay, to seize the body of the delinquent and imprison him, or upon such refusal or neglect, an application may be made to a court having jurisdiction of the person, and its payment enforced by attachment, fine and imprisonment.

There is no lien on real estate for taxes due on personal property, the poll tax or licence tax, unless it is created by express statute.

When the collector fails to make the tax on real estate from the goods and chattels of the person charged, it is usual to provide for the sale of the real estate, or so much thereof as will provide for the payment of the tax. But sometimes a harsher mode is adopted, and the land is declared to be forfeited to the State. In Louisiana the forfeiture is accomplished by sending the delinquent-list to the auditor, then it is filed and recorded. The recording is considered a seizure of the land. In some of the States, as Ohio, North Carolina, and Illinois, the forfeiture is consummated in a different mode. When land is sold for non-payment of taxes, if no one bids a sufficient amount for the whole tract to pay the taxes, it is struck off to the State; and when these lands thus owned by the State have accumulated, they are sold. Where lands are forfeited they may be redeemed.

In New York, taxes on real property not paid for two years, from the 1st of May following the date on which the tax was laid, are enforced by sale.

Lists of such lands are sent to the county and city officers eighteen weeks before the sale, and published weekly for ten weeks previous to the sale in two newspapers of the county where the land is situated; and notice of sale, which always takes place at Albany, is published for twelve weeks preceding, in county newspapers. Sufficient of each parcel of land to pay taxes, interest, and expenses of sale is sold ; the surplus, if any, is held in trust for the former owner. The purchaser at the sale receives a certificate describing the property and the amount paid therefor ; and if no previous redemption, he is entitled to a deed at the expiration of two years from the last day of sale. The officer must publish, in two newspapers of the county, a description of the land, and the amount necessary to be paid for redemption, weekly for six weeks ; the last notice must appear at least eighteen weeks before the expiration of the time for redemption. Land may be redeemed within two years from the time of sale on payment of the amount paid by the purchaser, with 10 per cent. interest ; if no redemption, the controller then executes a conveyance vesting in the purchaser the absolute estate in fee simple. If at the time of such conveyance the lands are in the immediate occupancy of persons other than the purchaser, the latter must serve notice upon such persons of the sale and conveyance, within two years after the time for redemption expires. At any time within six months after such notice, the occupant, or any other person, may redeem, on payment of the consideration mentioned in the conveyance, with 37½ per cent. interest on such sum, and charge of executing the deed.

Within two years of the time of the tax sale, mortgagees must file a record of their mortgages in the proper office, or else they will be deemed to have abandoned their claim upon the land, and the purchaser takes free from mortgage. The purchaser at any time after receiving his conveyance can serve a notice on such mortgagees as have filed their records, requiring them to reedem the lands within six months by payment of the purchase price with interest. If payment is made, it is deemed to be included in the mortgage ; if not made, the purchaser takes free from mortgages.

The Boards of Equalisation before referred to, have been long established in the United States, and it is now sought to introduce the system into the United Kingdom, where many defects exist in the unequal distribution of the public burdens.

In the United States the roll or tax list is usually open for inspection and correction of errors for a certain period, while in the hands of the assessors, and then an appeal is allowed to some local tribunal invested with jurisdiction over such matters. In some of the States, no period is allowed for correction by the assessors after the roll is completed, but application is made at once to the tribunal designated by statute for relief. In some of the States, the supervisors of the county are vested with the power of revising and correcting the roll, in others it is a board of county commissioners, or the county court, and in others a board of equalisation; but whatever be the name of the tribunal, its powers and the errors which it can correct are of a similar nature.

The functions of those boards are twofold; they are sometimes vested with the powers of a board of review in addition to other powers, but when not invested with such powers, their duty is to equalise the assessments of a county so that all the towns of a county may bear the burden of taxation equally, or to equalise the assessments of a State so that each county may bear its proper portion of the burden. In the latter case it is called a State board of equalisation. The boards of equalisation for counties are generally composed of some local officers of the county, and have not only the authority to equalise by adding a percentage, but they are also vested with the power to review and correct the assessments made by the assessors.

The manner in which the assessment is equalised is different in different States. In Iowa, New Jersey, Illinois, and Ohio the board add to or deduct from the aggregate valuation of property in the roll such per centum as will raise or reduce it to the proper valuation. These boards cannot assess land or other property omitted from the roll by the assessors. Their function is to increase or diminish the valuations, or correct the errors as to property on the list. While they have the power to correct the valuation of particular individuals on application, they cannot increase the valuation on the property of a taxpayer without notice to him. Where it appears that the assessors have valued rents reserved on leases to non-residents at their full value, while other property in towns of the county is assessed at not over one-third of its value, this is such an equality as the board has power to correct, and if they refuse they may be compelled to act by mandamus.

BETTERMENT.

IN a previous chapter we referred to the system of local assessment or " betterment " which prevails in the United States.

In the opening of streets, the grading and paving of streets, the constitution of sewers, the laying of water-pipes in cities, and in the construction of drains and levels in agricultural districts, the expense of such works is very generally defrayed, not by a general tax on the whole State, or even on the whole of the political sub-division in which the works are constructed, but by a tax on all the real estate in a smaller district, created by the legislature as a taxing district. The tax thus laid is called an assessment, or more generally a local assessment.

In New York State itself every city within the territory, and many even of the villages, have had powers of this kind conferred upon them for making roads or paving streets, or laying sewers, or draining marshes, or providing public parks, or other improvements for the general convenience; and while in most cases the special tax is laid only on owners of property actually abutting on the improvement in the measure of their frontage, in some it has been laid on all real estate benefited by the improvement in the measure of the benefit received.

The power of defining the taxing district is often delegated to the council of the city, or other local officers of the State, or commissioners appointed for the public improvement which is authorised. In such cases the statute indicates the principle on which the local officers are to ascertain the limits of the district in such expressions, as on

all the real estate "benefited," or on all in the
"vicinity" or on "adjoining property," or some
similar expression. The equity of the tax has
been again and again discussed by the judges of
the supreme courts of the several States, and invariably with the same result of an affirmative
finding. The question has been raised before them
in various ways, but usually either by an ordinary
abutting owner who contends that the tax is discriminating and violates the principle contained in
most of the State constitutions that all the taxation
must be equal and uniform, or by a church or
university claiming immunity from the tax on the
ground of a special privilege granted them by
statute of exemption from all taxation. The
answer has been very much to the same purport in
all the different States. The judges have taken
their stand on the broad principle that they who
reap the benefit of a public work ought to bear the
burden of it, and where the benefit is discriminating,
the burden, to be equal, must be discriminating
likewise. "A local assessment," cites Mr. Bur-
roughs, in his "Law of Taxation," "is an equivalent
or compensation for the enhanced value which the
property of the person has received for the improvements. 'Tis only because of specific benefit that
specific property is taxed for a specific purpose.
The assessment on property is therefore laid with

reference to the benefit which such property is supposed to receive from the expenditure of the money."

The limit of local assessment clearly appears, therefore, to be the benefit received. Any tax beyond that is an exaction from the owner of more than his just share of the public burden. It ceases to be taxation, and becomes a taking of private property for public use without just compensation.

Some States expressly protect the local owners from excessive exactions by imposing a maximum limit on these assessments.

The doctrine which has been laid down by the American courts in dealing with those cases, is that a local improvement possesses always more or less of a private character, notwithstanding that it may be undertaken under public authority; but whatever doctrine or reason is laid down, the decisions always substantially rest on the equitable consideration that the sphere of benefit ought to be the sphere of burden, and that just as it would be wrong to tax individuals alone for improvements from which all alike benefit, so it would be equally wrong to tax all alike for the improvements from which particular individuals receive the lion's share of advantage.

The benefits taken into account must be direct, and not remote. In considering benefits with a view to a set-off in compensation cases, they exclude contingent, consequential, prospective, and general benefits, such as the property shares with all other property in the town. Where the expense is directed to be placed "upon the adjoining property" in case of a street assessment, the courts of New York claim that it only applies to property contiguous to the street, and not to property adjacent but separated from it; and a lot separated from a street by a narrow strip is not considered as fronting on the street, so as to be assessed; but an owner whose lot fronts on a street cannot withdraw it from liability to assessment by conveying away a ribbon fronting on the street, after the ordinance for the improvement of it has been passed.

The benefit received is usually determined by a board of commissioners, or assessors, who view the premises, ascertain what will be the increased value of all the property in the designated district, and what is the increased value of each lot of land. The increased market value of the lands is the true rule of assessment, and it is proper to consider all the circumstances which give increased value by reason of the improvement.

As a general rule, the assessment is solely made upon land, and not on personal property. If the district is defined definitely, all land in the district is liable, without reference to the use or purpose to which it is devoted. Neither as a rule can the owner be personally assessed. Where "the city engineer was directed to assess the cost of improvements, make out certified bills against each lot in the name of the owner, which were to be delivered to the contractor for the work, who should proceed to collect the same by ordinary process of law in his name, each certificate to be a lien on the lot of ground described therein," this statute was construed not to authorise the contractor to sue the owners of the lots. " Ordinary process of law " as to local assessments was held to mean such process as is adopted to enforce a lien or specific charge upon the property specially assessed. " The sole object," says Justice Bliss, " of a local tax being to benefit local property, it should be a charge upon the property only, and not a general one on the owner. The latter, indeed, is not what is understood by a local or special assessment, but the very term would confine it to property in the locality ; for if the owner be personally liable, it is not only a local assessment, but also a general one as against the owner."

If there can be a personal assessment, or the owner can be made personally liable for the tax which is imposed upon a lot of land, upon the theory that its pecuniary value is increased by the improvement, the lot may be sold, and if there is a deficiency the owner may be required to pay it; or, in other words, for the benefit conferred on the property the property may be confiscated, and the owner, for the privilege of having it confiscated, may be required to pay a tax into the City Treasury.

Upon the whole, this system of local assessment has been found to work fairly well. It undoubtedly facilitates improvements, because it is one of the least burdensome methods of meeting the cost— always the chief difficulty in their way. The mere fact of its general adoption among a people so shrewd and practical, and containing so large a proportion of proprietors as the Americans, is a sufficient proof that it has given satisfaction.

CHAPTER VII.

FRANCE.

BEFORE inquiring into the local taxation of this country, it may be as well to give a short description of its divisions and form of local government so as to make the system of taxation clear.

French territory is divided into eighty-six departments. The departments are sub-divided into 262 arrondissements; these, in turn, into 2,868 cantons; and, lastly, the cantons into 36,097 communes. These divisions form a graduated hierarchy of local administration. No other divisions conflict with them. The canton is more judicial than administrative. The representative and agent of the central power in the departments is the Prefect. In each arrondissement there is a Sub-Prefect, and in each commune a Mayor. The Sub-Prefect and Mayor stand towards their divisions more or less in the same position as the Prefect does towards his department.

The Municipal Councils are elected by universal suffrage, and for three years, and in communes of more than 500 inhabitants it must not include persons of a near degree of relationship; an example of the extreme wariness against undue influence of every description characterising most French institutions. With the sole exception of the Council of Paris, the Municipal Councils are elected by *scrutin de liste*—that is to say, the electors vote for as many candidates as there are vacancies. The capital under its special *régime* elects its eighty councillors by *scrutin d'arrondissement*, each voter naming only one candidate for his quarter.

In theory, Paris is but one of the 36,097 communes of France, though it contains a fifteenth of the whole population of the country. In Paris the sectional mayors are appointed by the Government, and there is no central mayor at all—in a word, the organisation of the capital of the country is entirely exceptional. Till lately, Lyons was another exception, but Lyons is now governed like the other chief towns. The twofold election of the Municipal Council by the citizens, and of the Mayor by the Municipal Council, is the cornerstone of a free municipal system. The Paris mayoralty is really in commission, the Prefect of the Seine and the Prefect of Police performing the duties of the office between them. These, again, are appointed by the Government, and they are absolutely irresponsible to the Municipal Council.

L

The Council is merely a deliberative body, the executive being entirely in the hands of the two prefects. It debates the civic budget, but it has no power to refuse the essential supplies or to order new credits.

The annual municipal expenditure of Paris is of colossal proportions, and its control is only nominally in the hands of the Council. The Prefect of the Seine appoints the *personnel* of most of the great spending departments. The Director of Public Works is named by the Government, and is independent even of the Prefect. The Director of the Public Charities is likewise a Government nominee. All the Council can do, after voting the money, is to offer a " suggestion " as to the way in which it shall be used ; the Director and the Prefect between them may spend it as they like.

The object of the exceptional treatment of the capital is, of course, to clip its wings for such attempted flights over France as she took in 1789 and 1792, to say nothing of 1870. The City tried to usurp authority over the country, and in revenge the country denies her authority over herself.

The Commune is the administrative unit, the molecule of the great structure of State. The real executive officer is the Prefect. He appoints to many offices, and, with the help of his own Council, he prepares the budget of his department for the Council-General (Conseillers Généraux), a Parliament of the department.

The department levies no special rates, and has no special fiscal officers for assessment or collection. Its revenues are ingathered with the State direct taxes. These are four in number—the land, the personal, the door and window, and the trade taxes. As regards the first three of these, the total amount to be derived from them is fixed by the Budget Act beforehand, and apportioned among the departments. The General Council (Conseillers Généraux) of the department in turn sub-divides its share among the arrondissements, and the Arrondissement Council further sub-divides its share among the communes. The fourth tax—the trade tax—is of fixed amount, and its yield is dependent on the number of persons carrying on trade. The revenues of the department are derived from a percentage added to these four State taxes. This percentage is known as the "centimes additionnels"—i.e., to every franc of the "principal" a certain number of "centimes" or hundredths are added on for county or municipal purposes, according to their respective wants, and within certain limits determined by law. The "centime" equals the hundredth part of the total annual estimate of the four direct taxes levied in France generally, in the department or in the commune, as the case

L 2

may be. Thus, supposing in a commune the original total of these four State taxes is put at 20,000 francs, the centime is worth 200 francs, and in this form of centime all additions to taxation are made for local or other purposes. The collecting of the rates is undertaken gratuitously by the receivers of the taxes in the service of the State, so that, on the one hand, it costs the department nothing, and, on the other hand, the ratepayers have to deal with but one single tax-gatherer for all their rates and taxes.

These centimes are divided into three classes—(1) ordinary or Parliamentary (législatif) centimes; (2) extraordinary centimes ; (3) special centimes. The Parliamentary centimes are voted annually by Parliament, and place the administration of the department beyond the risk of being brought to a standstill through the vagaries of any general council. The General Council, however, decides the mode of employing them. Parliamentary centimes are added to the land and personal taxes only. The extraordinary centimes, on the contrary, are levied by virtue of a decision of the General Council, and are raised on all four taxes. The maximum is annually fixed by Parliament, and can only be exceeded by sanction of an Act of Parliament.

The special centimes are an additional percentage, authorised by Parliament for special objects, as the construction of new roads, etc.

Subsidies may be granted out of the State Exchequer to needy departments, a fund of £160,000 being annually appropriated for this purpose. The departments whose rates are insufficient to meet the local requirements in an adequate manner, and which have to resort to the distribution of this fund, lie mostly in the mountainous parts of France.

We thus see that the local taxation is in the main based upon the imperial direct taxation, and, the incidence being the same, we will state shortly the nature of the four taxes before referred to.

1. *Contribution foncière*, which is divided into two sections—the tax on lands and the tax on buildings. The distribution of the land and house tax is very different in different parts of France, and the " centimes additionnels " are variously imposed. For the purposes of valuation the land is divided into five classes, to each of which corresponds a fixed tax payable to the State at so much per hectare (2½ acres). For instance, for good arable land the land tax may be two or three francs a hectare ; for an enclosed park or garden four or five francs, and inferior land in proportion, with, of course, as we have stated, the " centimes additionnels " added on for local purposes.

These taxes are imposed upon all lands and buildings not especially exempt by law, and are based upon the average productiveness of the property in produce or rents during a series of years. As regards the land, the tax is levied on the net revenue, that is to say, what remains to the owner after deducting from the gross produce the cost of cultivation, sowing, gathering of crops, and maintenance.

The net revenue for property in houses and buildings is the surplus accruing to the owner after deducting from the letting value or rent the amount of expenditure requisite to prevent deterioration and cost of maintenance.

The French law does not for land name the exact proportion to be deducted from the gross produce ; but for houses it fixes it at a quarter of the annual rent or letting value, and for factories, warehouses, etc., at a third, it being considered that the repair of buildings devoted to trade and industrial purposes is more costly than that of private houses.

In forming an estimate of the taxable revenue of arable land, the assessors ascertain the nature and quantity of the crops produced without labour or expense, in conformity with the usual custom of the locality. The yield is averaged by the production of fifteen years, excepting, however, the two most abundant and the two most inferior yields. The ordinary yearly yield having been established, the expenses attending planting, cultivation, and harvesting are deducted, and the remaining amount is the revenue taxed.

Gardens are rated at their renting value, which is estimated on the same basis as that of arable land, but in no case can they be rated higher. Lands devoted to ornamental purposes, such as parks, avenues, etc., are rated as superior tillable land.

The estimated value of the production of vineyards is arrived at by the same method employed in arable land valuation. A deduction of 15 per cent., besides the expenses attending cultivation, gathering, and pressing the grapes, is made. This deduction is allowed in view of the extra outlay for annual trimming of the vines, partial replanting, and necessary labour during the years that the vineyards are nonproducing. When the vines only live a certain number of years, and replanting is possible or removal necessary, to allow the ground to rest for other agricultural purposes, the valuation is based on the following :—

I. The quantity and quality of the wine produced.

II. The quality of the land on which the vines are planted, and the crop the land might produce if cultivated as arable land.

III. The life of the vines.

IV. The number of years that the land produced no vines.

House property is estimated in two ways. First
according to its superficies at the rate of the best
agricultural land, and secondly according to the
annual letting value of the buildings, deducting the
previous estimate of the agricultural value of the
extent of the surface they occupy. The average
letting value for ten years (deducting the two
highest and two lowest returns) is then taken for
the purpose of estimating the net imposible
revenue. However, buildings are not subject to
the tax until the third year after their completion.
The Chambers have recently passed a measure for
the exemption of sheds and agricultural outhouses
of a less annual value than £2 from taxation, even
when used as habitations, and the Government
house tax throughout France is now fixed at the
rate of 3·20 per cent. In the application of the
rate of 3·20 to the total annual value of a house, a
deduction of a quarter is always allowed for costs
of repair and maintenance, so that on the letting
price of a house of 100 francs, 2 francs 40 centimes,
and not 3 francs 20 centimes, will be claimed by
the tax-gatherer for the Government tax, with the
" centimes additionnels " for local purposes.

The real property tax, being thus a tax upon

the revenue derived from a certain property in land or buildings, is due only from the person in the enjoyment of that revenue; but any agricultural tenant may be held liable for one year's taxes left unpaid by his landlord.

The different revenues for which the real estate tax has been fixed, at the time the cadastre or tax-roll has been prepared, cannot be altered whatever the improvements or deteriorations of the property may have been by either the industry of the proprietor or his negligence. However cadastral revenues of land, covered or not by buildings, may be modified when in any community assessed for at least thirty years, the Municipal Council, with the assent of the General Council, makes application at communal expense for a revision and renewal of the tax-roll (cadastre). The valuation of the taxable revenue of houses and workshops may be revised every ten years. This revision is made with the authorisation of the Prefect, and is made by the assessors assisted by the controller. The mayor has to inform the taxpayers that he proceeds to the renewal of the valuation of houses and workshops, and that they may apply for a reduction within three months of the publication of the tax list from the valuation of their property.

2. *Contribution personnelle et mobilière* (the personal and personal property tax) is made up of

two elements, one fixed and the other variable. The first is a small poll-tax of what is considered equivalent to three days of labour. This is payable by every Frenchman in France, and every foreigner of either sex who is in the enjoyment of citizenship and is not a pauper. Even minors having sufficient means of subsistence from their own fortune or employment, although when living with their parents, are liable for the tax.

The General Council fixes the average price of a day's labour in each commune or municipality, but it has no power to fix it below fifty centimes or above a franc and a half. Thus the minimum of this tax is one and a half francs, and the maximum four and a half francs.

It is due in the commune of the taxpayer's domicile. In case of having two domiciles, it is to be paid where the taxpayer lives most of the time —where he has his principal residence, or where he follows his profession or occupation.

The other element of this tax is imposed on all those liable to the poll-tax. It is a direct annual levy of a fixed percentage upon the rental paid for all furnished apartments or dwellings inhabited by all except those exempt by law.

Though this is in its main features an income-tax, it is a tax which certainly falls more on the owner of house property than on him who derives

his income from sources other than houses and
land. The latter, moreover, may occupy an apartment in no way commensurate with his income.

3. *The door and window tax* is levied and assessed on all doors and windows opening into
streets, courtyards, and gardens of houses or
workshops. In general, all openings giving air or
light to houses and buildings for human habitations,
shops, workshops, sheds, warehouses, etc., are taxable whatever their shape, dimension, or fastening
may be. The object of this tax, like the one
previously described, is to make all individuals
participate in the expenses of the State and local
divisions in proportion to their fortunes, as mani-
fested by the importance of their dwellings—an
importance considered, or sufficiently expressed, by
their number of windows and doors.

The openings to new buildings become taxable
as soon as the buildings become habitable. If at
the time of the making of the tax-roll some rooms
of a new house are not yet habitable, the openings
of such rooms are for the time exempt. If the
entire front of a room or atelier consists of windows,
the number of windows to be taxed is determined
by their solid divisions of either iron, stone, or
wood. The tax is graduated according to the
number of inhabitants and the nature and number
in which the doors and windows are arranged.

Doors and windows of manufacturing establishments are not taxable, except those in the dwelling part.

The door and window tax is levied by repartition between the departments, arrondissements, communes, and taxpayers according to the subjoined tariff, excepting contingencies.

IN FRANCS.

Population of cities and communes.	For houses with					For houses with six or more openings.		
	One opening.	Two openings.	Three openings.	Four openings.	Five openings.	Carriage doors vehicles and warehouses.	Ordinary windows ground floor, entresol, and first and second stories.	Windows, third storey and above.
Below 5,000	·30	·45	·90	1·60	2·50	1·60	·60	·60
5,000 to 10,000	·40	·60	1·35	2·20	3·25	3·50	·75	·75
10,000 to 25,000	·50	·80	1·80	2·80	4·00	7·40	·90	·75
25,000 to 50,000	·60	1·00	2·70	4·00	5·50	11·20	1·20	·75
50,000 to 100,000	·80	1·20	3 60	5·20	7·00	15·00	1·50	·75
Over 100,000	1·00	1·50	4·50	6·40	8·50	18·80	1·80	·75

In cities and communes of over 5,000 inhabitants the tax corresponding with the number of population applies only to the dwellings within the octroi lines; those outside are classed as rural communes.

The Councils-General apportion the contingent

amount due by each department among the communes through the councils of arrondissement.

The director of the direct taxes prepares every year a table giving (1) the number of taxable openings of each class; (2) the product of the taxes according to the tariff; and (3) the projected apportionment. In large cities and towns it must, of course, be a source of considerable revenue. The tariff in each commune rises and falls in proportion to the amount fixed as the quota of the commune. Though the occupier is legally liable for this charge, it is sometimes borne by the landlord, and it thus becomes an addition to the property tax in certain cases, quite out of proportion to the value of the house-property concerned, large and small openings on each storey being taxed equally. This latter evil in Paris has, since 1852, been dealt with, and there has been more justice in the allotment of this tax, the letting value of the house being taken into consideration, and the size and nature of the doors and windows. In Bordeaux as well as Paris exceptional tariffs are now in force.

(4) The *contribution des patentés* is the tax upon trade. Every individual Frenchman or foreigner in France engaged in commerce, trade, industry, or a profession not embraced in the exemptions provided for by law, is obliged to take

out a licence. The different licences for professional or business purposes are divided into several categories, according to the nature of the business and the population of the city, and the tax levied in proportion to the importance and presumed profit of the trade. If an individual owns several establishments he has to pay for one of them at the highest rate of the categories in which his business is placed, but only one-half out of the rate for each of the remaining establishments. This tax comprises a fixed and a proportionate tax. The reason of this combination is evident, for were a fixed duty only to be levied on all the followers of one same class of industry, the tax would then affect unequally the rich and the poor ; whereas with the addition of a proportionate duty a proper equilibrium is established between the amount required from all the holders of licences.

The fixed taxes are regulated by law according to Schedules A, B, C, and D, which modify the taxes previously levied. The taxpayer must belong to one of these four different categories ; the fixed tax is then regulated by the general tariff, and according to the population of the commune, or according to the population and the situation of the commune, by an exceptional tariff, or, finally, without regard to the population, but according to the elements of production.

Commercial, industrial, or professional avocations not specified in the tables are nevertheless subject to the licence tax, which is regulated according to similar industries.

The categories into which persons liable to this tax are placed are as follows :—

(A) Retail merchants and wholesale and retail merchants and artisans who employ workmen ; (B) bankers, brokers, and negociants—*i.e.*, wholesale traders, importers and exporters ; (C) manufacturers ; (D) liberal professions, viz., lawyers, physicians, etc.

Schedule A in this classification is the most important and complicated of the four divisions under the licence law. Under this head are classed retail merchants and artisans who employ workmen (and who are classified entirely apart from the manufacturers in Schedule C). Taxpayers in Schedule A are divided into eight sub-classes, according to the nature and supposed lucrativeness of their business. These sub-classes are again divided into nine categories, according to the population of the commune in which the licentiate is located.

Thus a merchant (Sub-class No. 1) pays in Paris a fixed licence tax of 400 francs ; in Marseilles, 300 ; in Toulon, 240 ; and so on down to 35 francs in a commune having less than 2,000 inhabitants.

A coal-dealer (Sub-class No. 5) would pay in the same cities 50, 40, 30, and 7 francs respectively, as will appear from the following table :—

IN FRANCS.

	Class 1.	Class 2.	Class 3.	Class 4.	Class 5.	Class 6.	Class 7.	Class 8.
In Paris	400	200	140	75	50	40	20	12
In communes of more than 100,000	300	150	100	75	50	40	20	12
50,000 to 100,000	240	120	80	60	40	32	16	10
30,000 to 50,000	180	90	60	45	30	24	12	8
20,000 to 30,000	120	60	40	30	20	16	8	6
10,000 to 20,000	80	45	30	25	15	10	8	5
5,000 to 10,000	60	40	25	20	12	8	5	4
2,000 to 5,000	45	30	22	15	9	6	4	3
2,000 and less	35	25	18	12	7	4	3	2

All this relates to the fixed element of the licence tax, which is imposed equally upon all persons exercising their avocations under the same conditions.

In establishments where the fixed tax is regulated according to the number of hands employed, the hands below sixteen years of age or over sixty years count only for half.

The proportionate tax is levied upon the rentable value of a dwelling-house, as well as warehouses, stores, shops, workshops, sheds, or any other locality in connection with the exercise of a taxable profession. It is due the same if the dwelling or building is occupied rent free. The proportionate tax from workshops and industrial establishments is levied on the tenant value in their entirety and furnished with all the materials of production.

According to this law, which, with the exception of gas manufacturers, is applicable almost exclusively to taxpayers of Table C, not only the rentable value of the building, but also the rentable value of the machinery, and all industrial appliances, such as motive power and accessories, are taxable.

The proportionate tax is payable in all the communes where the warehouses, stores, etc., are situated.

If a taxpayer owns more than one dwelling-house, he pays the proportionate tax only on the one where he exercises his industry and where he trades.

The proportionate tax is fixed at the twentieth part of the rentable value for all taxable professions, on trades, with the exceptions stated in Table D, which are somewhat numerous.

Everyone paying a licence tax receives a certificate free of stamp duty, which is to be produced whenever the mayor, commissary of police, or other judiciary officer asks for it. Goods sold without a licence can be seized and held at the expense of the seller until a licence is obtained.

These are the direct State taxes, which form

M

the basis of the local taxation : but besides the addition for local purposes of the " centimes " to the State taxes, the municipalities have other means of relieving their citizens of their superfluous wealth.   A dog tax is levied, and, independently of the duties collected at the entrance of important cities on behalf of the State, there are others called " municipal taxes," the collection of which is secured by the service of the " régie " or by that of the " octroi."

Each commune can levy a tax on dogs of not less than one or more than ten francs a head. Dogs are divided into two classes. The highest tax is paid for dogs of luxury or sport, and the lowest for such as may be used by blind persons, shepherd or watch dogs. The tax must be paid for the entire year ; and if the owner dies during the year the unpaid proportion of the tax is a charge upon the heirs.

The "octroi" is a kind of custom house on a small scale. In order to raise additional revenue for large towns, the agents of the octroi are posted at the entrances of the towns, and all persons, carriages, and carts entering the town are stopped and duties demanded upon numerous articles, no matter where produced. The "régie" is the administration which collects in the interior of towns certain special taxes.

Each commune or city of 4,000 inhabitants or over may levy an octroi for home consumption, and goods can only be delivered after such duty has been paid ; the hours within which delivery can be made are regulated by law.

Cities having an octroi may claim an authorisation to add to it a part of their quota of personal and mobiliary tax, in order to be able to exempt rents below a certain amount. This is always done in Paris, where rents marked less than 500 francs are exempt, adding from $7\frac{1}{2}$ to $11\frac{1}{2}$ per cent. to all rents taxable above 600 to 1,000 francs.

This octroi tax is particularly disagreeable, and the very sight of an octroi barrier with its different implements for probing the waggons, boxes, boring casks, measuring, weighing, and testing produce subject to the tax is unpleasant. They have and exercise the right to examine all travellers on foot or mounted. Nor is this the worst feature ; by increasing the cost of the necessaries of life, which the articles charged usually are, they decrease the buying capacity of the workman, and consequently diminish his capacity for work. The expense of collecting this tax is necessarily great. At Amiens it is about 11 per cent. ; elsewhere nearly 20 per cent. At Rouen it is 17 per cent. ; but the reason of the excess here is, there are so many different modes of entering Rouen, both by land

M 2

and water, many more offices and officers are required.

Communes may have such further special municipal revenue as they think proper, as rents from markets, fairs, and slaughter-houses ; for the stands of public vehicles, for superintendence of the streets, etc. ; for communal tolls, weighing, measuring, etc. ; and fees for special services, privileges, etc. ; income from public funds or from capital invested with individuals. Every commune can hold public funds, and can also place its disposable funds with individuals by way of mortgage.

We have before us a list of the special municipal taxes of Nantes, and marvel how the inhabitants are content to bear them. If they make any sort of repairs to their houses, or even petty repairs to the cornice of a house, a tax must be paid. Likewise, if openings are made in a wall for a door or window, and again, if old doors or windows are closed up. If you have a small balcony in front of your window, or projecting steps, lanterns or hooks to exhibit goods, or even reflectors to front lights, tribute must be paid to the local Cæsars.

In addition to a large number of indirect taxes, such as the fiscal and protective duties, and revenue derived from stamps registration, donations or sales of property, etc. etc., the State has monopolies in the manufacture of tobacco, powder, matches, the postal and telegraphic service, coining of money and medal department. The Government also attends to business not covered by a monopoly, such as the forwarding of money and newspapers equally performed by railroads and other companies.

State industries, outside of a monopoly are such as, since 1878, working of some State railways, establishments for instruction and learning, of the manufacture of objects of art, like Sèvres china and Gobelin's tapestry; of the publication of newspapers, books, etc., and also of banking and insurance operations, etc.

The assessment of the direct taxes is entrusted to a special service composed of: (1) director-general at Paris, (2) eighty-six divisions distributed in the different departments, but under the control of the director-general. Each division is comprised of a superintendent, one inspector, and several controllers. The duty of the controllers is to collect necessary information for preparing the assessment lists. The inspector supervises the controllers. The director transmits all orders from the director-general to the inspectors and controllers, directs the service, regulates the work, and prepares the tax lists.

The authorities who prepare the matricular lists, together with the tax commissioners, are the mayor and communal assessors, of whom there are seven,

namely, the mayor, the adjunct or substitute, and
five taxpayers on real estate, of whom two at least
must reside in the communal.   Besides these, there
are five substitute assessors, nominated by the sous-
prefect on presentation by the mayor.   No less
than five assessors form a quorum.

The collection of the taxes is a separate service
under the control of the director-general of accounts
at Paris, with the following officers in each department :—Treasurer ; paymaster-general, residing in
the principal city of the department ; receiver of
the taxes, residing in the principal town of the
arrondissement ; and collectors whose duties are to
collect the taxes enumerated in the tax lists.
These special officers receive aid and assistance
from the authorities of the departments and
communes.

The direct taxes become due every month, or
the twelfth part of the yearly tax.   The proprietors
or principal lessees of houses are bound to require
their tenants or sub-tenants to produce their tax
receipts a month before their moving away, else they
will become themselves liable.   If the tenants refuse to produce their receipts to the proprietor, he
must immediately inform the tax-collector, and get
from him an acknowledgment of the receipt of
such notice, when he is released from further
liability.   We think we have given a sufficient review

of the French system of taxation. It is graphically described in a report by the United States consul at Bordeaux as follows :—

"Taxation in France is comparable to an insatiable monster, with its covetous eye upon every possible taxable thing. From the poorest creature struggling for daily bread to those enjoying the luxuries of wealth, each pays his mite or portion. Nothing that the City can tax—no industry, profession, trade, or act—is exempt. Every traveller indirectly pays for the privilege of seeing France. There is not a hotel at which he stops, no article of food or drink supplied him, even the very bed he sleeps upon, but which pays its tribute. The agricultural class bears the heaviest burden of taxation. First of all, the land pays its heavy tribute, every beast of burden, all cattle, vehicles, and implements are taxed. Nothing that is produced on the farm but is met at the city entrances by the collectors of the 'octroi.' Among the principal of the numerous causes of taxation in France is the standing army, averaging one soldier to every twenty inhabitants, maintained, armed, and paid by the Government ; the forcing of all youths over eighteen years of age to undergo from three to five years' military service ; and the compulsion of all able-bodied men under forty-five years of age to spend annually from twenty-eight days to six weeks in military drill, thus depriving the country of the services of the best producers at the very period when they are most valuable and capable."

According to statistics, land in France consists of some 28,000.000 holdings, divided amongst 5,000,000 proprietors, and each one of these 28,000,000 can be sold or let at the good pleasure of the proprietor. Entail does not exist in France, and children share alike the real and personal estate of the parents.

With respect to the selling or letting of property, the provisions of the French law are equally applicable to urban and rural property, and considerable latitude is allowed to vendors and lessors as regards the conditions they may desire to attach to sales or leases, provided always that these conditions do not in any way interfere with police, municipal, or State regulations, and do not contravene either servitudes and prescriptions, or infringe the rights and privileges of neighbours.

In France, property can be sold, and is not unfrequently sold, in small lots, so as to enable persons to build houses on it. These sales may be unconditional, in which case the purchase is bound by such restrictions only as are made in the public interest.

Instead of being sold in building lots, land is sometimes let for a term of years upon condition that houses are built upon it ; that an annual or other periodical rent is paid by the lessee ; and that at the end of the term the houses shall become the property of the landlord. With respect to the length of such leases, it is usual to calculate it on the probable income to be derived from the houses. The calculation is based on the principal that the lessee shall not only obtain an annual income, varying from 4 to 6 per cent. of the capital expended, but that the money laid out on the buildings should be redeemed.

It is, therefore, very difficult to fix an average for the duration of this kind of lease, much depending upon the commercial, industrial, and social conditions of a particular locality.

CHAPTER VIII.

GERMANY.

THE German Empire affords us as an example of the absence of uniformity in the mode of assessing local taxation. Each federal state has its own system, and even some towns in the same state have different ways of augmenting their local exchequer.

The public revenues of Germany are imposed and collected partly by the Empire, partly by the separate states, and partly by the different local authorities.

The Empire has entire control of the customs and excise, and it may be said that for imperial purposes no direct taxation is levied. The various states, however, impose direct taxation, and it will be found that the income principal is the most characteristic feature.

This variety will, no doubt, show us the different ways and means by which German politicians hope to meet the demands necessitated by the multi-

farious wants of large cities and communities, by
evading at the same time apparent injustice or
impartiality in the imposition of taxes.

PRUSSIA.

The Prussian provinces are sub-divided into
" Kreises " — *i.e.*, circuits or counties, and every
kreise is again sub-divided into "communes," being
either towns or communes of the country (Landge-
meinden).

Large cities constitute kreises of their own.
Only Berlin occupies an exceptional position in
Prussian Monarchy. It constitutes a city, kreise,
and province combined.

Though it will furnish a good example as to
the local taxation paid by a Prussian inhabitant,
yet the high standard of its tax percentages can
hardly be regarded as typical for other places ; its
position as the capital of the German Empire requiring a number of expenses for public works and
for facilities of trade and traffic which smaller
places may, without injury to the interests of their
occupants, dispense with.

For cities and hamlets not exceeding 2,500
inhabitants in number a simplified constitution is
applicable. The control of a city is under : (1) the
Burgomaster (Mayor) ; (2) Magistracy (Magisterial
Senate) ; (3) Board of Aldermen. The Magistracy

is a body charged with the administration of the
city property. The Board of Aldermen represents
the burgesses and controls the administration. The
Mayor directs and superintends the entire run of
business and is responsible for the current administration of affairs.

To defray the expenditure for local purposes,
the communes are under law permitted to collect
certain taxes on houses, rentals, incomes, dogs ;
tolls on macadamised roads, bridges, ferries, or
(which many cities do) to levy an excise, laid on
articles of food (mill-ground articles, cattle, meat,
etc.) entered for consumption (octroi).

Municipal revenue is raised either by : (1) the
surtaxes (Ausschlage) based on the rates of certain
specified State direct taxes, or (2) by special sanction from the State to impose certain specified
taxes, direct or indirect. The former one is the
one generally adopted by Prussian municipal and
provincial communes, having no independent communal revenue for real property.

The amount of these surtaxes, of course, varies
in each commune, according to its means and wants.
In some provinces the special sanction of the State
is necessary to impose a communal surtax higher
than 5 per cent. of the rate of the State tax, but in
the case of the majority of provinces such sanction
is only required when the communal surtax is

higher than 50 per cent. of the State rate. In very few communes the surtax is as high as 300 and 400 per cent. of the State tax. Some few wealthy communes are in a position to dispense altogether with the assistance of direct taxation.

The State taxes which are employed as bases for these surtaxes are : (1) on real property, (a) the land tax and the (b) house tax ; and (2) personal, as (a) the class-tax on personal net annual incomes under 3,000 marks (£150); and (b) classified income tax on annual net income above that amount ; and (c) the trading tax.

The land tax and the surtax is levied on all productive land. The amount to be raised is distributed for collection among the different kreises ; within these it is again distributed among the individual communes and independent manors of the kreise, and by those among the rateable properties (Siegenschaften), and proportioned equally on the basis of their ascertained net annual yield to the cultivation. The net annual yield is the surplus of the average gross yield of each separate plot of land remaining after deducting farming costs. For the purpose of assessment each lot of land is classed under one or other of the following descriptive categories : (1) arable, (2) garden, (3) meadow, (4) pasture, (5) woodland, (6) water, (7) waste ; and in each category under one of eight classes denoting its net annual valuation. The rate of taxes collected for land is about 9½ per cent. from the estimated value of its yield.

There are different modes of assessing the several State taxes. As regards the land tax, the Secretary of the Treasury stands at the head of the land-appraising authorities of the whole State. Immediately subordinate to him are the commissioners-general, whose duty is to direct and to supervise the execution of the required land-appraising work, and to see that equitable results be secured within the borders of the State. A central commission is formed consisting of four land experts, and of several members from each province, one-half of the provincial members being chosen by the Upper House, and one-half by the House of Representatives. This central commission has to fix the tariff of classification and to settle the final results of assessment. A commission, appointed for each province and supported by technical experts, directs and controls the execution of the necessary assessments and appraisements. Each province has also a board presided over by the provincial commissioners and a commission of assessment assisted by an assessing board, to superintend and execute the work of assessment, and to fix or revise the tariff of appraisement within their district, and to perform all other duties connected with the office. The costs of assessing and collecting the land tax is fixed at from 3 to 4 per cent. from the amount actually collected and received.

The house tax and surtax is assessed on all permanent buildings, inclusive of the grounds upon which erected, and of the yards and gardens belonging thereto : providing that the area of the gardens does not exceed 2 roods 20 perches. Gardens of a larger size are subject to the land tax. It is, properly speaking, a separate category of the land tax, and the individual assessments are similarly recorded in the land registers. For the purpose of assessment, all taxable houses and buildings are placed in one of two categories. The first in which the assessment is 4 per cent. of the occupancy value, includes all buildings designed especially for dwelling houses, or to satisfy personal requirements, also theatres, private schools, etc. The second category, taxed at the rate of 2 per cent. of the annual occupancy value, embraces all buildings exclusively or principally used for trading or industrial purposes. These annual values, in case of towns and villages with a large proportion of letting houses, are assessed on the basis of ascertained average letting values. In districts where no such basis is obtainable, rules are laid down to guide the assessors in fixing the gross annual value of the occupancy; these rules appear to take into consideration the material structure of the buildings and the circumstances of the locality. An increase of the building tax, in consequence of additional improvements, only comes into force two whole years after the alterations have been made.

The classification of houses and buildings liable to this tax, is as follows:—

ASSESSMENT TARIFF FOR HOUSE TAX.

Class.	Yearly valuation.	Annual rate of tax.				Class.	Yearly valuation.	Annual rate of tax.			
		At 4 p.c.		At 2 p.c.				At 4 p.c.		At 2 p.c.	
	Marks.	Mks.	Pf.	Mks.	Pf.		Marks.	Mks.	Pf.	Mks.	Pf.
1	12	0	·40	0	·20	23	675	27	·00	13	·00
2	18	0	·60	0	·30	24	750	30	·00	15	·00
3	24	0	·80	0	·40	25	825	33	·00	16	·00
4	36	1	·20	0	·60	26	900	36	·00	18	·00
5	45	1	·80	0	·90	27	975	39	·00	19	·00
6	60	2	·40	1	·20	28	1,050	42	·00	21	·00
7	75	3	·00	1	·50	29	1,125	45	·00	22	·00
8	90	3	·60	1	·80	30	1,200	48	·00	24	·00
9	105	4	·20	2	·10	31	1,350	54	·00	27	·00
10	120	4	·80	2	·40	32	1,500	60	·00	30	·00
11	135	5	·40	2	·70	33	1,650	66	·00	33	·00
12	150	6	·00	3	·00	34	1,800	72	·00	36	·00
13	180	7	·20	3	·60	35	1,950	78	·00	39	·00
14	210	8	·40	4	·20	36	2,100	84	·00	42	·00
15	240	9	·60	4	·80	37	2,250	90	·00	45	·00
16	270	10	·80	5	·40	38	2,400	96	·00	48	·00
17	300	12	·00	6	·00	39	2,550	102	·00	51	·00
18	364	14	·40	7	·20	40	2,700	108	·00	54	·00
19	420	16	·80	8	·40	41	2,850	114	·00	57	·00
20	480	19	·20	9	·60	42	3,000	120	·00	60	·00
21	540	21	·60	10	·80	43		132	·00	66	·00
22	600	24	·00	12	·00						

Up to 6,000 marks each further class rises by 300 marks, and after that by 600 marks.

The rental value of buildings is appraised by a commission chosen by the building owners of the district at a meeting held for that purpose. The commissioners perform their duties under the direction of the chief magistrates of the respective districts.

The cost of assessing and collecting the class taxes is fixed at from 3 to 4 per cent. from the amount actually collected.

The class tax (Classensteuer) and surtax are levied off all persons having their own household, and all persons supporting themselves by their own means, independent of the head of the family or household they may belong to. Only to physical persons as such, or to the individual, this class tax attaches; it has no bearing upon firms, corporations, societies, etc. It will be noticed that as this class income tax is payable by persons having a net income from £21 a year and under £150 a year, a class of taxpayers is reached who are entirely relieved from the payment of income tax in the united kingdom.

The class taxpayers are divided into twelve distinct classes, formed on the basis of the annual income, those included in each class being liable to a different rate from those in another class. Incomes under £45 a year are exempt from State taxation, although liable to communal taxation on the basis of a fictitious State tax equal to 1s. 6d.

N

per annum. Incomes from £45 to £150 are
entitled to relief from one-fourth the annual State
tax. The classification and the normal annual
tax of each class are as follows :—

CLASS TAX.

Annual net incomes ranging between 420 marks
and 3,000 marks are divided into 12 classes, thus :

Class.	Income.			Annual tax.
	Marks.		Marks.	Marks.
I.	Above 420 to and inclusive of 660			3
II.	,, 660	,,	,, 900	6
III.	,, 900	,,	,, 1,050	9
IV.	,, 1,050	,,	., 1,200	12
V.	,, 1,200	,,	,, 1,350	18
VI.	,, 1,350	,,	,, 1,500	24
VII.	,, 1,500	,,	,, 1,650	30
VIII.	,, 1,650	,,	,, 1,800	36
IX.	,, 1,800	,,	,, 2,100	42
X.	,, 2,100	,,	,, 2,400	48
XI.	,, 2,400	,,	,, 2,700	60
XII.	,, 2,700	,,	,, 3,000	72

The classified (graded) income-taxes and surtax
are levied on all persons having an annual income
over and above £150 a year. They are classified
for assessment into forty classes. Even foreigners
staying in Prussia more than one year must pay
the tax upon their net income, although the sources
of such income may be elsewhere and in a different
country. Such strangers are liable to the communal or municipal taxes after the third month of
residence.

The classification, with the annual tax assessment upon each class, is as follows :—

CLASSIFIED INCOME TAX.
Assessment Classes.

Class	Above (Marks)	to (Marks) Inclusive	Annual tax (Marks)
1	3,000	3,600	90
2	3,600	4,200	108
3	4,200	4,800	126
4	4,800	5,400	144
5	5,400	6,000	162
6	6,000	7,200	180
7	7,200	8,400	216
8	8,400	9,600	252
9	9,600	10,800	288
10	10,800	12,000	324
11	12,000	14,400	360
12	14,400	16,800	432
13	16,800	19,200	504
14	19,200	21,600	576
15	21,600	25,200	648
16	25,200	28,000	756
17	28,000	32,400	864
18	32,400	36,000	972
19	36,000	42,000	1,080
20	42,000	48,000	1,200

Class	Above (Marks)	to (Marks) Inclusive	Annual tax (Marks)
21	48,000	54,000	1,400
22	54,000	60,000	1,620
23	60,000	72,000	1,800
24	72,000	84,000	2,160
25	84,000	96,000	2,520
26	96,000	108,000	2,880
27	108,000	120,000	3,240
28	120,000	144,000	3,600
29	144,000	168,000	4,320
30	168,000	204,000	5,040
31	204,000	240,000	6,120
32	240,000	300,000	7,200
33	300,000	360,000	9,000
34	360,000	420,000	10,800
35	420,000	480,000	12,000
36	480,000	540,000	14,400
37	540,000	600,000	16,200
38	600,000	660,000	18,000
39	660,000	720,000	19,800
40	720,000	780,000	21,600

N 2

And for every additional 60,000 marks an additional tax of 1,800 marks. In assessing the communal supplements, only half of the official salaries of Government officials is taken into account for the class and income tax ; accordingly, an official salary of 1,500 marks would be assessed on the basis of the State tax on an income of 750 marks, *i.e.* on 6 marks instead of 24 marks. The pay of persons in the standing army is exempt from State taxation, and was until recently equally exempt from local taxation ; but it has now been made liable to the latter taxation.

The municipal authorities are required to keep a correct record of persons liable to the income tax. The assessment is made by a district assessing board presided over by the Chief Magistrate of the district.

The board is constituted by a certain number of persons, of whom one-third are appointed by the district or municipal authorities, and two-thirds by the taxpayers of the various income classes.

The classification and assessing are done by the board upon information and evidence obtained and examination had. The parties assessed may appeal from the decisions of the board to an administration tribunal organised for that purpose, and whose jurisdiction is final.

In absence of authentic proof to establish the

amount of annual income, circumstantial and hypothetical evidence is admitted. The style of dwelling and living is taken as a basis upon which to calculate the income, and the annual expenditure of a person is accepted as sufficient proof of a corresponding income.

The Prussian tax and fiscal authorities understand it well to bring reticent, evasive, and unwilling taxpayers to terms, amicably if it can be, peremptorily if it must be. The costs of assessing and collecting the classified income taxes are fixed at three per cent. on the amount actually received.

The trading tax and surtax are assessed in a most complicated manner. The trades and occupations for the purposes of taxation are divided into classes and each class into sections, and the tax for each class and section is fixed by law.

Companies and firms are subject to the tax the same as individuals ; but apart from what the individual may think in Prussia, the professions of physician, lawyers, actors, painters, etc., are not regarded as pursuits for gain, and consequently not subject to the tax.

We think it will be unnecessary to give the classification of the different trades and occupations. Every party affected participates in its distribution. Wholesale dealers, merchants, and the smaller grades of industrials, by their repre-

sentatives elected for that purpose, co-operate with
the authorities and have their say. The conflicting
interests and opinions of the various occupations
are thereby sought to be reconciled. The practice
is attended with equitable results, inasmuch as the
several trades are best qualified to judge as to the
proper distribution of the burden.

The costs of assessing and collecting the trade
and occupation taxes are fixed at 4 per cent. on
the amount actually received. Before entering on
a business, the person must give notice to the local
authority so as to be placed in the proper class and
section.

Such is a sketch of the general nature of the
State taxation of Prussia, which forms the basis of
the municipal taxation generally. But, as has
been already stated, the local taxation system of
Berlin is not an example of that adopted in other
towns, but shows how various the systems may be
even in the same country.

Unlike any other city in Prussia, Berlin, as
stated before, has the rights and duties of a
province, and from its multiple character the tasks
imposed upon its local administrations are considerable, and exceptional legislation has been
enacted for it. There is no "Octroi" collected in
Berlin, although certain communes are permitted
to levy an excise laid on articles of food entered

for consumption. The city derives its income for
municipal purposes from—

1. A house tax paid by the owners of the
houses, generally at the rate of 2⅓ per cent. of the
amount of rentals received.

2. A rental tax, which is paid by the tenants at
the rate of about 6⅔ per cent. of the amount of the
rental paid.

3. A municipal income tax collected mostly at
the rate of 100 per cent. of the amount of the class
or State income tax. Reference has already been
made to the different classifications of the incomes
liable to the State and this municipal income tax.

4. A dog-tax of nine shillings each dog per
year. The number of the canine breed within
Berlin may be ascertained when this tax generally
returns about £15,000 a year.

No mention is made here of the other strictly
speaking non-municipal taxes which a Prussian has
to bear, such as the church tax and school tax,
although the communes have to provide for the
organisation of schools, subject to the control of
the State. Neither has been included what Berlin
house-owners have to pay to have their houses
connected with the system of sewerage, and for gas
and water consumed within their houses. For
primary schools no special school-money is collected in Berlin.

In Frankfort-on-Main the levy upon the class and income tax is ninety per cent. added to the State classified income and class tax combined. The assessment on house rent is different there, being 4 per cent. annually from the annual rent stipulated. The tax on income submitted by the State is 3 per cent., and inasmuch as the city has added ninety marks to every hundred marks of State tax, it results that the percentage levied on the income of persons residing in the city as a municipal tax is 5·9 per cent. A water rate of 4 per cent. on the rental value is also charged for the water supply.

The local taxes are payable either in monthly or quarterly instalments, which is a source of great convenience to the ratepayers. Like ours, none of the taxes constitute a charge on the property, being merely a personal liability of the individual, and yet the losses in collection seem to be of little importance. This appears to be accounted for by the fact that arrears are not permitted to run up. If the tax is not paid within three days after demand a levy is made.

In Prussia, and practically throughout Germany generally, house property is invariably held in freehold tenure, and the system of letting land on long building leases is practically unknown. Property is usually sold in small lots, so as to

enable persons to build houses thereon ; but in
each case a fixed price in one sum must be given.
Yearly rents or other periodical payments are not
admissible. The only restriction to which the
purchaser would be subject who was desirous of
building on such lots in country as well as in town
districts would be :—(1) Legal restrictions, in the
case of buildings for commercial or industrial
purposes and the like, imposed for the purpose of
preventing any prejudice to the convenience, safety,
or health of the public ; (2) police restrictions,
imposed with the object of securing proper access
to the dwelling-house, and its proper sanitary condition, and further to provide for the arrangements
of the structure being kept strictly within the limits
of any plan which may have been fixed or approved
by the municipal authority ; (3) private restrictions
arising out of any such covenant or agreement
which may have been entered into between vendor
and purchaser as to the description of building to
be erected, or the use to be made of the ground
sold.

WURTEMBERG.

Here, as in the other kingdoms, the local taxes
are levied by adding so much per cent. to the State
direct tax according to the requirements of the
local authorities.

These requirements vary enormously ; in some communes scarcely any taxes are necessary, owing to their possessing large communal properties, but in most cases the additions to the State tax for local purposes far exceed the amount of the tax for national purposes.

In Stuttgart, the capital, the city authorities levy percentages added to the State :—

(*a*) Land tax, which, for national purposes, is 3'9 per cent. on the yearly average net yield of the land, as assessed by official appraisers, making with the local percentage of 5'8 per cent. an average tax of 9'7 per cent. on the " cadastrial value."

(*b*) House tax, which is estimated by considering 3 per cent. of the full value as the net revenue upon which a tax of 3'9 per cent. is levied, the local percentage, being in this case 5'8 per cent., also making a similar average tax of 9'7 per cent. on the cadastrial value of buildings.

(*c*) Trade tax, the mode of assessment of which is most complicated. The tax includes every kind of industrial and commercial enterprise, except farming. Merchants and tradesmen have to state the amount of capital invested in their business, and the number of assistants. An estimate is then made of the annual revenue from the capital invested and the value of the merchant's personal activity, which value is considered as the merchant's personal earnings, the sum total forming the amount on which the tax is levied. Any capital less than £35 is not subject to the tax, and of personal earnings only an amount exceeding £170 is subject to the full tax, while of minor amounts only the following proportions are counted :—

Up to 850 marks		one-tenth.
From 850 to 1,700 marks	...	two-tenths.
„ 1,700 to 2,550 „ ...	... ...	four-tenths.
„ 2,550 to 3,400 „ ...	... ...	eight-tenths.

(d) On the revenue from investments in stocks, bonds, etc., and on all kinds of salaries exceeding £17 per annum, a tax of 4·8 per cent. is levied for State purposes, and for municipal purposes 1 per cent. of the revenue assessed for Government taxation.

(e) A residence tax, due from every self-dependent person residing in Stuttgart. Male persons pay 4s. per annum ; females 2s. per annum.

(f) Taxes on the consumption of beer, meat, and gas.

SAXONY.

The local taxation of the kingdom of Saxony, urban and rural, is very diversified. The principal direct imposts are :—

A house tax levied on the basis of the "taxation units" of the State, "grundstener"; a land tax assessed on local measurements of real estate; a property tax; a poll tax on households; taxes on rental, and on the capital value of land and houses; a local income tax. These are applied in various forms and combinations.

The towns and rural communes of Saxony are, as a rule, owners of the real and funded property; gasworks, waterworks, and other sources of income from which local expenditure is partly defrayed to the extent, possibly, of half of the whole or more, one locality being thereby altogether exempt from municipal taxation. Again, the relative amount raised by the house and building tax is not constant, but varies from place to place according to the nature of the local taxation, which follows very dissimilar patterns of assessment.

Let us take the capital, Dresden, as an example of a moderately taxed Saxon town. Chief among the civic resources is the rent tax, which (for Saxony) is peculiar to Dresden. It occurs also in Berlin, as we have seen. It is, as its name implies, assessed on the rental, and is paid by the occupier. The rate for houses is 12 per cent., and 1 per cent. for church expenditure, making in all 13 per cent. on the rental, or, as we should say, 2s. 7d. in the pound. For shops, warehouses, etc., half rates are charged ; for gardens, etc., one-fifth rate. Dwellings rented at £5 8s. or under are exempt ; from that level up to £7 10s. half rates only are charged.

Next in importance is the Dresden tax on the capital value of building and land. The rental is appraised on moderate terms, one-third is then deducted, and the remainder taken at twenty years' purchase. The sum resulting is the capital value, which is charged with a rate of 36 per 10,000. This impost appears to fall more lightly on owners of detached houses than on houses on flats.

According to Mr. Mill, a rate on house rent is one of the fairest of taxes. " The amount paid in rent," he observes, " is the best criterion of a man's means, and it bears, on the whole, a pretty constant proportion to general expenditure." With their practical experience of this tax, the Germans have come to an opinion removed, *toto cælo*, from this. They observe that a person with an income of about £30 has to disburse a full quarter of his revenue, or 25 per cent., on his rent ; that, as revenue rises, the proportion expended on rent rapidly diminishes, so as to be only 3 per cent. on incomes of more than £1,500 per annum, and on the larger incomes a mere vanishing fraction of their amount. These being the facts observed in Germany (in Berlin the contrasts observed are even more notable still), it is natural that there should be a prevalent conviction of the extreme unfairness of the house tax.

These taxes are supplemented by a tax on burgesses and residents, who pay four shillings as the maximum ; a dog tax of 10s., a tax of 12s. on caged nightingales, and an octroi duty on such articles of food as flour, beer, game, poultry, fish, meat, and tolls on beasts. The octroi duties, it has been calculated, only lay a charge of about 2s. 10d. per head on the inhabitants of Dresden.

A percentage is also added to the State income tax, the incidence of which is significant. The Saxon income tax is levied on incomes in excess of £15 a year. The incomes are divided into classes, and the rates of taxation are progressive, and increase in proportion to the amount of the income. Thus, on incomes from 300 to 400 marks (£15 to £20), the State tax is a half-mark, or sixpence. On incomes £125 to £140 the State tax would be £2 8s., and so until on the higher incomes the State tax would amount to fully 4½ per cent. It is important to observe also that " income " here includes all value received. Thus, in the fiscal language of Saxony, the income of a servant consists of wages, together with the appraised worth in money of his or her lodging, food, livery, or other emoluments.

Class.	Income.						Tax.				
	Marks.				£		Marks.	£	s.	d.	
1	300	—	400	...	15	— 20	½	...	0	0	6
2	400	—	500	...	20	— 25	1	...	0	1	0
3	500	—	600	...	25	— 30	2	...	0	2	0
4	600	—	700	..	30	— 35	3	...	0	3	0
5	700	—	800	...	35	— 40	4	...	0	4	0
6	800	—	900	...	40	— 45	6	...	0	6	0
7	950	—	1,100	...	47	— 55	8	...	0	8	0
8	1,100	—	1,250	...	55	— 62	11	...	0	11	0
14	2,500	—	2,800	...	125	— 140	48	...	2	8	0
19	4,800	—	5,400	...	240	— 270	136	...	6	16	0
20	5,400	—	6,300	...	270	— 310	162	..	8	2	0
21	6,300	—	7,200	...	310	— 360	189	...	9	9	0

For all the succeeding classes the tax is 3 per cent. on the minimum amount of the class ; up to 12,000 marks (£600) the rise is 1,200 marks ; for higher classes the groups are larger. At the top of the scale the progression is by advances of 5,000 marks; thus all incomes from 60,000 to 65,000 marks would pay 3 per cent. on the minimum, *i.e.* on 60,000 = 1,800 marks, or £90.

The low limit of income (£15) at which the Saxon tax begins is worthy attention, remembering that our income tax does not touch incomes below £150, and that up to £400 there is abatement for £120. The persons with incomes between £15 and £150 form, it appears, in Saxony, about 90 per cent. of all the tax-payers, and about 40 per cent. of the entire tax is extracted from them.

With us all this class would be exempted. If we were to compare the local taxation of Dresden with that of our own cities, we would find that upon premises of equal valuation in each place the Saxon would have only to pay a sum equivalent to one-third the local taxation on a citizen of, say Dublin. The pattern of fiscal moderation set by Dresden is by no means followed in the provincial towns of Saxony, which, as a rule, have the capital, building, and land tax combined, with some species of progressive income tax, which is very general.

In Leipzig the town income tax commences with 11d. for an income of £15 to £20, and attains the maximum rate of 3 per cent. with incomes of £7,500. The capital valuation for the ground and building tax there is computed by taking fifteen times the net income; the percentage is lower than in Dresden, making for £150 rental value £4 10s. against £7 4s. (for owners) in the capital. The State has transferred the levying of its direct taxes to the various towns, and allows them for the expense of collection 3 per cent. of the amount collected. In Chemnitz this three per cent. does not cover the cost of collection, though the cost of collecting the municipal taxes is not proportionally so great. The reasons for this are, (1) the amount collected is larger; and (2) the municipal taxes are levied by citizens who are not paid for their services.

The municipal taxes in Chemnitz are assessed in this way. The General Commission of Assessors apportion out the work to smaller commissions from among the citizens of the town—one for hosiery manufacturers, one for curtain weavers, and so on, so that all of the same business are taxed by the same assessors. A member of the Town Council presides over each sub-committee. Anyone refusing to act or neglecting to attend a meeting without sufficient reason is fined from 15 to 300 marks ; but if a member or any of his relatives is being assessed, he is obliged to temporarily absent himself. The committee has power to put into a different class those who have a large family of children, or who support poor relatives, or who have incurable sickness, or those who have met with some great misfortune. By this arrangement the authorities of Chemnitz are enabled to effect an equitable levy of the town taxes with the least possible cost upon the citizens.

BAVARIA.

In the kingdom of Bavaria many of the municipal authorities own forest land and let shooting and fishing. About 970,000 acres of the forest land of Bavaria belong to communes, and return a considerable amount in aid of the taxation necessitated by local requirements.

O

The larger proportion of the communes levy
no direct taxation, but augment their revenue from
property by the imposition of tolls on roads and
bridges, and some local duties on articles of consumption. A very small number of communes—
mostly of what we would call villages—have had
often to assess their taxation at over 500 per cent.
of the direct State taxes. The direct communal
taxation appears to be higher in the Palatinate
than in the seven provinces east of the Rhine.

The power is vested in the various communal
unions—*i.e.* divisions, districts, and communes—
of levying local taxes, forming percentages of all
the State direct taxes, as explained as regards
Prussia generally.

There is no limit to the legal maximum of the
percentage, which is, of course, regulated by the
necessities of the local authority.

The State direct taxes forming the basis for
these local percentages are : (1) the land tax, (2)
house tax, (3) trades tax, (4) income tax on capital,
as bonds, shares, etc., and (5) income tax on salaries,
pensions, professions, etc. ; but the first two are the
principal sources of revenue.

The Bavarian land tax, in which is included the
tax on forests, is not levied either upon the value
of the land in a given year or on the true annual
production of the land, but is calculated from its

superficial area and its natural productive power, as shown by its average production. To calculate the average production, an average agricultural working power is presupposed, and also that every three years the land lies fallow for a season. It is also only the principal products which are taken into account in striking the average of production, by products being left out of account.

The average yearly production is then measured out by the old unit of area called "Tagewerk" (equal 0·3407 hectares), and divided into classes according to the quality. For arable land the average yearly production of one-eighth of a "Scheffel" corn (equal 27·7947 litres) constitutes one class, each class differing from the next by that amount. In other sorts of culture, the principle that each class differs from the next by the value of one-eighth Scheffel also holds good, and one-eighth Scheffel corn is taken as equal to one gulden, or 1·75 marks.

The land tax, therefore, is assessed on the basis of the combination of the area of the land expressed in "Tagewerks," and the quality thereof which remains unchanged as long as the land is cultivated. The standard of production taken as unity is one-eighth Scheffel corn, or an average yearly return of 1 mark 71 pfennigs.

Each finance law for each biennial period

O 2

determines the number of pfennigs or fractions of
a pfennig to be levied from each one-eighth Scheffel
for the land tax. For many years past 8·4 pfennigs have been regularly levied on each standard
of unity—as land tax. Consequently, when once
the amount the land can yield is determined as
above, the percentage equivalent of the tax is
$\frac{8 \cdot 4 \times 100}{171} = \frac{840}{171} = 4 \cdot 9$ per cent. The real income derived
from the land may, of course, be very different,
and, consequently, the percentage thereon which
the tax composes may also be different.

The Bavarian house tax is neither calculated
upon the current market value of the house nor
upon the annual rent actually produced from it.
The standard by which the tax is determined is
the rent-producing power of the house, as shown
in the case of houses under lease by the actual
rent, and in the case of houses not under lease by
a revised estimate calculated by comparison with
other similar houses paying rent. When, however,
in the case of non-rented houses, no proper means
of comparison and estimate exist, as is frequently
the case in out-of-the-way country districts, the
tax is calculated at the rate of 5 marks (5s.) per
"are" of the space occupied by the house and
courtyard space. This is called the "areal" tax.
The minimum tax payable, however, whether the
rent or "areal" tax, is in either case 15s. The

maximum "areal" tax is 125s., but for rent tax
there is no maximum. Once the yearly rent-
producing power is fixed in marks for the purpose
of the house tax, the finance law for each biennial
finance period determines how many pfennigs and
fractions of a pfennig per mark must be levied.

For many years past the amount of the house
tax has been 3·85 pfennigs per mark of the rent-
producing power, and this, therefore, amounts to a
house tax of 3·85 per cent. It is obvious that in
many cases the tax must amount to a different
rate from this on the actual rent paid, and, therefore, to that extent varies from the above-mentioned
percentage. But, whenever possible, the rent-
producing power is calculated as near as may be to
the actual rent ; and further, in communes where
rent tax is paid, a new determination or assessment of the tax is made every ten years, on the
application either of the State authorities or of the
taxpayers.

FREE PORTS.

The systems of taxation in Hamburg are peculiar as compared with those of the other commonwealths of the German Empire, on account of the
relations which subsist between Hamburg as a free
port and the Imperial Government. In Hamburg,
State and local taxes are jointly taken from the
people. No separate account is kept of the State

and local taxes ; the joint receipts form a general
fund, and the State and municipal Treasury are
the same. The principal sources of revenue to the
Imperial Government are import duties and the
taxes upon articles of consumption ; Hamburg
being a free port and exempt from direct taxes to
the Imperial Treasury; still it appears the standard
of expenditure is higher and the cost of living
dearer than in Berlin, and far exceeds the prices
paid for the same commodities in South German
cities.

An inhabitant of Hamburg has to pay to the
local authority:—(1) A ground tax. The assessment
is one-half per cent. on the estimated value of the
property. On small buildings and lodgings the
assessment is diminished by one quarter. The
estimated value of the houses let for lodgings is
ascertained by converting the rent into an interest
upon the capital. The valuation is obtained at a
rate of $4\frac{1}{7}$ per cent. for smaller dwellings, and at
$6\frac{1}{2}$ per cent. for larger ones. The taxes on a house
paying 1,000 marks rent would be $11\frac{22}{33}$ per cent.
of the rent. The tax of one-half per cent. on the
valuation is considered a heavy incumbrance on
property in Hamburg. Hence house-rent is
high. (2) An income tax. This tax is levied upon
every person having an income of £25 and over.
It is progressive, and varies from 12s. per cent. to

3½ per cent. income. The head of a family has a right to demand a reduction of his taxes, which is generally liberally granted. (3) The victual tax, which is a duty demanded at the entrance of the city upon wholesale imports of meats and other consumables; (4) Stamp duties; (5) Declaration custom duty; (6) Port dues; (7) Tolls on roads and bridges; (8) Inheritance tax. The taxes on inheritances are as follows:—

Two and one-half per cent. for relations of the second and third degree; adopted children, 5 per cent.; relations of fourth degree, 7½ per cent.; relations of more distant degree, or non-relatives, 10 per cent. The following inheritances are exempt from such taxation: From parents to children, from husband to wife, to charitable institutions, estates of less than 4,500 marks, legacies of 360 marks and less as long as one person is not left more than 360 marks, also amount left to executors as long as it does not exceed the sum of 4,500 marks. (9) Dog tax, of 10s.; and (10) a brand tax upon all measures. Under the methods of taxation, the wealthy pay the bulk of direct taxes, but here, as elsewhere, this burden is shifted through trade and interchange until it eventually reaches the shoulders of the poor.

The burden of taxation in Hamburg is to be

found in the ground tax. On account of this tax
house rent is comparatively high—in fact, higher
by 10 per cent. than in any other city in Germany.
The consequence is that every artisan and tradesman demands a higher price for his articles and
produce.

The expense of collecting the several taxes is
light. For the collection of the ground and income
tax few officers are required, as the citizens do the
greater part of the work themselves. Printed
blanks are sent to each taxpayer, with a notice
that taxes are due, and must be paid at a particular
time at the respective offices. They are required
to appear in person at the offices, and render their
assessments and pay the taxes. Non-compliance
with the order is followed by a seizure of a sufficient
amount of the property to cover fines, taxes, and
cost of collection. The actual cost of collection is
difficult to ascertain, as the officers have other
official duties to perform, and the different methods
are not kept separate; but it may be safely admitted
that the greater part of the expense is the collection
of the indirect taxes.

The local taxation of Bremen, one of the other
free ports, is so dissimilar that we are forced to
give it, especially as it shows how the water and
lighting tax is divided between owner and occupier.
The authorities derive their income from an income

tax, often reaching fully 4 per cent. of the income ;
a poor tax, being about 1 per cent. on the income,
and collected with the income tax ; tax on land of
$5\frac{1}{2}$ per cent. of net receipts therefrom ; tax on
buildings of 2·1 per mille on assessed value ; water
tax payable by (1) owners of buildings at $\frac{1}{2}$ per
mille on assessed value, (2) owners of land (ground)
$\frac{1}{4}$ per cent. on net revenue therefrom, (3) lessee at
1 per cent. on amount of rent paid by him ; lighting tax payable by (1) owners of buildings at $1\frac{1}{20}$
per mille of assessed value, (2) owners of land
(ground) at $2\frac{3}{5}$ per cent. on net revenue, (3) lessee
at 5 per cent. on amount of rent paid ; tax on
business transactions of firms ; retail liquor tax,
octroi on articles of food and necessaries of life,
death duties, stamp duties ; auction tax of $\frac{1}{2}$ per
cent. of net receipts ; taxes on clubs, societies,
billiards, public halls, pleasure vehicles, horses, dogs,
nightingales, insurance policies, turnpike and canal
tolls.   Of the cost of collecting all these various
taxes, that of the octroi is the most expensive,
requiring as many officials as the customs.   It is
the most oppressive tax on the poor people, making,
as it does, the necessaries of life more costly.   There
is, however, the consolation that articles of luxury
are highly taxed, which is commendable.

CHAPTER IX.

AUSTRIA.

HERE, as in other Continental countries, the imperial taxes furnish the principal basis of all local taxation, which is levied in the form of an addition to the State tax as the "centimes additionnels" are levied in France for the requirements of the department and communes.

There are in Austria various units of local self-government—the province, the county (Bezirk), the schools district, and the " Gemeinde," or commune or township. Each of these defrays its wants principally by charging some percentage on the State taxes, varying in different provinces from 25 to 37 per cent. on the State tax. In Bohemia, for instance, the provincial tax is 36 per cent. ; in Lower Austria 30 per cent. In most provinces this additional percentage is laid equally upon the several imperial direct taxes, but in Moravia and Lower Austria the percentage on income and earnings taxes is a little lower than upon the taxes on real property.

The State taxes upon which this additional

percentage is levied for local purposes are the taxes on real property and the taxes on personal property.

The taxes on real property are divided into taxes on proceeds or profits of realty (agricultural lands, forests, vineyards, etc.), and taxes on the proceeds or profits of buildings (rents). The taxes on personal property are divided into taxes on manufactories, on industrial, mercantile, and professional occupations (erwerbsteuer licence), and taxes on income derived either from such industrial, mercantile, or professional occupations, or from invested capital. A manufacturer, for instance, if he owns the building in which he carries on business, pays taxes first on the rental value of the building; secondly, a high licence tax for the privilege of carrying on his business; and, thirdly, an income tax on the net profits derived from his business.

The taxes on real property are (1) land tax and (2) house tax.

1. The land tax. Every tax district has its own permanent record of the dimensions, character, and average producing capacity of all parcels of land within the district. This permanent record (Kataster) has existed for a long series of years, and the tax is levied upon the basis of the estimated producing capacity as shown in this

record. From time to time new estimates are
made, and the owners of realty have the right to
protest if they think the estimate is too high.
The question is decided by the finance officers of
the district, and in certain cases an appeal lies to
the Minister of Finance ; but no appeal operates as
a stay of proceedings in the collection of the tax.

According to the Kataster records the taxable
area of land in Austria amounted to 32½ million
acres, classified as (*a*) agricultural lands, (*b*)
meadows, (*c*) gardens, (*d*) vineyards, (*e*) pasture,
(*f*) alps, (*g*) forests, (*h*) lakes, swamps, and ponds ;
and the quantity of each and its average net
producing capacity is duly recorded.

Under the law of 7th June, 1881, the total
amount of taxes to be imposed upon the producing
capacity of taxable lands was fixed at a certain
sum per annum for a period of 15 years, and the
percentage of such average net produce to be paid
by the owners was also duly fixed. The local
additional percentage varies periodically according
to the records of the municipality.

In case of default in payment of this tax at the
time fixed by law, the party making default must
pay interest at the rate of 1½ kreutzers per day
for each hundred florins due. If the tax is not
paid within four weeks after it becomes payable,
execution issues for the amount of taxes and

interest against the personal property of the delinquent.

If the personal property levied upon is insufficient to pay the tax, an execution issues against realty.

II. The house tax. The theory of this tax is that it is imposed upon the profits of the capital invested in the buildings. It is considered a fair and safe form of taxation by the Austrian Government, for the reason that it is quite impossible to conceal the real amount of capital invested in the buildings, and, following the views of Adam Smith, the authorities advocate the justice of this tax as a combination of a tax upon the realty and upon the improvements situate thereon. The tax upon buildings is divided into two classes, viz. :—(*a*) a tax upon the net amount of rent received, or upon the rental value, called the " house-rent tax " (hauszinssteuer), and (*b*) the tax upon dwelling-houses graduated according to the number of dwelling-rooms, the houses being divided into a certain number of classes, called the " house-class tax " (hausclassensteuer).

(A) The house-rent tax is not by any means uniform throughout the empire, but is only levied in certain cities and localities particularly mentioned in the law, and wherever the house-rent tax is not levied, the house-class tax is imposed. The most noticeable characteristic of this law is its total want of uniformity.

In order to arrive at the net amount of rents received for the purpose of assessing the house-rent tax, a deduction of from 15 per cent. to 30 per cent. is made from the gross amount to cover the necessary repairs, etc. Upon the balance the percentages for the State and municipality are imposed. These two percentages are frequently so large that they receive considerable attention in dealings between landlords and tenants. For instance, in Vienna, the total amount of the house-rent tax, State and local, is .45 per cent. of the net amount of rents received.

(B) Since 1882 the house-class tax is levied in proportion to the number of inhabited or habitable dwelling-rooms, without reference to the cost or value of the building, and without regard to its style of architecture or purpose. Palace and peasant's hut come under the same rule and classification. However, the tax is not a certain amount for each room, but sixteen taxable classes are established, for the lowest of which, containing one room, a certain tax is payable, which is graduated and increases according to the higher classification in which the building is placed. The highest classification is a building containing from 36 to 40 dwelling-rooms.

As before stated, under this classification all rooms which are or can be inhabited are taxed; barns, stables, and out-houses are exempt. Ante-rooms, halls, assembly-rooms, and writing-rooms also fall within the classification, but kitchens, cellars, and garrets (the latter only if not occupied), are excluded.

It matters not whether the rooms are furnished or not, or whether windows or doors are broken; they are all taxable if they can be made fit for dwelling without rebuilding. Certain workshops are also taxable. The workshops of tailors, shoe-makers, weavers, and cabinet-makers, etc., sale-rooms of merchants, offices of druggists and surgeons, fall within this classification, because, as a commentator on this law remarks, all these buildings require but little change to make them habitable.

The dwelling-rooms, bed-rooms, offices and storage-rooms of factories, also come within this provision.

If a house is destroyed by water or fire, the house-class tax is abated for the year within which the damage took place.

In the following cases, both the house-rent tax and the house-class tax are totally abated for the term of 12 years:—

(1) If a new building is erected upon ground

not theretofore built upon ; (2) if a building is torn
down to the ground and rebuilt ; (3) if a building
is enlarged by erecting a new storey or storeys, the
new storeys are exempt from taxation for the
period aforesaid ; (4) if separate storeys or parts of
buildings are torn down and rebuilt, the new part
is exempt in the same manner.

The term of 12 years begins to run the day
of occupation of the building. It must, however,
not be supposed that these tax-free buildings are
entirely free from taxes because the law just
quoted so provides. Special enactments have
brought these buildings within the reach of the
tax-collector. In Vienna, for instance, tax-free
buildings pay the State and municipality 20 per
cent., while buildings not tax-free pay 45 per cent.
of the rental value as house-rent tax.

III. The tariff of the licence tax on proceeds of
personal property and business contains 4 principal
classes, under which all pursuits and employments
subject to this tax are classified, viz. : —

(1) Factories ; (2) commercial ventures, with a
separate classification for wholesale business; (3)
arts and industries (including retail merchants and
dealers and pedlars) ; (4) employment, (a) for
instruction, teaching, etc., (b) brokers and commission agents, attorneys, etc., (c) carriers.

The tax is payable semi-annually in advance.

The estimate of the amount of earnings is based upon the average earnings of the three previous years. In assessing this tax the tax officers find little difficulty to ascertain the net earnings of factories and wholesale merchants, because they gain the required information from the balance-sheet to be furnished by these establishments, under the provisions of the Income Tax Law and commercial regulations. In order to gain definite data as to the proper amount of tax due from the other taxable classes, the law instructs the tax officers to take into consideration the amount of capital invested, the nature of the business, its location, the number of workmen and clerks employed, the machinery and apparatus used, etc. The amount of house-rent paid by a business man is to be considered in arriving at his net earnings. In judging from all these facts and circumstances, the tax officers decide to which particular class and sub-division of a class the taxpayer belongs. The law fixes the number of classes and sub-classes of taxpayers subject to this licence tax, and also provides for the amount of tax to be paid by each class and sub-division thereof, in the several cities and localities; but it omits entirely to fix the precise conditions (*i.e.*, the precise amount of net earnings) under which a taxpayer is to be enrolled in any one particular class or sub-class, but leaves

P

the decision upon this point to the tax officers of the several districts, and requires them to be guided in their decision by the declarations to be made by the taxpayer and by the estimate of the local authorities.

There are certain exemptions from payment of the licence tax, and they include—(*a*) the agricultural industry so far as it is confined to the raising of raw products; (*b*) all workmen who work for wages or by the job; (*c*) all common day-labourers; (*d*) all Government officers; (*e*) all authors and artists; (*f*) all teachers in towns having less than 4,000 souls; (*g*) all mines (except smelting works); (*h*) dealers in tobacco, stamps, and lottery tickets; (*i*) fisheries in coast districts; (*j*) savings banks; (*k*) physicians, surgeons and midwives.

IV. An income tax has existed in Austria since the beginning of the nineteenth century. It was repealed in 1829 and re-enacted in 1849. This tax is divided into three classes :—

First Class.—Under the first class the following income is taxed : (*a*) the income derived from all those trades and occupations which are subject to a licence tax ; (*b*) the income of mining and smelting works; (*c*) the profits made by the tenants of agricultural lands, of tolls, and of consumption-tax districts.

Second Class.—Income from services rendered

or labour performed in occupations not subject to a licence tax ; (*b*) annual income or dividends paid by life-insurance or other companies. Servants are only taxed under this class if their total income exceed 630 florins per annum.

Third Class.—Under this class are embraced : Interest from loans, interest from invested capital ; income from savings banks and life-insurance companies. Benevolent and mutual assistance corporations and stipends are also included in this class.

In addition to the percentage added to the foregoing State direct tax, the Municipality of Vienna derive a share from the consumption tax collected on the line of the city. The tax is collected partly on behalf of the State and partly on behalf of the municipality. The tariff as established is high. Almost all provisions, beverages, eatables and commodities, alive and dead, are subjected to this tax.

Every vehicle drawn by horses, and every horse that crosses the line into the city, pays an octroi tax of four kreutzers for each horse.

All other so-called "Closed Cities" have a similar tariff, though the rates are not so high as those of Vienna.

The taxpayer of Vienna has also to support the local Chamber of Commerce, which acts as the

P 2

advisory board to the Minister of Commerce, and
has the commercial and industrial interests of the
city in charge. Certain general taxes are levied
for its support and maintenance.

Unquestionably the Austrian tax system
favours the capitalist and the great real estate
owner, and the heaviest tax burden is borne by the
merchant and business man of limited means.

The capitalist may invest his millions in tax-
free securities, and thus escape taxation almost
entirely. If he dwells in a palace within a closed
city, he pays a house-rent tax on its rental value ;
if his estates are situated in the open country, he
pays the house-class tax, and in this case it is to be
noted that the wealthy owner pays no higher rate
of taxation on a marble edifice containing, say,
forty rooms, than the owner of a common brick
tenement house in the neighbouring village with
the same number of rooms, because, as already
stated, the house-class tax is levied according
to the number of inhabited or habitable rooms,
without reference to the character or cost of the
building. The most expensive stables and out-
buildings, though they cost thousands upon
thousands, are free of tax the same as the straw-
thatched barn of the peasant. A millionaire,
therefore, may enjoy the possession of a grand
establishment in the country—a castle containing

forty rooms—by paying the comparatively small tax of 220 florins per annum, exactly the same amount which the landlord of the village inn has to pay if he happens to be in the use and occupation of the same number of habitable rooms. But it should be remembered that the landlord of the village inn pays a large licence tax and an income tax besides, both of which the man in the castle escapes because he invested his millions in tax-free securities, and is not compelled to carry on business to support himself and family. If a large park surrounds the castle, that, too, in most cases, is free of tax, because it is unproductive, while the garden patch in the rear of the village inn certainly produces something, and is therefore subject to the usual levy for that class of property.

It is quite superfluous to carry the comparison any further; it is evident that, as to the two cases mentioned, there is little uniformity in the system of taxation under consideration. But the tax-payer who carries the heaviest burden, is the small merchant and business man generally, who carries on business in one of the "closed cities" like Vienna.

First of all he pays indirectly a house-rent tax of 45 per cent. of the actual rental value of his dwelling, because the owner of the tenement building takes good care to place his rent high enough, so that he can afford to pay the tax of 45 per cent. to the Government. And it is a notorious fact, that, especially in Vienna, the rents of the small flats fit for dwellings of the middle classes are unreasonably high.

Next he pays his licence tax, to be fixed by the tax officers at a rate decided by them; then he pays a tax on his net income, amounting to from 10 to 20 per cent., again as the tax officers may decide; then the Chamber of Commerce comes in for its share of taxes, and after this follow the indirect taxes, principally the consumption tax, which raises the price of his meat, his bread, his candles, his beer, his wine—in fact, everything he puts upon his table or into his kitchen, even the oats and hay on which he feeds his horse (if his business requires him to keep horses), down to the straw for their bedding, is raised in price by the consumption tariff line drawn around these so-called " closed cities."

The United States Consul General at Vienna thus expresses himself as to the social condition of the citizens of that city consequent upon the heavy burden and unequal incidence of the taxation : " Vienna is to-day one of the most expensive cities on the Continent of Europe. Many necessaries of life, in the shape of good healthy food, are so dear that they are placed

beyond the reach of the man of moderate means.
A mechanic, or a clerk, or a public functionary,
with a salary of barely 1,000 florins per annum,
rarely sees a roast on his table. It is self-
evident that the high prices of rents and provisions
have been the principal factors in shaping the
habits and mode of life of the people. Among the
middle and lower classes there is little home life.
The dwellings are so small and pinched that
family gatherings and invitations to friends are
impracticable, and the coffee-house and cheap
restaurants and public gardens are resorted to
for social intercourse as well as for the evening
meal, and thousands manage to make a supper
out of a glass of beer and a slice of bread, because
more than one substantial meal at their own
houses is quite beyond their means. These, and
many other unavoidable deductions, may be drawn
from that dry line of figures giving the statistics
of taxation in the Empire of Austria."

CHAPTER X.

SWITZERLAND.

SWITZERLAND presents the rare picture of a State which, possessing only a population of something over two and a half millions, and divided in parts by high mountain chains, yet contains members of three great civilised nations. They are not chained together by a despotic power, but united by the firm conviction that this relation is more to their advantage than would be a union with their great parent nations.

Each of the twenty-five cantons being sovereign in so far as its sovereignty is not limited by the federal constitution, regulates its own internal affairs according to its own judgment, and accordingly every variety of condition is met with. Notwithstanding, the principle is everywhere recognised that the nation shall govern itself according to its own judgment and requirements.

All officials, even the judges, are chosen from among the people, and this only for a fixed period.

There are, therefore, no official castes, no high
salaries, no pensions; and yet peace and order
rule here in a higher degree than in any other
country.

Every able-bodied citizen, property owner, and
resident in the several cantons, is subject to payment of two distinct classes of taxes, viz. : —

(1) Those imposed by the cantons.

(2) Those imposed by the respective townships
composing them.

Both are collected by the town authorities,
but at different times. The cantonal taxes are
turned over to the treasurers of the cantons, and
the towns are generally allowed to retain 1 per
cent. as payment of their collection.

The Federal Government derives its revenue
largely from custom duties and postal telegraph
service—and the residue from a few special taxes,
as citizenship, railways, on banks of issue, registration of trade marks, and of commercial houses,
gunpowder manufactures, and military tax. The
military tax is payable by every Swiss of the age
of military service, from twenty to forty-four years
old, living in the territory or out of the territory of
the confederation, and who does not personally
perform military service.

This special tax consists of a personal tax of
six francs, and of an additional tax on property

and income, the amount exacted from any one taxpayer not to exceed 3,000 francs per annum.

In many of the cantons a tax is levied on property without any distinction being made between real estate and personalty, and in those cantons in which a separate tax is levied on real property, lands and buildings appear to be subject to the same assessment.

The systems of assessment differ also in the various communes or townships of each of the twenty-five cantons.

As the cantonal authorities execute many works properly belonging to the municipal or city authorities, a description of the sources of their revenue is necessary to fully understand the Swiss system of local taxation. We will take the systems adopted in Berne and Zürich respectively.

The law regulating the taxation of the Canton of Berne recognises the following taxes as direct : (1) property tax ; (a) ground tax ; (b) capital tax.

There is a division of real estate into several classes, viz.—ground property (without forest) ; forests and improvements.

Then there is another division as to kind of cultivation : (1) gardens, orchards, meadows, arable lands ; (2) pasture grounds ; (3) vineyards.

There is also a sub-division of these three classes as to value, viz. :—Forests are valued according to (1) yield of wood ; (2) market price of wood ; (3) climatological conditions resulting from topography.

Buildings are classed and valued according to the construction of the walls and roofing, material, stone, brick, wood, or framework, filled with broken stones or butts ; and for what purpose used—dwelling, barn, granary, store, or manufacture.

The tax is two francs for each thousand francs of assessed value. Of this 1.70 francs are for general administration, and 30 centimes for pauper fund.

The assessed value is reached by deducting debts for which the property is made liable by mortgage, lien, or other legal process. But this provision excludes debts, though secured as above, which are due to the confederation, or to creditors not within the jurisdiction of the canton.

The exemptions to the property tax are :—

(1) Buildings and ground the property of the State used for public purposes ; (2) churches, parsonages, school-houses, hospitals, asylums, roads, rivers, and lakes ; (3) grounds incapable of cultivation or pasturage ; (4) establishments under federal administration ; (5) railway stations and appurtenances ; (6) real estate under 100 francs value.

The *Capital tax* covers personal property, stocks, rents, annuities, etc. If the creditor of stocks, bonds, or rents for which property is bound, resides out of the jurisdiction of the canton, the owner of the property must pay the tax ; but it is considered as being paid on behalf of the creditor, and he is authorised to retain the amount so paid from the interest or rent so paid by him.

The assessment of the tax on stocks, etc., is arrived at by fixing a value of twenty-five-fold the amount of annual interest or rent or dividend, and of this each 1,000 francs is taxed the same per cent. as the real estate, or 2 francs per 1,000.

The ground property pays tax in the district where it is located and listed, personating where the owner is domiciled or claims domicile.

The *Income tax*. The persons subject are : —

(1) All persons established in the canton, including Swiss citizens of other cantons and foreigners ; (2) temporary residents beyond six months ; (3) all companies, corporations, etc., licensed to do business.

The tax is divided into three classes :—

(1) Income from professional pursuits, trades, or employments which carry with them salary, wages, fees or emoluments, and income from industry, commerce, and manufacture. This class pays three per cent.

(2) Income from annuities, pensions, etc. This class pays four per cent.

(3) Incomes from interests, stocks, bonds, shares, deposits (not subject to the tax on property in the canton). This class pays five per cent.

From the first class is exempt the sum of 600 francs, and 100 francs from the second and third classes.

This exemption can be made only once, and cannot be claimed by a party who may be engaged in two distinct pursuits or businesses, as deductable from each one ; and although husband and wife may be engaged in separate business and keep separate accounts, the allowance is only made for one. In addition, however, to the 600 francs allowed in the first class, there is 10 per cent. additional permitted for expense in producing income—that is, the net income is sought to be taxed.

Persons whose official positions entitle them to receive certain privileges and perquisites of value— such as parsons, teachers, policemen, and employés in certain establishments who may be furnished with firewood, free lodgings, and small tracts of ground, must add the same to their gross income according to a certain stated scale of value.

The indirect cantonal taxes are :—

(1) Tax on inheritance, legacies, and donations ; (2) on markets, traffic, hawking, etc. These can be taxed only so far as space, stalls, and extra expense of police, fire department, and sanitary

purposes may be involved. (3) On public-houses
and retailers of spirits. These are divided into
(a) houses that lodge, board, and sell spirits;
(b) houses that sell food and spirits, and do not
lodge. The first pay according to a list of eleven
classes ranging from 300 to 2,000 francs per annum.
The second embraces eight classes, and runs from
300 to 1,600 francs. Ten per cent. of the amount
realised from this tax is given to the commune or
township where the houses are located for school
and paupers. (4) On the manufacture of brandy
and spirits for trade. (5) For cantonal fire insurance. This is the most unique responsibility
which municipalities have undertaken. Switzerland is so far the only Continental country which
has undertaken the municipal insurance of property
against fire, lighting, explosion, or damage by
water in extinguishing a conflagration.

The insurance tax is obligatory for four-fifths
of the taxable value, and is conducted under the
restrictions and regulations usually pertaining to
fire insurance, and precludes any other insurance
upon the property.

In case of fire the indemnity is made in proportion of the sum insured to valuation. Single
houses isolated, without a fireplace, and under
500 francs value, are exempt from this law; and
powder-mills, laboratories for fireworks, depositories

of powder or dynamite, and chemical manufactures, are excluded.

Additional premiums for insurance are imposed in the following cases :—

(*a*) Houses with wood or partly wood roofs 20 centimes per 1,000 francs ; (*b*) when the wall in whole or part consists of material not fire-proof, from 10 to 20 centimes per 1,000 francs, according to its distance from other buildings ; (*c*) where there is special risk from character of business carried on.

The fire-insurance tax varies according to the loss that may be suffered in a year. It is generally about one and a half francs, with small additional assessments for some small townships.

The collection of the insurance tax is, as in other cases, intrusted by the canton to the several communes, which retain a small percentage (4 centimes per 1,000 francs) for expenses of collection.

For systematising the operation of the law the canton is divided into six appraisement districts, in each of which a commission consisting of three members is appointed by the cantonal council for a three years' term. This commission has for its duty the appraisal of the values at which all the buildings in the district are to be insured. The control of the entire system is vested in the direction of the police for the canton.

(6) *Stamp tax.* All unstamped instruments have no validity in law ; (7) State Church tax. All Protestant Swiss citizens who have not exercised the legal right to withdraw from the State Church are subject to a tax on a certain scale on their incomes and property ; (8) miscellaneous taxes or licences. There are a variety of other miscellaneous taxes or licences imposed by cantonal law, such as the right to hunt and fish, on travellers, hospitals conducted for profits, etc.

Such are the taxes imposed by the Canton of Berne. Those imposed by the City or Commune of Berne are the ground and capital taxes. These taxes on real and personal property are the same as in the canton, viz., 2 francs per 1,000 ; classification ; and other features similar also to cantonal.

The City income tax is 3, 4, and 5 francs per cent., regulated as the cantonal.

Water tax. Four francs for each room the house contains. The net profit annually to the city is about 15,160 francs.

Gas. One-half franc on the 1,000 of the house valuation.

Schools. Higher classes annually 60 francs, and lower classes 4 francs.

Dogs are charged for at 10 francs annually.

Burial tax. The Municipal authorities of Berne are also the burial board, and in return for certain stipulated fees supply graves, hearse, coaches, horses, and bury the dead.

Taxes are also levied for *permis de séjour* issued to temporary residents and foreigners.

Receipts are also had from spaces and stalls in the markets, from the use of the abattoir and its stable, and from the weighing of commodities.

A citizenship can be purchased in the Commune of Berne as well as in the canton and confederation.

It is somewhat strange that the practice which prevails, in giving in property for cantonal taxation, of deducting all indebtedness secured by mortgage where the creditors reside in the canton—(to deny the same having been decided by the courts to be double taxation, and in contravention of a provision of the federal constitution prohibiting double taxation)—has not been applied to the city or communal taxes. It is thought that as far as it is now applied, there is much fraud practised, and that fictitious mortgages are created for the purpose of evading just taxes. By permitting encumbrances in the beginning honestly made to continue after maturity, when the debtor is able to pay, secures their indefinite continuance at less cost than would follow from the additional tax which would result from the liquidation of the encumbrance.

The system of direct taxation in the Canton of

Q

Zürich is the most democratic and levelling to be met with. It is essentially progressive.

It eases the burden for the poor and the labouring classes, and places the greater weight upon the shoulders of those who are best able to bear it, and that, too, in proportion to their ability. The system, indeed, gives evidence of careful study and wise thought. While it cannot be said that the law actually hinders the acquisition of great fortunes or the diversion of wealth into the hands of a few, it yet inculcates the lesson that an increase in wealth brings with it increased duties and responsibilities towards the Government, which protects the individual in the possession of that wealth.

As an example of this progressive levy, the following may be given :—

Property tax. Of the property of individual taxpayers the following portions are assessed, viz. :—

					Francs.
Five-tenths per 1,000 on the first ...				...	20,000
Six-tenths ,,	,,	,,	next ...	...	30,000
Seven-tenths ,,	,,	,,	...	...	50,000
Eight-tenths ,,	,,	,,	...	...	100,000
Nine-tenths ,,	,,	,,	...	...	200,000
Ten-tenths ,,	,,	,,	on all above		200,000

Income tax. Of the taxable income of the individual, the following portions are assessed, viz. :—

Two-tenths on the first	...	...	1,500 francs.
Four-tenths on the next	...	...	1,500 ,,
Six-tenths ,, ,,	...	...	3,000 ,,
Eight-tenths ,, ,,	...	...	4,000 ,,
Ten-tenths on all above	...	...	4,000 ,,

Every hundred francs of income assessment pays two francs tax for every franc per thousand levied on property assessments.

Citizenship tax. The tax payable by all citizens entitled to vote amounts to one-third of the sum levied per thousand on property assessment.

The like progression is observed in the Zürich Cantonal inheritance tax, increasing not alone as the degrees in blood become more remote, but also as the amount of the bequest or inheritance is of greater value.

An admirable consolidation of tax is observed by the authorities of the City of Zürich.

For city purposes a direct tax is levied on property, on households, and on men who have passed their twentieth year.

The town regulations of Zürich to a great extent harmonise in their general tenor with the cantonal law, already given, pertaining to the levy and collection of direct taxes. A few distinctive features and details yet exist.

The town taxes are levied on property, household, and man, on the basis of so many francs per

Q 2

thousand on property, so many francs for every household, and so many francs for every man who has passed his twentieth year. A minor source of income are the receipts from the indirect taxes, viz., the various office fees, fees at fairs and markets, for use of slaughter-house, baths, fire police, etc. etc.

Toward the expenditure for the care of paupers of the township, all citizens of the same residing in the canton, either within or without the limits of the home township, are required to contribute by taxation.

For all other town charges the following persons are taxable, viz. :—(a) all citizens residing within the township or sojourning longer than three months in other towns of the canton (and not liable to taxation at the place of their sojourn) and settlers. From the taxable property is to be deducted that portion which under the provisions of (b) is subjected to taxation in other townships; (b Owners of land within the township limits who reside outside of the township, i.e., so far as such land has a value of at least 1,000 francs; (c) an owner or partner in any industry carried on in the township, but resident outside of the township, for a *pro rata* portion of its property; (d) corporations, stock companies, and endowments domiciled within the township, for that property upon which they, as such, are taxable by the canton; (c) stock companies, for the full value of their landed property lying within the township.

Lands for public revenues, as well as those portions of the township lands the yield of which is applied to the revenues, are taxable for all township expenditures.

The canton pays proportional damages to townships the roads of which have been materially injured by reason of hauling of wood from the cantonal forests or the carrying on of the cantonal mines.

Citizens of townships which are subdivided into several church or school districts are only taxable in the church or school district in which they reside. However, nobody is compelled to pay a tax specially imposed for the individual support of any religious society to which he does not belong.

If the system of Swiss local taxation is more democratic than ours, their laws and customs regarding the occupancy of land are also sufficiently up to date.

Our notions of degrees of estate in land are not only absent from the Swiss law, but are almost incomprehensible to the Swiss themselves.

Absolute ownership in the occupier is the only condition known to them, and they possess no idea of such tenures as exist in the United Kingdom, viz., leases of 99 years, copyhold, estate in tail, and so forth. Farm leases are a separate matter. These are, in general, originally made for short periods, and not unfrequently renewed from year to year. Leases of dwelling-houses are usually granted from year to year, or for a short term of years; but leases for long periods, such as 50 or 99 years, are not to be found in Switzerland.

Property may be sold in small or large lots, and the purchaser acquires full rights over it, to build upon it or not, as he chooses. There can be no reservation of rent from it, or of other annual or periodical payments. If the purchase-money be not paid in full at the time of sale, a mortgage is thereby created in favour of the vendor, the annual interest upon which is charged, not upon the land, but upon the capital. In case of the purchaser's failure to pay the full capital or the interest thereon, the vendor is not entitled to resume possession of the land, but must recover the money in the same way as an ordinary debt.

It would be contrary to the constitution in many cantons, and notably in Berne, to subject land to periodical and irredeemable payments, as savouring too much of feudalism.

CHAPTER XI.

BELGIUM, NETHERLANDS, DENMARK.

BELGIUM is neither a centralised country like France, and (to a certain extent) like the United Kingdom, nor a confederation like the United States and Switzerland. The provinces and townships (communes) enjoy a real autonomy, the rule as stated in the constitution of the kingdom being that provincial affairs are to be settled by the Provincial Assembly, and local affairs by the Communal Council (both being elected bodies) ; but, of course, a veto is vested in the central Government on matters which might be considered contrary to the interest of the State.

As a consequence, taxes are established and levied, not only by the State, but by the provinces and communes also, the only condition being that the creation of any local tax is subject to the approval of the Government. Taxes of all kinds are levied in some localities. Of course, they are not the same everywhere, and it would be impossible to give here, even by approximation, an idea of the innumerable objects some of these taxes touch. As a rule, however, the majority of the provinces, and especially communes, find it easier to add a few additional centimes to every franc of the State taxes. The State taxes, which generally form the basis of these additional centimes, are (1) the personal taxes, and (2) the tax on licences.

The State personal taxes of Belgium are based and levied on (1) the rental value of the property occupied ; (2) the number of windows and doors ; (3) the value of the furniture ; (4) the number of servants ; and (5) the number of horses.

The State rental tax is a tax of 5 per cent. on the gross annual rental of all houses and buildings, calculated on the average annual rental received during the preceding ten years. Government or local officials occupying premises by virtue of their offices are exempt from the tax.

The tax on windows and doors has been already explained when dealing with France. Here, however, it varies with the storeys on which the window or door may be constructed.

The State tax on furniture is 1 per cent. on the value of the furniture. It includes all things in the house for personal or domestic use, but clothing and implements used in trade and for personal adornment are exempt.

The State tax on servants varies with the

number of the servants, the nature of their duties, and sex. A supplementary tax of 10 francs is charged should a male servant have to wear a livery.

The State tax on horses also varies according to the use made of the horse and the profession exercised by the owner or keeper. However, horses exclusively employed in agriculture, factories, and by shopkeepers, are exempt from taxation.

The State licence tax is levied on all those exercising a profession or trade, with certain exceptions, as ecclesiastics and members of the learned professions, etc. For the establishment of this licence tax there are two tariffs, called " A " and " B." The first, " A," imposes the same licence for all the communes, and the second, " B," on the contrary, varies the tax according to the importance of the commune. Tariff " A," applicable to all communes, comprises seventeen classes, and the tax varies according to the classification of the profession or trade, the highest being 401 francs, and the lowest 170 francs. For the application of tariff " B," the law divides the communes into six grades, according to the population, and then distributes the professions and trades amongst fourteen classes, according to the importance they occupy in commerce and industry. Thus, a profession of the first class pays a tax variable, according as it is exercised in a commune of the first, second, etc., or sixth grade. A licence tax for foreign commercial travellers is 20 francs a year.

Space will only permit an example of the actual local taxation of the capital of Belgium. In Brussels the municipal taxes include (1) an addition of 95 per cent. to the State personal tax. (2) An addition of 15 per cent. to the State licence tax. (3) Tax on buildings temporarily exempted from the Government real estate tax ; buildings constructed or reconstructed after 1871 are not liable to the Government real estate tax until the second year of their occupation. This slight exemption, however, does not apply to the city, and it collects a municipal tax of 15 per cent. on the net rental. (4) Tax on drinking and tobacco traffic. Dealers in liquors and tobacco are divided into several classes, and taxed according to the amount of annual sales effected. (5) A city tax of 7 per cent. on the revenue from real estate. (6) A carriage tax of 50 francs for a two-horse carriage, and 30 francs for a one-horse vehicle. Any number of vehicles of the same class may be kept on payment of the tax for the first. (7) Dog tax, except on those belonging to blind persons. (8) A tax of 250 francs on every person exercising the profession of a stock or exchange broker or agent, and 15 francs on their clerks. (9) A tax of 25 francs on brokers of merchandise, and 10 francs on their clerks. (10) A tax on constructions or reconstructions. The city is divided into ten classes for the assessment of this tax. That for the first class is 1 franc per cubic metre for the first five metres of the height, 50 centimes from the height of five to ten metres, and 25 centimes above ten metres. The tax of each of the remaining nine classes is reduced one-tenth. The out-houses, stables, etc., pay one-fourth of the tax. This tax, however, is doubled if the street is opened at the city's expense, and it is one-half more if the street is widened for a length of thirty-five metres at the cost of the city. In the laying-out of new streets in Antwerp, the owners of the property fronting on such streets are required to bear all the expenses, each in proportion to the number of running metres along the front of his property. The amount due per metre is found in dividing the cost of the work by double the length of the street, thus covering both sides. For the expense of sewers 12 francs per running metre is collected from the proprietors of improved and unimproved property. The payment of these taxes for sewers and pavements is required but once and not yearly, even not again when repairs become necessary and are executed.

To all these samples of local taxation in Brussels, must, of course, be added the tolls received for space at the markets, and the use of the public slaughter-houses.

The additional centimes to the State taxes are collected by the State tax-collectors at a cost of 2 per cent. on the sum collected. The other local taxes are collected by the local collectors appointed by the local authorities, and receive, as a rule, a fixed salary. Although in some instances the rate of taxation in Belgium may seem high, yet it is levied upon assessments made so low that the amount of tax paid is comparatively small.

There exists no distinction in the system of tenure between urban and suburban dwellings in Belgium, as both are governed by the same rules and regulations. Houses are regarded as private property, which the owners let for a term to be determined by the parties interested. Leases which exceed nine years must be transcribed in the public registers, of which anyone may obtain extracts. Houses are, as a rule, however, freehold property. Leaseholds exist only to a very limited extent, and are tending generally to disappear. Of late years companies have been formed in the country for the construction of working men's dwellings, the tenant having the faculty of becoming the proprietor of the house which he inhabits by paying annually a sum as rent, comprising the interest and sinking fund of the capital representing the value of the ground and the cost of construction.

NETHERLANDS.

As in the case of Belgium, so in Holland the provincial municipal revenues are raised chiefly by additional centimes being added to the State direct taxes, called in the vernacular of the country " de heffing van oheentem op's Ryks directe belastingen." The State taxes, which are principally availed of for this purpose, are : (1) The land tax, (2) the personal tax, and (3) the licence tax.

The land tax is levied on all lands, whether cultivated or not, and on all improved and unimproved real estate. For the purpose of assessing the tax, the land is classified in accordance with its value, quality, and producing capacity ; and on city, town, and other property the tax is payable in accordance with the rent value of the premises. All lands which by draining and diking, etc., are first rendered cultivable, are exempt from this tax for a term of ten years. Likewise improvements on formerly vacant city and town property renders the same exempt for eight years.

Property belonging to the State, municipality, or recognised ecclesiastical bodies, is also exempt.

The personal tax, as we have seen in Belgium, has various subdivisions. This denomination stands for a tax which is levied on the rent value of all premises, on doors and windows, on hearths and fireplaces, on the furniture—or rather value thereof—on the number of servants employed, and on horses owned and used in business. This tax is paid by the inhabitants of the house, whether owners, tenants, or lodgers. Exemptions from the payment of this tax, or taxes, are provided for by different laws, the application of which extends to and relieves the great mass of the wage-earning population and most all other persons whose yearly income falls below, say, about £120.

The licence tax is levied upon persons engaged in different trades and occupations. They are grouped into classes, of which there are a large number, and in accordance with one or another of which each person is assessed, or is made to pay for his licence. The charge as to many kinds of business is very low, amounting only to about a half-sovereign per annum ; but in certain cases it runs up to as much as £80. It should be stated that licences are required by each member of a firm, or, in other words, one licence does not entitle any firm to carry on any business if it is composed of two or more partners.

Joint-stock companies and corporations pay to the State for their business 2 per cent. on their yearly net incomes. The professional classes, fishermen, seamen, journeymen, tradesmen, and servants are exempt, as also weavers when assisted in trade by their wives or children ; and recently the exemption was extended to widows who continue the pursuit of their late husband's former and certain occupations, so long as they employ only one workman.

Some localities derive a part of their income from taxes on dogs, on public entertainments, and all of them from a licence duty established a few years ago on the retail spirit trade. Besides, some localities make a source of income by working a gas factory for their own account, or by granting concessions to individuals for running the same, or a water-works within the municipality, payment being made in a share of the profits. On the same terms there has been granted in Amsterdam a concession for working tramways. In Amsterdam and some other localities a tax is levied, called street money, that is to say, a contribution from the houses for the maintenance of the pavement, the sewers, etc. ; but, after all, this is nothing but an indirect tax, for which the law or local administration fixes a maximum, thus rendering a direct increase of this tax, as local taxation, impossible.

Duties are also levied for the use of establishments destined to particular services, as port duties, sluice, bridge, and ferry tolls, markets fees, etc.

Next to England the Netherlands is the only country where the system of free trade has found an earnest and complete application. The tariff of import duties is purely a fiscal one, and rates are very low, and a great many articles are absolutely free. Local excises, or the French system of octroi, have been abolished in Holland, as well as the Government excises on most of the necessities of life. This action on the part of the authorities has been a step in the right direction, alleviating the burden laid by taxation on the working portion of the population.

In the Netherlands it may be assumed as a general rule that property in land or houses is held by the proprietor as a freehold, limited owner-ship being hardly known there, as the system of letting or hiring land or building leases finds no favour in that country.

DENMARK.

As all the towns in Denmark are guided by similar principles in raising local taxes to meet their expenditure, we will confine ourselves to the course pursued in the capital, Copenhagen. The sources of local taxation are not very complicated, being confined to (1) a local income tax, (2) tax on real estate, and (3) a paving tax.

In 1861 power was given for the first time to municipalities throughout the kingdom to levy an income tax, being restricted, however, to a maximum rate of 3 per cent. The tax at present levied is 2 per cent. on the ratepayer's income. Incomes below £25 are exempt, and a graduated abatement is allowed on incomes up to £75, when the liability to the full tax occurs.

Office expenses may be deducted to reduce incomes derived from trade sources, and each ratepayer is also allowed to deduct from this income such amount as has been paid by him in the preceding year for taxes to the State or to the municipality, the expenses of repairs on his real estate, and the interest of any mortgage debt he may have thereon.

The city of Copenhagen is divided into twenty-three districts, for each of which one tax-collector or more is or are appointed, who, at the close of each year, furnish the tax office with a list of the inhabitants, with accompanying information as to their social and pecuniary positions. The collectors are allowed 2 per cent. on the amount collected.

The real estate tax is divided into two classes :

R

(1) the "general ground" tax ; and (2) the "areal tax." The first is levied upon all ground, whether within or without the city walls, or built upon or not. Several years ago a measurement survey was made under the following procedure : all ground situated within the distance of 20 ells from the street lines, and which was designated "street ground," was taken in full in the survey admeasurement, whilst the remaining ground, designated " inner ground," was only assessed at one-sixth its real value. The ground thus found liable to taxation was valued and rated at fixed rates of 16 öre and 2·66 kroner per square ell, according to its situation. By multiplying such scales of taxes on the rateable area of ground, the tax value was obtained, and for each proportional amount of 160 kroner of such taxed value, the ground was rated for one portion of ground tax. To remedy the inequalities of this system of levying the tax, it was enacted that, when the ground was built upon, the value of the building should also be taken into account, so that every 10,000 kroner of the building's insurance should be rated at one portion additional.

This rating only applied to buildings within the city walls ; but as the building of dwelling-houses, with the rapid growth of population, was carried on to a very great extent outside the walls, the tax was fixed thereon as follows : The unbuilt-

upon ground was divided into three classes, and
valued at 1,200, 2,400, and 10,000 kroner per barrel
(56,000 square feet), according to the purposes for
which they were used, with its valuation for
business purposes. To this, again, a change was
made in 1861, which, on the whole, made a radical
alteration in the tax conditions of the city. This
law united all the tax, fixing the same at 15·66
kroner and 18·66 kroner for ground without the
city walls. By this law the ground-tax has
become a fixed one, and can only be increased
by the levying of a greater number of portions
on newly erected dwellings. In cases where
buildings may be deprived of some of the corporation's benefits, such as lighting, etc., a proportionate reduction in the tax is conceded.

The "areal" tax is levied upon all buildings
within the city. It was rearranged, and, as with
the ground tax, is now fixed at a constant rate of
13½ öre per square ell frontage, and at 9 öre per
square ell on the sides and back part of the
building. From it small dwellings, under 64
square ells, are exempt.

It is a presumption of the law that taxes on
buildings fall upon the lessees of the house; or,
supposing the owner does himself inhabit the
house, fall on him as occupier thereof, not as
owner; in other words, the building tax is a tax

R 2

on the consumption (that is, the use of the house),
and not a property tax. The paving tax is only
levied upon property within the city walls. It is
levied according to the length of the façade to the
street, and the width of the street.

CHAPTER XII.

ITALY.

LIKE some of the other Continental countries, the Italian system of administration is one of centralisation. In this system there are three financial units, namely, the State, the province, and the commune. For the support of the State the various kinds of imposts levied by the Government are briefly classified as follows : (1) Direct taxes ; (2) taxes on consumption ; (3) taxes on business ; (4) miscellaneous (State salt and tobacco monopoly). According to the Italian nomenclature, only those taxes which are levied on real estate, including buildings, and those levied on incomes (richezza mobile), are classed as direct taxes. All others are called indirect taxes.

Under the law regulating provincial and municipal taxation, the various provinces and communes are empowered within certain limits to assess taxes supplementary to the State taxes on lands and buildings. The communes are also empowered, within certain limits, to assess taxes supplementary to the State tax on articles of home consumption. As a matter of fact, the supplementary tax of this nature constitutes one of the most important sources of revenue in the Italian communes.

Generally speaking, the powers delegated to the communes are: (1) To assess taxes on provisions, drinkables, fuel and illuminating fluids, building material, forage, etc.; (2) to farm out, with right of working, public weights, public grain and liquid measures, and the privilege of letting public stalls and booths at times of fairs and markets; (3) to assess a tax for the occupation of public spaces and areas, etc.; (4) to assess a tax on draught animals, beasts of burden and dogs, when the last-mentioned animals are not used for guarding rural edifices or flocks; (5) to assess taxes supplementary to the direct taxes of the State as before mentioned. Taxation under the first four foregoing heads must not, however, exceed 20 per cent. of the value of the merchandise or interest taxed. The supplementary tax to the direct State taxes can never exceed 50 per cent. of the taxes imposed by the Government.

The value upon which the land tax is levied is that already established in the records of the kingdom, according to the nature, quality, and class of lands. But as the Italian records are not yet uniform, and there being at present a great inequality amongst the different records of the regions of Italy, the impost is not levied by a uniform and constant aliquot on the land-tax rent levied throughout the kingdom, but, instead, the impost is applied by a method called "distinct division," that is to say, the Government, fixing beforehand the total sum to be paid in the course of the year by the contributors, to whom an only and uniform yearly aliquot is fixed, which is obtained by dividing the proportion so estimated in the records of the department to which the contributor belongs.

In Rome, the State tax on land is 9·16 per cent. of the appraised value; in addition to this, lands pay the provincial tax and the municipal tax, the former of 3·20 and the latter of 4·89 per cent., making in all 17·25 per cent.

In Florence, the State tax on land is 18·10 per cent. on its net income, the provincial 7·05 per cent., and the commune 20·20 per cent., making in all 45·35 per cent

The tax on buildings is fixed on the basis of registered value. This is ascertained by officials called Agents of the Imposts, who estimate the precise value approximately, founded upon the proprietor's valuation. In Rome, the State tax on

buildings is 16·25 on the amount of taxes due;
in addition thereto come the provincial and
municipal taxes, the former being 4·94 per cent.,
and the latter 7·53 per cent., making a total of
28·72 per cent. on the amount of the taxes to be
paid.   The gross amount on which the assessment
is made for taxation on buildings is reduced by
one-third for workshops and manufactories, and
one-fourth for all other buildings.

In Florence the State tax on buildings is 16·25
per cent., the provincial 5·60, and the Commune
16·10 per cent., making in all 37·95 per cent.

In Rome there is a supplementary tax to the
State tax on the manufacture of spirits, beer, and
mineral waters.   To certain of the larger communes there is a restitution by the State of one-
tenth of the amount collected for income tax
within their limits.

Aside from the supplementary levies on the
foregoing State taxes, all other communal taxes
are classified under two heads, known as (1) taxes
discretionary to the communes, (2) communal
dues.

The following are classified under the first
head :—

1. *Taxes* on beasts of burden and draught
animals.   This tax is charged to the owners of
horses and all beasts of burden.   It is divided into

three categories. In the Commune of Rome they are as follows :—(*a*) all animals used by private persons pay about £3 per annum ; (*b*) all animals in public service, such as tramways, omnibuses, etc., about £1 4s. per year; (*c*) animals for carts and drays about 10s. per year.

2. *Cattle tax.* This tax is on the owners of cows, and every kind of farm animal ; like the tax on horses it is per head. It is an animal tax payable at the beginning of the agricultural season. This impost is classified under 13 heads, and is charged from about 6s. per horse to fourpence per sheep or lamb.

3. *Taxes on sales and industries.* The municipality of Rome does not assess a tax under the head of sales. There is, however, a tax on industries and professions (which should not be confounded with the State income tax). It varies from £2 to £80, and is assessed on persons exercising industries and professions, according to the importance of the same.

In 1870 each commune was empowered to levy a tax on all persons, both native and foreign, doing business or practising a profession within its limits. To carry into effect the said law, the communes of Italy were divided into six classes, according to their population, and a maxium tax fixed for each, viz. :—

(1) Over 80,000 inhabitants, maximum tax £12 10 0
(2)   ,,   40,000 to 80,000 ,,   ,,   ,,   10 8 4
(3)   ,,   20,001 to 40,000 ,,   ,,   ,,   8 6 8
(4)   ,,   5,001 to 20,000 ,,   ,,   ,,   6 5 0
(5)   ,,   2,001 to 5,000 ,,   ,,   ,,   4 3 4
(6) Under 2,001   ,,   ,,   ,,   2 1 8

The tax itself is graduated, and is based upon the estimated income of the person exercising the trade or profession. The following is a fair example of the scale in operation in Florence.

MUNICIPAL TAX ON DEALERS AND PRO-
FESSIONS, ETC.

Income.	Class	Tax.			Income.	Class	Tax.		
		£	s.	d.			£	s.	d.
Up to and over £2.500	1	12	10	0	Up to £280	14	1	9	2
,, £1,800	2	11	5	0	,, 220	15	1	5	0
,, 1,600	3	10	0	0	,, 200	16	1	0	10
,, 1,400	4	8	15	0	,, 180	17	0	18	4
,, 1,200	5	7	10	0	,, 160	18	0	16	8
,, 1,000	6	6	5	0	,, 140	19	0	14	2
,, 800	7	5	0	0	,, 120	20	0	12	6
,, 680	8	4	3	4	,, 100	21	0	10	0
,, 560	9	3	6	8	,, 80	22	0	9	2
,, 480	10	2	10	0	,, 60	23	0	8	4
,, 400	11	2	1	8	,, 40	24	0	5	0
,, 360	12	1	17	6	,, 30	25	0	4	2
,, 320	13	1	13	4					

4. *Tax on rentable value.* This is collected from persons having furnished houses or rooms to let. It is proportioned to the income therefrom.

The municipality of Rome does not assess this tax.

5. *Carriage tax.* This is collected from owners of private and public vehicles of all kinds used either in the transportation of persons or merchandise. This tax is doubled for all vehicles bearing coats of arms and heraldic insignia.

6. *Servants' tax.* In Rome, masters and employers are taxed per annum for male servants, five shillings; females, two shillings.

7. *Dog tax.* The tax on dogs in Rome is five shillings per animal per year. Shepherd-dogs are exempted from this tax.

8. *Family tax.* Rome does not assess a tax under this head. In those communes where it is imposed, it applies to all persons (not indigent) residing within the limits of the commune.

A family is understood to represent several individuals bound by family ties and residing together. If members of a family do not so reside, they are subject to tax as individuals. Persons residing together, but not relatives, are taxed separately. Minors are not exempt.

It is a fixed graduated capitation tax, families being classified according to their estimated income.

9. *Personal labour tax.* Neither is this tax assessed in Rome. Where it is imposed it consists

of an obligation for each head of a family, who, by reason of economical conditions, is exempted from certain other taxes, to furnish annually four days, work for himself and for each able-bodied male member of his family, and each draught animal with its respective vehicle owned or worked by the family. This personal labour tax, where enforced, may be substituted by a cash payment. It was originally instituted for the improvement of the country roads.

10. *Tax on signs*, show-cases and awnings. This is collected from masters of stores, shops, etc., and is divided into three classes, according to the desirability of the locality in which the business establishment is situate.

The following are known as communal dues:—

1. *Licences* for hotels, restaurants, cafés, drinking saloons, etc. In Rome, these licences are paid for at the rate of 5 per cent. on the amount of outlay for rent for the first year; for succeeding years the rate is one-tenth of the tax for the first year.

2. *Verification* of weights and measures. In Rome, no tax is assessed under this head.

3. *Rents* of booths and occupation of public spaces. This tax is levied according to the superficial area occupied, the position of the site, and is used on fair days.

4. *Butchers' tax.* Two kinds of taxes are levied

under this head. All animals destined for slaughter go first to the cattle market, and then to the slaughter-house, for both of which the taxes are obligatory.

5. *Scholastic tax.* As there is only one class of communal schools in Rome, this tax is about eight shillings per month, both for boys and girls.

6. *Mortuary tax.* The Italian cemeteries are, as a rule, owned and managed by the municipal authorities. The hearse service with fixed rates is also a monopoly of the municipalities.

7. *Tolls.* In Rome there are two toll bridges, on which the municipality exacts one halfpenny for each pedestrian, and twopence-halfpenny for each vehicle.

8. *Civil Registrars' Acts.* Certified copies of all original documents have to be paid for.

9. *Miscellaneous.* Under this head the municipal authority assesses an annual water tax on three separate water supplies, the assessment varying according to the desirability of the water, furnished in one-inch pipes. However, one of the best water supplies in Rome has been ceded to a private stock company for a term of years, and which charges special rates. The average revenue in Rome from this source is about 6,938,366 lire.

The octroi or internal consumption tax in Rome is upon so varied and numerous a class of commodities that it is unnecessary to give them here in detail. This tax is the most important source of revenue to Italian communes, and is levied on articles of common consumption or utility even upon which there may be no State tax. The average annual revenue from this source alone to the municipality of Rome is about 15,027,265 lire. The rate of taxation on each article varies in the different cities of the kingdom.

In Florence traders have to pay an additional tax, as the chambers of commerce of that city, apart from the municipal authority, are empowered to levy upon natives and foreigners engaged in trade, professions, or industries a tax in proportion to the income derived from such trade, profession, or industry, based upon the items of the Government income tax, and subject to the same system of collection.

The only taxes collected directly by the Government are the duties on imports and exports, and the taxes on business ; other direct taxes are collected in the following manner :—

The public officers or administrators prepare the tax lists, and their collection is farmed out for periods of five years to private enterprises or associations called esattore e ricevitore delle imposte dirette (exactors and receivers of direct taxes). The cost of collections under this system varies

considerably in the different parts of the kingdom.
These associations receive a commission on the
amounts collected. It is not paid by the Government, but is added to the amount of taxes to be
collected, and is paid by the taxpayer. In Rome
the commission is usually £2,$\frac{1}{10}$ per cent. of taxes
due. The right to collect taxes is in some instances
even purchased from the Government.

In like manner the collection of the direct taxes
of provinces and communes is usually farmed out.
The collectors of direct taxes on account of the
province of Rome usually add to the charge of the
taxpayer the same rate for collection as to the
State tax. For the direct taxes of the municipality
of Rome the rate is £1,$\frac{4}{12}$ per cent. of taxes due.
The cost of the municipality for the collection of
its indirect taxes is about fourteen shillings per
cent. of taxes due ; also 4 per cent. of amounts
collected as arrearages. This rate of 4 per cent.
for arrearages is equal for the whole kingdom.

Since the octroi tax or duties are partly of the
State and partly of the municipality, to avoid a
double set of officers the municipalities usually
collect them, and pay to the State a regular sum
agreed upon. The municipalities in their town
then either collect these duties by their own agents,
or farm them out to individuals or companies. In
other cases the State collects the Government and

communal octroi duties, and allows the municipalities a fixed portion. This last mode is adopted in the city of Naples, and under the arrangement between the State and the municipal authorities the former collects all the excise taxes, and pays to the municipality annually the net amount of 10,000,000 lire as her share.

According to the Italian Civil Code, property in land and buildings consists in the right of enjoyment and disposal thereof in the most absolute way. But the system of stipulating a rent or other annual or periodical payment has been very much abandoned, and owing to facilities afforded by the laws of the country for redeeming such rents, which are called "conone" or "cense," it is generally the practice to pay off these rents created in former times, so as to make the property freehold.

The stipulations under such contracts, called "emphiteosis," depend upon the covenants made by the parties ; or, in the default of special covenant, the general rules laid down in the Civil Code are applied.

Inasmuch as the Italian law enables tenants under an "emphiteosis" to redeem the rent by paying an amount of money equivalent to twenty times the amount of the yearly rent—and, if the rent is payable in kind, the value is to be calculated at the average market price of the produce during ten years then preceding—it follows that a contract of "emphitcosis" which was originally intended for the amelioration of the property, by building or otherwise, is reduced to the simple payment of a certain yearly interest at 5 per cent. on a fixed sum of money, which sum of money is not easily to be realised by means of conveyance; it will not increase in proportion as the value of the property may be rising, and it will be liable to depreciation in proportion as the value of money decreases.

Long leases, in the ordinary form, for any period above thirty years, are not permitted.

The tendency in Italy is to make all property freehold and easily transmissible.

S

CHAPTER XIII.

SWEDEN AND NORWAY.

TAXATION in the kingdom of Sweden has as a foundation so many remote usages and ancient conditions of life, that it is most difficult to elucidate the existing methods and obsolete terms, which are but little understood by the present generation of taxpayers themselves. The system may be embodied in two general divisions: (1) national (Staten); and (2) local (Kommunal).

The local tax is derived from the following:—

(1) Real estate: (a) income tax from capital or labour.

(2) Church tax, on basis of State tax *per capita.*

(3) Liquor licensing tax.

From the tax on real estate and income by capital or labour is derived the greater part of the amount raised for the expenses of the community.

The amount levied by the State on real estate and income is used as a basis or foundation of the local or kommunal tax in cities and towns, which amount is called " bevillning " (contribution).

The city or town authorities ascertain the amount necessary to meet the expenses of the year, and after deducting any income the city or town may have, find the relative value the amount bears to the amount collected by the State from real estate and income, and use it as a multiple for their assessment.

Real estate is divided into two classes :—

(1) Agricultural real estate, which is taxed for State purposes 3 öre on every 100 kroner of its assessed value ; (2) other real estate, which is taxed for State purposes 5 öre on every 100 kroner of its assessed value.

All incomes from capital or labour exceeding 500 kroner per annum, are taxed 1 per cent. with certain deductions until the income is 1,800 kroner. In exceptional cases, such as numerous family, accident, long-continued illness, the authorities can raise the exemption from taxation up to 700 kroner.

The assessors, in estimating the income, use the amount of house-rent paid by each taxpayer as a gauge by which to calculate the probable amount of income, as follows: Should the yearly rent amount to from 300 to 500 kroner, the income is esti- mated at least three times the amount ; 500 to

S 2

1,000 kroner, four times the amount; 1,000 to
5,000 kroner, five times the amount; above 1,500
kroner, six times the amount.

The "bevillning" tax, being the only one
where annual value is considered, may be said
to be assessed in this way : If a property in the
country, including necessary buildings, be worth
£1,000, and have a building upon it also worth
£1,000, but which is not necessary to agriculture,
such as a saw-mill, it is taken at 3 per cent., equal
to £30, and the "bevillning" at 1 per cent. on
the £30, equal to six shillings, while the revenue
from the saw-mill is taken at 5 per cent., equal
to £50, and the "bevillning" at 1 per cent. on
the £50, equal to ten shillings, so that the property would pay sixteen shillings per annum to
the State.

Now if the "bevillning" (amount of State tax
on real estate and income) in the city or town
was 100,000 kroner, and the amount to be raised
in the town was 400,000 kroner, then every taxpayer, for every kroner paid to the State on real
estate and income, is assessed four kroner by the
city or town.

Church tax, on the basis of the building, is
a tax levied for the support of the State Church,
and is expended for building and repairing
churches, or parish buildings, salaries of priests, etc.

The tax is apportioned on the foundation of the bevillning also, the estimated expenses of the State Church for the year being divided among the taxpayers by certain rules on the basis of the bevillning. The amount of the bevillning is also used as a foundation for the local tax in the country.

Church tax *per capita* (kyrkoskatt) consists of a personal tax, irrespective of age and sex, of fifty öre *per capita*.

There is considerable dissatisfaction over the tax for the maintenance of the State Church and clergy, which is especially felt by all those belonging to other denominations, who, in addition to the State Church tax, have their own clergy and houses of worship to support.

The receipts from the provincial liquor licensing tax are divided thus: one-fifth goes to the budget of the province, one-fifth is paid to the Government Agricultural Society, three-fifths are paid into the municipal chest if the money has been raised in towns, but if it has been raised in the country it is divided among the parishes according to their population.

Personal property of every description is exempt from taxation in Sweden. It can hardly be wondered at, therefore, that complaints are made against the pressure of taxation upon real

estate owners, who are the occupiers as well, and
particularly on the farming community, partly
owing, it is said, to disproportionately high assessments. Another explanation may be, that personal property being exempt, the tax burden falls
upon real estate and income, and the latter, as
is well known, being more difficult to reach, the
real consequently bears the greater weight of the
taxes.

In the country districts, there is a distinctive
feature in the Swedish system of taxation worthy
of noting, different from any that has as yet been
considered, and which brings back to our mind
our own old feudal system. It lies in certain
burdens of land coming more under the denomination of rent than taxation, and being, moreover,
paid in kind as much as in money.

These burdens are for military service, a large
part of the Swedish army, the so-called " Indelta "
or tenemented army being supported by persons
who hold their lands on the tenure of providing
soldiers. This they do partly by money payments
to the soldiers, partly by gifts and provisions of
various sorts, but chiefly by setting apart portions
of land, which are enjoyed rent free by the above-
named soldiers.

Sweden is divided into districts for this purpose,
and both cavalry and infantry are furnished by the

country districts, though, oddly enough, not by
the towns. Some look upon this as a system of
taxation, others as a system of land tenure.

In the consideration of the burden of taxation
upon the farming community, should also be taken
into account, besides their taxes and their share
of the protective tariff with comparatively little
benefit from the same, the high latitude of their
lands and short summers, which naturally are
more detrimental to agriculture than to other
industries, coupled with their competition with
the farmers of other countries much more advantageously situated.

The tenure of dwelling-houses in this country
is usually freehold. The system of letting land
on long building leases cannot be said to prevail
to any great extent in Sweden. In the larger
towns, where houses are built and let in flats, the
system does not exist, the houses being built on
freehold plots. In the country leases are not
uncommon, but usually for large lots for agricultural purposes ; the tenant has the right at the
end of his lease to remove any buildings erected
by him, all other improvements (in cultivation,
planting, fencing, etc.) falling to the ground-land-
lord. The natural tendency of this is, if the
buildings erected be useful and substantial, to
bring about an agreement between the landlord

and tenant for the former to take them over from the latter at a valuation.

The only cases in which leases for building dwelling-houses are common in this country are those of plots in the neighbourhood of towns, and in summer resorts, sea-side and lake-side bathing places, etc., for the erection of villas.

The usual term of a lease is fifty years, but shorter periods are of frequent occurrence, and everything may be said to depend on the wording of the contract.

If a plot is held on lease, the lessee has no right to transfer it to a third person without the landlord's special permission, unless the lessee has had this right specially reserved to him in his contract.

NORWAY.

In Norway a somewhat more healthy state of things exists than in Sweden. When Denmark ceded the country to Sweden in 1814, the Norwegians did not allow themselves to be thus bartered. They adopted a free constitution for themselves, and after a few encounters with the Swedish troops, a treaty was agreed to, the principal article of which is the modified constitution of 1814, in accordance with which Norway is a free and independent State under the King of Sweden.

All Norwegians are equal in the eye of the law ; constitutionally there is no longer any nobility in existence. A decree of 1821 decided that exemption from taxation should cease at the death of the then existing feudal owners.

Norway shows what a country, very scantily endowed by Nature, may become by means of advantageous national arrangements.

It is well known how barren the soil is, and that the yield of corn is far from sufficient for home consumption. Manufacturing industries are few ; likewise are the roads. Thus the population are principally confined to navigation and fishing.

The country was in a lamentable condition when it obtained its independence. Then the peasantry were the actual rulers, and although they were only plain, simple people, yet there were among them many practical, common-sense men. They have now not only promoted the material well-being, but art and science also. The printing press has found its way into the extreme points of Finland. Middle schools and good parish schools, in which the education is free, exist in most of the towns.

Loans have been obtained and expended upon productive services, such as construction of harbours, high roads, lighthouses, railways, mortgage banks, and others of a like national character. The proceeds of the customs, which have considerably increased, are the chief and main support of the Government.

The local taxation on real estate (lands and houses), and on capital and income, and from the licensing of the spirit and other trades, are somewhat similar to that levied in Sweden.

The condition of the country, both as regards simplicity and solid practical tendencies, is very much similar to that of Switzerland.

Land is let at an annual ground rent for building purposes, either for a term of years or in perpetuity. On the expiration of the terms of a lease for a specific number of years, the tenant, as in Sweden, remains the owner of the house, which he is at liberty to remove.

Under the common law, a landlord can resume possession of his property, and by application to the "Foged" (King's bailiff), eject the tenant or put the property and the buildings up to public auction if the rent or periodical payments be not paid. The same course can be adopted in the event of any breach of agreement, but in such case only by recourse to the competent tribunal.

CHAPTER XIV.

RUSSIA, POLAND, SPAIN, TURKEY AND GREECE.

THE Russian Government derives its revenue from a capitation and land tax, excise and customs duties, various licences and fees; succession and deed-of-gift duties, passports, duties on express railway traffic; tax on fire-insurance policies, on increase of salaries of public officials; royalty dues on mines, mints, post-office and telegraph; receipts from domain lands, mines and railways; and other miscellaneous sources of revenue. These indirect taxes are very numerous, and that which forms the richest source of revenue is the duty on liquors, or, in reality, the brandy duty. It practically yields one-third of the imperial revenue.

The unit of local government in Russia is the Commune. The communal institutions are unique in their way. Each commune includes all its members in a very peculiar socialistic body. The Russian system excludes the autonomy of the separate individual. The community owns its lands under a mutual obligation of the persons belonging to the place, to pay the taxes and furnish recruits.

These peasant republics are found from Smolensk to Viatka—from the Onegabai to the Cossack Settlements on the Don ; but they are unknown in Finland, the Baltic Provinces, Astrakhan, Kasan, Siberia, Kiev, Podolia and Ukrania. Since the emancipation of the peasants, however, the idea which is the natural consequence of it, viz., of turning the property of the commune into private property (the first condition of a thorough cultivation of the soil) meets with constantly increasing approbation.

The cantonal system is an extension of the patriarchal system of the commune for the sake of convenience. The district assembly is elected partly by the district town, partly by the communes, and the remainder by the landed proprietors. This latter body deals with (1) district communication, (2) schools, (3) sanitary matters, such as drainage, vaccination, and cattle disease, etc. The Provincial Assembly is elected from the district assemblies, and decides questions above the power of the district assembly, such as (1) main roads and railways, (2) general education, (3) famine, epidemics, hospitals, etc.

Town councils are now established in most of the chief towns of the empire. In many parts of

Russia, land pays more (sometimes four or five times as much) in local taxation than capital in the hands of a merchant pays in imperial and local taxation together.

Great difficulty has been experienced in obtaining information as to the financial conditions of the different Russian territories, but from the importance of the capital of the kingdom of Poland, the manner of raising municipal supplies there may be taken as the best example that can be given of the system generally adopted.

In Warsaw the municipal authorities collect the following kinds of taxes :—

Tax on immovable property. (1) This is in the nature of an income tax. All private immovable properties yielding a revenue, whether liable or not to the Government hearth tax, bear this tax upon their gross revenue.

It is assessed at the following rate :—

Revenue under 500 roubles (£78), 2 per cent.
   ,, over 500 to 1,000 roubles (£78 to £156), 3 p.c.
   ,, over 1,000 to 2,000 ,, (£156 to £312), 4 p.c.
   ,, 2,000 and over ,, (£312 and over), 5 p.c.

Vacant properties or properties yielding no income are assessed ¼ per cent. on the appraised value.

On Government buildings, and on those belonging to the various Government institutions, 5 per cent. on the gross revenue is levied; (2) the municipality collects an additional hearth tax to the hearth tax levied by the Government authorities. This tax is computed according to the value of each building, and is an equal percentage ratio to the amount at which the building was estimated by virtue of the ukase of the mutual government. It is collected at the rate of 1·25 per cent. of the gross annual value.

(3) *Industry tax.* A tax is levied upon commercial certificates and licences, authorising the carrying on of a trade or industry. These licences are divided into various classes according to the nature of the different trades, and a fixed charge levied for each.

(4) *Hackney-coach tax.* Hackney coaches and omnibuses bear a tax of 10 roubles 80 copecks (about £1 14s. 2d.), and sledges 1 rouble 80 copecks (about 5s. 8d.).

(5) *Excise licence tax.* The municipal tax is 50 per cent. of the price for the excise liquor licence. These licences are also divided into various categories, according to the class of liquor to be sold and the nature and proportion of the business premises.

(6) *Miscellaneous taxes.* Under this head a capitation tax is levied on each dog and horse ; also a tax on sojourn certificates, authorising the inhabitants of other towns to freely reside at

Warsaw; on foreign passports, and on the attestation of various acts and documents of the municipal authorities.

Owners of places of amusement and shows have to pay 3 per cent. on the gross revenue.

Gas rate is 3 copecks per 1,000 cubic feet. Successful litigants have to pay 1 per cent. of the litigious amount, and certain scrivenery charges.

Turnpike tolls are levied, and the same tax is collected from the railway companies at certain rates regulated per passenger, per animal, per weight of luggage, etc.

Each portion of the Russian Empire possesses its own distinctive laws and customs respecting the tenure of houses and the system of letting land.

In Russia, and especially in towns, tenements are usually freehold. The same applies in Poland. In cases where property is let, instead of being sold, to persons for terms of years, the conditions are generally that houses are to be erected thereon, an annual rent paid, and it is usual to stipulate that at the end of the term the houses become the property of the landlord. In Finland and in the Baltic provinces, however, the owner of the house is at liberty to remove it at the expiration of the lease, or sell it to the landlord at a valuation.

Although letting for a term is unknown, still,

where it is resorted to, Russian law prescribes that immovable property is not to be let for a period longer than twelve years, with the exception of two cases, in which the term may be as long as thirty years, viz., when waste land is let for the purpose of (1) establishing factories, or (2) constructing country houses within seventeen miles of the two capitals (St. Petersburg and Moscow).

In Poland twelve years is also the usual term ; in Finland from ten to fifty years, and in the Baltic provinces the term is variable, the average length being about twenty-four years.

Land-owners in Poland, as a rule, farm their own land, whatever its extent, either personally, through their sons or other relative, or by agent.

SPAIN.

THE taxes paid by the people of Spain to the general government or to the municipalities are called "contributions," and the mode of assessing and collecting them is rather a novel one.

The Government financial authorities at Madrid call upon each province for a certain sum to be collected from the merchants and tradespeople, the amount to be paid by each trade, profession, or occupation is stated—so much from the bankers, so much from the merchants, tailors, bootmakers, butchers, and so on, even to the smallest dealer,

everything or anything. Each kind of business has
its allotment, or what is termed in Spain its
"cuota." This cuota is estimated according to the
population of the city, town, or village in which the
occupation or trade may be carried on.

Thus, for example, the cuota for a merchant is
put down at :—

Madrid or Barcelona per annum	...	2,645 pesetas.
Cadiz, Malaga, Seville, Valencia	...	1,955 ,,
Alicante, Ameria, Coruna, etc.	...	1,610 ,,
Other capitals of provinces and seaports of 16,000 and upwards in population ...	...	1,000 ,,
Towns of 10,000 to 16,000 ...	...	700 ,,
Towns of 2,500 to 10,000 ...		500 ,,
All others pay	...	400 ,,

The cuota for each district having been fixed,
the Government allows them to distribute the total
sum required amongst themselves, so long as the
aggregate is forthcoming; therefore, three merchants are selected by the Government and three
others by the merchants themselves to represent
them. These meet together and make an assessment against each firm doing business in the city,
according to the amount of business done by each,
the largest firm paying the most, and so on down
to the smallest concerns. Each merchant is notified

T

the amount at which the committee has assessed him.

They have a right to appeal to the committee, and from thence to the Government, but generally some satisfactory arrangement is come to before the Government is appealed to.

To the cuota fixed as above is added 18 per cent. as an annual tax to the city or municipality in which the merchant or tradesman is located, and another 6 per cent. off the total is paid for the expenses of collection.

In every city, town, or village in Spain a " Consumos" duty is collected upon everything consumed —that is, anything to eat, drink, or burn.

TURKEY AND GREECE.

THE fiscal condition of the Ottoman Empire is hidden from the public gaze. Its total revenue is an unknown quantity, no figures being published, and no information given confidentially. It is impossible to obtain information even as to such items as the amount produced by the taxes on land and buildings. These were formerly calculated as a percentage on the revenue of the property. Proofs of revenue were comparatively easily obtained, and the incidence of the tax was said to have been reasonably fair. A new system has, however, now been adopted, under which the tax is calculated on the gross value of the property. This, it is said, gives rise to much injustice and dissatisfaction, as proof of gross value is difficult to establish, and the decisions of local valuers are frequently arbitrary and unjust.

Practically speaking, all taxes in the empire are raised for national purposes, no taxes, not even in important towns, being permitted to be directly devoted to local purposes.

Each vilayet, and towns like Constantinople, are called upon to pay over the whole revenue collected to the State Treasury, which, on the other hand, approves an annual budget from each administrative centre, and permits the application of such funds as may be temporarily found in the local treasury to the payment of approved local demands.

The following are, so far as can be ascertained, the nominal rates of taxation on the different classes of land and house property; but the nominal and real rates are frequently widely divergent :—

1. Land on which no building exists, 4 per 1,000. Agricultural land pays, in addition, the tithe of the produce ("dime"). Vineyards which do not pay tithe pay 10 per 1,000. Gardens and orchards pay 10 per 1,000.

2. Houses valued at less than 5,000 piastres

T 2

(£45) are exempt from taxation when inhabited by the owner.

3. Houses valued over 5,000 and under 20,000 piastres (£180) pay 5 per 1,000 when inhabited by the owner.

4. Houses valued over 20,000 (£180) pay 8 per 1,000 when inhabited by the owner.

5. All houses rented pay 10 per 1,000.

6. All shops and warehouses pay 10 per 1,000.

7. Small houses in vineyards pay 8 per 1,000 when inhabited by the owner, and 10 per 1,000 when rented.

8. Fishing stations pay 4 per 1,000.

9. Ecclesiastical property (" Evkaf "), and property of which the revenue is specially devoted to religious or charitable purposes, pay 4 per 1,000.

An additional $\frac{1}{2}$ per 1,000 is levied on all property in land for the support of Mussulman schools.

GREECE.

THE country that produced a Pericles must have indeed retrograded when its administrators have to acknowledge that statistics are not kept, and this important criterion of the present condition and future prospects of the nation absent from its archives.

Liberty and political sagacity found a nursery in the old Greek commonwealths—commonwealths, and not mere municipalities, such as we are used to in modern times. However, their gradual extinction was the necessary consequence of the changes which followed on the centralising and despotic tendencies of the late Roman Empire, and the subsequent westward march of civilisation appears to have sapped the older country of its energy and prosperity.

It is, therefore, difficult to fathom the distribution of taxation, but it is believed that the poorer classes pay far more in proportion to their income than the rich or well-to-do classes.

The relations between indirect and direct taxation in national matters are as $2\frac{1}{2}$ to 1, the principal source of the national revenue being collected in the Custom House by taxation of imports.

In Piræus the principal revenue of the local authorities is also collected at the Custom House. It receives 5 per cent. on the sum charged as Customs dues by the Government on all goods imported for sale or use in the town. The other sources of civic revenue are the rents from corporate property; 10 per cent. of the tax collected by Government as licence to trades and on all kinds of business in the town; 10 per cent. of the Government house-property tax in the town; and the tax on vineyards and vegetable gardens, etc., in the township.

APPENDIX.

APPENDIX I.

TAXATION IN BRITISH COLONIES.

(Being Extracts from Parliamentary Return No. 181—1891).

RETURN compiled from Replies to Circular Despatch, showing—
1 TAXATION ON LAND : (*a*) The Percentage on the Annual
Value which the Rate levied amounts to ; (*b*) The Total
Amount raised, the Totals for Local and National Purposes
being stated separately ; (*c*) The Percentage which the
Amount raised by Taxation of Land bears to the Total
Taxation. 2 TAXATION OF BUILDINGS : (*a*) The Percentage
on the Annual Value which the Rate levied amounts to ; (*b*)
The Total Amount raised, the Totals for Local and National
Purposes being stated separately ; (*c*) The Percentage which
the Amount raised by Taxation of Buildings bears to the Total
Taxation.

	Percentage on the annual value which the rate levied amounts to.	Amount raised.			Percentage which amount raised bears to Total Taxation.
		Total.	Local Purposes.	National purposes.	
		£	£	£	
Gibraltar	Nil	Nil	Nil	Nil	Nil
Malta	,,	,,	,,	,,	,,
Sierra Leone ...	,,	,,	,,	,,	,,
Gambia	,,	,,	,,	,,	,,
Gold Coast ...	,,	,,	,,	,,	,,
Lagos	,,	,,	,,	,,	,,
Jamaica	·85	15,658	15,658	,,	2·8
Bahamas	Nil	Nil	Nil	,,	Nil
St. Lucia	,,	,,	,,	,,	,,
St. Vincent ...	6d. per acre	1,268	,,	1,268	4·47
Antigua	Not ascertainable	2,980	2,980	Nil	8¼
St. Kitts and Nevis	,,	4,400	4,400	,,	10·99
Virgin Islands ...	,,	131	131	,,	10·73
Dominica	2	1,938	1,938	,,	9
Montserrat ...	On lands and buildings jointly ; estimated 7½ town. 10 country	Not stated	Not stated	Not stated	Not stated
Bermuda	·118 on assessed capital value of lands and buildings jointly	1,259	1,259	—	4·43
Barbados	2s. 8d. to 4s. 10d. per acre	25,804	21,713	4,181	14·42
Ceylon	Nil	Nil	Nil	Nil	Nil

Note.—The Paddy Tax, which is virtually a land tax, yielded in 1883 Rs. 8·3,900 (national purposes), or 9·39 per cent. of the total taxation.

	Percentage on the annual value which the rate levied amounts to.	Amount raised.			Percentage which amount raised bears to Total Taxation.
Straits Settlements	5	831,846	Not stated	Not stated	·83
Hong Kong ...	Nil	Nil	Nil	Nil	Nil
Mauritius (Port Louis)	Lands and buildings jointly; three-fifths, with an additional ·50 thereon for 1890	Rs. 181,837	Rs. 181,837	,,	Not stated
		£	£		
Falkland Islands	½d. per acre = ·52 on annual value	1,476	1,476	,,	30
St. Helena... ...	Lands and buildings jointly, 1·1	941	941	,,	15·8
New Guinea ...	Nil	Nil	Nil	,,	Nil
Basutoland ...	,,	,,	,,	,,	,,
Bechuanaland (Vryburg) ...	Lands and buildings jointly, 27·08	897	897	,,	11·5
Zululand (Entonjaneni District)	1	115	—	,,	·3
Fiji : Suva Town ...	12·08	153	153	,,	·73 on total taxation; 10·89 on local taxation.
Levuka Town	7·5	209	209	,,	
		362	362		

	Percentage on the annual value which the rate levied amounts to.	Amount raised.			Percentage which amount raised bears to Total Taxation.
		Total.	Local Purposes.	National purposes.	
		£	£	£	
Gibraltar	7½	10,829	10,829	Nil	5·33
Malta	Nil	Nil	Nil	,,	Nil
Sierra Leone ...	,,	,,	,,	,,	,,
Gambia	3	410	410	,,	Not stated
Gold Coast ...	Nil	Nil	Nil	,,	Nil
Lagos	,,	,,	,,	,,	,,
Jamaica	13·2	54,400	54,400	,,	9·6
Bahamas	5	700	700	,,	1·5
St. Lucia	Not exceeding 8	2,400	2,400	,,	Not stated
St. Vincent ...	3·5	805	805	,,	2·84
Antigua	4·5	760	760	,,	2
St. Kitts and Nevis	4	570	570	,,	1·43
Virgin Islands ...	7·5	67	67	,,	5·25
Dominica	1	912	Not stated	Not stated	4·5
Montserrat... ...	See land				
Bermuda	See land				
Barbados	5	5,887	5,887	Nil	3·27
Ceylon...	3·37	Rs.295,300	Rs.295,300	,,	3·14
Straits Settlements	11	$430,653	Not stated	Not stated	11·24
Hong Kong ...	Victoria, 13; Hill districts, 8 75; Kowloon and villages, 7	$375,000		$375,000	31·25
Mauritius	See land				
Falklands	1·66	£60	£60	Nil	1·39
St. Helena... ...	See land				
New Guinea ...	Nil	Nil	Nil	,,	Nil
Basutoland ...	14s. per hut	18,674	,,	£18,674	·02
Bechuanaland ...	See land				
Zululand	14s. per native hut	28,000	Not stated	Not stated	73
Fiji : Suva Town ...	17·03	2,368	2,368	Nil	6·02 on total taxation ; 8·71 on local taxation.
Levuka Town	7·5	599	599	Nil	
		2,967	2,967		

CANADA.

PROVINCE OF ONTARIO.

In the province of Ontario taxation on land and buildings is for municipal and school purposes only.

Land and buildings are included in the term "real property," and separate valuation is not required by the Assessment Act.

For the purpose of assessment, real property is estimated at its actual cash value, as it would be appraised in payment of a just debt from an insolvent debtor, and the rate is levied upon such valuation.

The following table presents the assessment statistics of the province by townships, towns and villages, and cities, for the year 1887, being the last year for which the returns have been compiled :—

Classes of Municipalities.	Value of Personal Property.	Taxes Imposed.	Rate of Taxation.
	Dollars.	Dollars.	Mills.onDols.
Townships	428,614,636	4,157,562	9·7
Towns and Villages ...	91,014,414	1,729,274	19·0
Cities	132,839,465	2,444,246	18·4
Totals ...	652,468,515	8,331,082	12·77

(Signed)   A. BLUE,

Deputy Minister of Agriculture.

MANITOBA.

MEMORANDUM AS TO SOURCE OF REVENUE AND SYSTEM OF TAXATION IN MANITOBA.

(A.) The revenue of the province is derived from the following sources, viz. :—

Subsidy from the Federal Government, fines, marriage licences, liquor licences, etc, etc.

There is no direct national tax levied, all levies on lands or buildings being expended for local purposes only.

(B.) All lands in rural municipalities improved for farming or gardening purposes are assessed at the same value as such lands would be assessed if unimproved, but lands improved for other purposes than the above, the value of the improvements are added to the assessments of the lands.

(C.) All produce from lands occupied as farms or gardens are exempt from taxation ; live stock and farming implements, the property of a farmer, are also exempt to the value of 1,000 dollars.

(D.) In villages, towns, and cities the assessment of lands is ma'e according to the actual value.

AUSTRALIA.

NEW SOUTH WALES.

Neither land nor buildings are taxed for national revenue in New South Wales. For local purposes the Municipalities Act (31 Vict. No. 12), provides that municipalities may levy rates of not more than one shilling in the £ for ordinary purposes, and not more than one shilling in the £ for special purposes. The assessment is made in the following manner, viz. :—

Upon nine-tenths of the fair average rental of all buildings and cultivated lands, or lands which are, or have been, let for pastoral, mining, or other purposes, whether such land or buildings be actually in occupation or not, and upon five per cent. of the capital value of the fee-simple of all unimproved land.

Land is not taxed separately from buildings unless it be not improved (that is in effect un-occupied); it is therefore impossible to distinguish, as this return requires, taxation on land from taxation on buildings.

The attached statement shows the valuation of lands and buildings for purposes of local taxation and the amount of taxation for the year ended February, 1890.

VALUATION OF LAND AND BUILDINGS SUBJECT TO MUNICIPAL TAXATION IN NEW SOUTH WALES.

	Capital.	Annual.
	£	£
Value of unimproved land	15,665,508	783,275
Value of improved lands, buildings, &c.	111,546,538	7,009,075
Total	127,212,046	7,792,350

TAXATION.

	£
For general local purposes	383,426
For lighting	47,283
For water and other rates	24,069
Total	454,778

The area of the colony within municipal boundaries comprises only 1,384,926 acres, the remainder of the colony being 197,463,074 acres. The value of lands outside municipal limits is approximately £120,000,000, and the value of improvements thereon, £61,000,000 ; total, £181,000,000. No tax is levied on either land or improvements.

VICTORIA.

TAXATION ON LAND AND BUILDINGS.

	Percentage of Annual Value.
Taxation by General Government on land only ...	7·0
Taxation by Local Government on land and buildings	5·7
Taxation by Local and General Government on land and buildings	— 5·8
	£
Amount raised annually for national purposes on land only	124,308
Amount raised annually for local purposes on land and buildings	732,324
Total amount raised annually on land and buildings ...	£856,632
	Per Cent.
Proportion which the amount raised annually by the General Government by means of taxation on land bears to the total taxation by the General Government	3·3
Proportion which the amount raised annually by the Local Government by means of taxation on land and buildings bears to the total taxation by the Local Government	80·0
Proportion which the amount raised annually by the General and Local Government by means of taxation on land and buildings bears to the total taxation by the General and Local Government	— · 18·4

NOTE.—The General Government taxes land held in large blocks, viz.:—7,080,968 acres in all, but does not tax blocks under 640 acres in extent, or any blocks not worth £2,500, or any buildings. The tax is upon the capital value, and no return is made of the annual value, but for the purpose of this table the latter has been assumed to be five shillings per acre. The Local Government, which taxes both land and buildings, does not separate the two, and therefore it is not possible to give a statement for the taxation on the one apart from that on the other.

(Signed)   H. H. HAYTER,
Government Statist.

Office of the Government Statist, Melbourne,
26th June, 1890.

SOUTH AUSTRALIA.

RETURN SHOWING, FOR YEAR 1889, IN SOUTH AUSTRALIA.

1. *Taxation on land*—

(*a*) The percentage on the annual value which the rate levied amounts to = 4½th per cent.

	£
(*b*) The total amount raised for local purposes*	122,369
For national purposes†	67,877
Total	190,246

(*c*) The percentage which the amount raised by taxation of land bears to the total taxation = 9½ per cent. on land only (for national purposes).

2. *Taxation of buildings*—

(*a*) The percentage on the annual value which the rate levied amounts to = 4⅞ per cent. on lands and buildings combined (for local purposes only).

	£
(*b*) The total amount raised for local purposes*	122,369
For national purposes	nil.
Total	122,369

(*c*) The percentage which the amount raised by taxation of buildings bears to the total taxation = 7½ per cent. (estimated) for local purposes only.

Memorandum.—The Land Tax Act, 323, of 1884 (herewith) imposes for national purposes ½d. in the £ on the value of the fee-simple, less the value of

* On lands and buildings.
† On unimproved value of land.

U

the improvements thereon. The total assessment is £32,580,000.

Acts 190 of 1880 and 419 of 1887, the Municipal Corporations and District Councils Acts (herewith) regulate the rating, for local purposes, upon an assessment of the annual rent, including both land and buildings. The rate is usually 1s. in the £. The total assessed annual value is £2,520,112.

The value of the buildings, and of the land, cannot be distinguished.

(Signed)   L. H. SHOLL,

Under-Secretary and Government
Statist.

Chief Secretary's Office, Adelaide,
12th September, 1890.

QUEENSLAND.

RETURN SHOWING THE ANNUAL VALUE OF LANDS AND BUILDINGS IN THE COLONY OF QUEENSLAND FOR THE YEAR ENDED 31ST DECEMBER, 1889.

	£
Annual value of rateable property in divisions and municipalities for the year ended 31st December, 1889	3,982,799
Rates levied on the above	240,519
Percentage on the annual value which the rates levied amount to	6·04

The above taxation is for local purposes only, there being no taxation by the State on lands and buildings in Queensland.

The Treasury, Queensland, 30th June, 1890.

ESTIMATED NET ANNUAL VALUE OF RATEABLE PROPERTY (LANDS AND BUILDINGS) IN THE COLONY OF QUEENSLAND FOR THE YEAR ENDED 31ST DECEMBER, 1889.

	Capital Value.	Annual Value.	Rates Levied for Local Purposes.
MUNICIPALITIES AND SHIRES :—	£	£	£
Total Rateable Property	26,836,905	1,778,361	—
General Rates... ...	...	...	88,926
Separate Rates ...	...	...	45,074
Special Rates	...	...	20,182
			154,182
DIVISIONS :—			
Freehold	24,586,073	1,629,216	64,963
Selections and Home-steads	4,037,212	267,532	9,381
Lands Leased for pastoral purposes ...	4,643,291	307,690	11,993
	33,266,576	2,204,438	86,337
Total ...	60,103,481	3,982,799	240,519

MODE OF RATING

Town and suburban land, improved. ...	Two-thirds of the rent, but not less than 5 per cent. on capital value.
Town and suburban land, unimproved. ...	Not less than 8 per cent. nor more than 10 per cent. on capital value.
Country land... ...	Not less than 5 per cent. nor more than 8 per cent. on capital value.
Pastoral leaseholds	The annual value to be taken at rent payable under the lease.
Mines	The annual value to be estimated on surface value and buildings only.

The Treasury, Queensland, 30th June, 1890.

U 2

SOUTH AFRICA—CAPE TOWN.

THERE is no land tax in the form of a general rate for national purposes in this colony, and there is no complete and reliable valuation of land, either for national or for local purposes.

There is a valuation for Divisional Council purposes, but it is a partial one, not taking in land in native locations, the Division of Herschel, and the native territories ; and there is a valuation for municipal purposes of land and tenements in towns and villages.

The only source of information as to these partial valuations and the taxations thereon, is the Statistical Register, and the figures given for 1889 are as follows, viz. :

	£
Council purposes - -	35,436,046
Municipal purposes -	13,529,569

Total amount of assessment (not stated).

Total amount of taxation received :

	£
Divisional Councils - -	88,330
Municipalities - - -	166,514

There is no taxation at present either for general or for local purposes of buildings. Up to 1888 there was a direct taxation on buildings for national purposes, but the Act was repealed last year.

Taxation for local purposes is levied not on buildings alone, but on buildings and land, valued as one.

The last valuation of buildings in 1888, for national purposes, gave :

				£
Valuation	-	-	-	16,152,590
Taxation	-	-	-	101,106

Percentage of taxation on total taxation of colony :—

£1,595,457	·	-	-	6·34

The figures given, however, will not admit of comparison with returns from other countries and colonies.

NATAL.

RETURN SHOWING THE TAXATION OF LAND AND BUILDINGS IN THE COLONY OF NATAL.

Public Body levying the Tax.	Percentage on the Freehold Value of Land and Buildings which the Rate levied amounts to.	Total Sums raised during the last Financial Year.		Remarks.
		For Local Purposes.	For National Purposes.	
		£ s. d.	£ s. d.	
Corporation of Pietermaritzburg	1 9/32 per cent.	*16,689 13 0	Nil	*Including Water-rate of ½d. in £. General rate 2¼d. in £ on £1,265,023. Water-rate ¾d. in £ on £1,053,406.
Corporation of Durban ...	1¼ per cent.	22,092 14 5	Nil	Excluding Water-rate.
Newcastle Local Board ...	1 15/16 per cent.	411 5 10	Nil	ditto.
Ladysmith Local Board ...	1¼ per cent.	1,288 17 6	Nil	ditto.
Verulam Local Board ...	19/32 per cent.	165 0 0	Nil	ditto.

Note.—The Municipalities and Local Boards in Natal levy their rates on the freehold value of properties, the land and buildings being valued together; statistics of the taxation of land separate from the taxation of buildings cannot therefore be furnished.

| Colonial Government ... | 14s. per native hut, irrespective of value. | Nil | 76,004 12 0 | With the exception of native hut tax, no tax is imposed by the Government on land or buildings. |

Colonial Secretary's Office, Natal,   (Signed)   F. S. HADEN,
Pietermaritzburg, 15th October, 1890.   Colonial Secretary.

*ities of th*h*, and*
s Consuls

Value Liable ...cipal ...tion.	Num hous t... Mu pa...	Observations.
0,864	20	
1,840	58	...clude that of Water Trustees.
6,296	100	...sets, includes those from Gas and Water Works, &c.
8,244	19	
5,955	47	...sets, includes those from Gas, Water, Electricity, &c.
8,980	24	...penditure, includes £25,000 raised for School Board.
9,805	8	
0,724	49	...ssets includes Water rents, those from other sources not
5,439	106	
0,167	548	
4,635	5	...only. Table not including Accounts of Commissioners of
	(Inha... onl...	...rs of London.
4,086	105	
6,000	22	
0,000	45	
5,904	10	
5,360	69	...er sources includes Water Rents and Rates, &c.
8,000	14	
6,918	27	...er sources includes Gas Rents, &c.
-	50	...xclusive of Water and Gas Debts.
4,916	142	
4,625	1,	
6,068 [1]	84	...erty means total Cadastral income, not yearly value of ...ty as in United Kingdom. Exchange 25 francs to £. The ...ts of 1892 were £11,219,928, with the extraordinary receipts, ...al estate, or immovable goods, borrowed, &c., the amount ...18; with the balance of previous year, the amount was ... The ordinary expenses were £10,767,485; with the extra- ...nses, £11,232,870; with other expenses, £13,363,375. ...d is maintained for great works and expenses on same of
5,720 [2]	31	...ne, not yearly value. Exchange 25 francs to £.

value on roll, not yearly value of property. Exchange, 25 Lire

ange. Numbers of houses and families those included in Census

change.

families only approximate. House and Land taxes—Lire 65.76
l rate added to every 100 Lire of Government Tax. Government
estimated in 1892 [1] for lands, total Lire 935,127 in reason of 10.11
every 537 Lire estimated value ; [2] for houses total Lire 5,866,189
. of 16·25 for every 100 Lire of taxable income, viz., ¾ of assessed
Income Tax (Ricchezza Mobile) o, $\frac{1}{10}$ of Government Tax on
nal incomes only cat. B. and C. yield 190,000 Lire in favour of

20 marks to £. Yearly value column shows amount on roll for
.come and class tax, &c.

all houses are locked at 10 p.m., and by universal custom 10
are paid by everyone seeking admission after that hour. Exchange,
; to £.

10 florins to £.

25 francs to £.

12 florins to £.

ange.

five suburbs have been annexed to Zürich, increasing the popu-
· 105,000.

other cities the assessment is made on the capital and not yearly
See text.

18 Kroner to £.

1 rouble to 3s. 2d.

ange.

alue, not yearly value, taxed.

ing note.

ote.

ote.

ote, Total receipts principally from taxation.

J. J. O'MEARA.

PRINTED BY
CASSELL & COMPANY, LIMITED, LA BELLE SAUVAGE,
LONDON, E.C.

Illustrated, Fine-Art, and other Volumes.

Abbeys and Churches of England and Wales, The: Descriptive, Historical, Pictorial. Series II. 21s.

A Blot of Ink. Translated by Q and PAUL FRANCKE. 5s.

Adventure, The World of. Fully Illustrated. In Three Vols. 9s. each.

Africa and its Explorers, The Story of. By DR. ROBERT BROWN, F.L.S. Illustrated. Vols. I. and II., 7s. 6d. each.

Agrarian Tenures. By the Rt. Hon. G. SHAW-LEFEVRE, M.P. 10s. 6d.

Anthea. By CÉCILE CASSAVETTI (a Russian). A Story of the Greek War of Independence. *Cheap Edition.* 5s.

Arabian Nights Entertainments, Cassell's Pictorial. 10s. 6d.

Architectural Drawing. By R. PHENÉ SPIERS. Illustrated. 10s. 6d.

Art, The Magazine of. Yearly Vol. With 12 Photogravures, Etchings, &c., and about 400 Illustrations. 16s.

Artistic Anatomy. By Prof. M. DUVAL. *Cheap Edition.* 3s. 6d.

Astronomy, The Dawn of. A Study of the Astronomy and Temple Worship of the Ancient Egyptians. By J. NORMAN LOCKYER, F.R.S., F.R.A.S., &c. Illustrated. 21s.

Atlas, The Universal. A New and Complete General Atlas of the World, with 117 Pages of Maps, in Colours, and a Complete Index to about 125,000 Names. Cloth, 30s. net; or half-morocco, 35s. net.

Awkward Squads, The; and Other Ulster Stories. By SHAN F. BULLOCK. 5s.

Bashkirtseff, Marie, The Journal of. *Cheap Edition.* 7s. 6d.

Bashkirtseff, Marie, The Letters of. 7s. 6d.

Beetles, Butterflies, Moths, and Other Insects. By A. W. KAPPEL, F.E.S., and W. EGMONT KIRBY. With 12 Coloured Plates. 3s. 6d.

"Belle Sauvage" Library, The. Cloth, 2s. each.

Shirley.	Adventures of Mr.	Jack Hinton.
Coningsby.	Ledbury.	Poe's Works.
Mary Barton.	Ivanhoe.	Old Mortality.
The Antiquary.	Oliver Twist.	The Hour and the Man.
Nicholas Nickleby (Two Vols.).	Selections from Hood's Works.	Handy Andy. Scarlet Letter.
Jane Eyre.	Longfellow's Prose	Pickwick (Two Vols.).
Wuthering Heights.	Works.	Last of the Mohicans.
Dombey and Son (Two Vols.).	Sense and Sensibility. Lytton's Plays.	Pride and Prejudice. Yellowplush Papers.
The Prairie.	Tales, Poems, and	Tales of the Borders.
Night and Morning.	Sketches. Bret Harte.	Last Days of Palmyra.
Kenilworth.	Martin Chuzzlewit	Washington Irving's
Ingoldsby Legends.	(Two Vols.).	Sketch-Book.
Tower of London.	The Prince of the	The Talisman.
The Pioneers.	House of David.	Rienzi.
Charles O'Malley.	Sheridan's Plays.	Old Curiosity Shop.
Barnaby Rudge.	Uncle Tom's Cabin.	Heart of Midlothian.
Cakes and Ale.	Deerslayer.	Last Days of Pompeii.
The King's Own.	Rome and the Early	American Humour.
People I have Met.	Christians.	Sketches by Boz.
The Pathfinder.	The Trials of Margaret Lyndsay.	Macaulay's Lays and Essays.
Evelina.	Harry Lorrequer.	
Scott's Poems.	Eugene Aram.	
Last of the Barons.		

Biographical Dictionary, Cassell's New. 7s. 6d.

Birds' Nests, Eggs, and Egg-Collecting. By R. KEARTON. Illustrated with 16 Coloured Plates. 5s.

British Ballads. With Several Hundred Original Illustrations. Half-morocco, *price on application.*

British Battles on Land and Sea. By JAMES GRANT. With about 600 Illustrations. Three Vols., 4to, £1 7s.; *Library Edition,* £1 10s.

British Battles, Recent. Illustrated. 4to, 9s.; *Library Edition*, 10s.

Butterflies and Moths, European. With 61 Coloured Plates. 35s.

Canaries and Cage-Birds, The Illustrated Book of. With 56 Facsimile Coloured Plates, 35s. Half-morocco, £2 5s.

Capture of the "Estrella," The. A Tale of the Slave Trade. By COMMANDER CLAUDE HARDING, R.N. 5s.

Cassell's Family Magazine. Yearly Vol. Illustrated. 9s.

Cathedrals, Abbeys, and Churches of England and Wales. Descriptive, Historical, Pictorial. *Popular Edition.* Two Vols. 25s.

Catriona. A Sequel to "Kidnapped." By ROBERT LOUIS STEVENSON. 6s.

Celebrities of the Century. *Cheap Edition.* 10s. 6d.

Chips by an Old Chum; or, Australia in the Fifties. 1s.

Chums. The Illustrated Paper for Boys. First Yearly Volume. 7s. 6d.

Cities of the World. Four Vols. Illustrated. 7s. 6d. each.

Civil Service, Guide to Employment in the. 3s. 6d.

Climate and Health Resorts. By Dr. BURNEY YEO. 7s. 6d.

Clinical Manuals for Practitioners and Students of Medicine. A List of Volumes forwarded post free on application to the Publishers.

Colonist's Medical Handbook, The. By E. A. BARTON, M.R.C.S. 2s. 6d.

Colour. By Prof. A. H. CHURCH. With Coloured Plates. 3s. 6d.

Columbus, The Career of. By CHARLES ELTON, Q.C. 10s. 6d.

Combe, George, The Select Works of. Issued by Authority of the Combe Trustees. Popular Edition, 1s. each, net.

The Constitution of Man.	Science and Religion.
Moral Philosophy.	Discussions on Education.
American Notes.	

Cookery, A Year's. By PHYLLIS BROWNE. 3s. 6d.

Cookery, Cassell's Shilling. 384 pages, limp cloth, 1s.

Cookery, Vegetarian. By A. G. PAYNE. 1s. 6d.

Cooking by Gas, The Art of. By MARIE J. SUGG. Illustrated. 3s. 6d.

Cottage Gardening, Poultry, Bees, Allotments, Food, House, Window and Town Gardens. Edited by W. ROBINSON, F.L.S., Author of "The English Flower Garden." Fully Illustrated. Halfyearly Volumes, I. and II. Cloth, 2s. 6d. each.

Countries of the World, The. By ROBERT BROWN, M.A., Ph.D., &c. Complete in Six Vols., with about 750 Illustrations. 4to, 7s. 6d. each.

Cyclopædia, Cassell's Concise. Brought down to the latest date. With about 600 Illustrations. *Cheap Edition.* 7s. 6d.

Cyclopædia, Cassell's Miniature. Containing 30,000 subjects. Cloth, 2s. 6d.; half-roxburgh, 4s.

Delectable Duchy, The. Some Tales of East Cornwall. By Q. 6s.

Dickens, Character Sketches from. FIRST, SECOND, and THIRD SERIES. With Six Original Drawings in each by F. BARNARD. 21s. each.

Dick Whittington, A Modern. By JAMES PAYN. In One Vol., 6s.

Dog, Illustrated Book of the. By VERO SHAW, B.A. With 28 Coloured Plates. Cloth bevelled, 35s.; half-morocco, 45s.

Domestic Dictionary, The. Illustrated. Cloth, 7s. 6d.

Doré Bible, The. With 200 Full-page Illustrations by DORÉ. 15s.

Doré Don Quixote, The. With about 400 Illustrations by GUSTAVE DORÉ. *Cheap Edition.* Bevelled boards, gilt edges, 10s. 6d.

Doré Gallery, The. With 250 Illustrations by DORÉ. 4to, 42s.

Doré's Dante's Inferno. Illustrated by GUSTAVE DORÉ. With Preface by A. J. BUTLER. Cloth gilt or buckram. 7s. 6d.

Doré's Dante's Purgatory and Paradise. Illustrated by GUSTAVE DORÉ. *Cheap Edition.* 7s. 6d.

Doré's Milton's Paradise Lost. Illustrated by DORÉ. 4to, 21s.

Dorset, Old. Chapters in the History of the County. By H. J. MOULE, M.A. 10s. 6d.

Dr. Dumány's Wife. A Novel. By MAURUS JÓKAI. 6s.

Dulce Domum. Rhymes and Songs for Children. Edited by JOHN FARMER, Editor of "Gaudeamus," &c. Old Notation and Words, 5s. N.B.—The words of the Songs in "Dulce Domum" (with the Airs both in Tonic Sol-fa and Old Notation) can be had in Two Parts, 6d. each.

Earth, Our, and its Story. By Dr. ROBERT BROWN, F.L.S. With Coloured Plates and numerous Wood Engravings. Three Vols. 9s. each.

Edinburgh, Old and New. With 600 Illustrations. Three Vols. 9s. each.

Egypt: Descriptive, Historical, and Picturesque. By Prof. G. EBERS. With 800 Original Engravings. *Popular Edition.* In Two Vols. 42s.

Electricity in the Service of Man. Illustrated. *New and Revised Edition.* 10s. 6d.

Electricity, Practical. By Prof. W. E. AYRTON. 7s. 6d.

Encyclopædic Dictionary, The. In Fourteen Divisional Vols., 10s. 6d. each; or Seven Vols., half-morocco, 21s. each; half-russia, 25s.

England, Cassell's Illustrated History of. With 2,000 Illustrations. Ten Vols., 4to, 9s. each. *Revised Edition.* Vols. I. to VI. 9s. each.

English Dictionary, Cassell's. Giving definitions of more than 100,000 Words and Phrases. Cloth, 7s. 6d. *Cheap Edition.* 3s. 6d.

English History, The Dictionary of. *Cheap Edition.* 10s. 6d.

English Literature, Library of. By Prof. HENRY MORLEY. Complete in Five Vols., 7s. 6d. each.

English Literature, Morley's First Sketch of. *Revised Edition.* 7s. 6d.

English Literature, The Story of. By ANNA BUCKLAND. 3s. 6d.

English Writers. By Prof. HENRY MORLEY. Vols. I. to X. 5s. each.

Etiquette of Good Society. *New Edition.* Edited and Revised by LADY COLIN CAMPBELL. 1s.; cloth, 1s. 6d.

Fairway Island. By HORACE HUTCHINSON. With 4 Full-page Plates. *Cheap Edition.* 3s. 6d.

Faith Doctor, The. A Novel. By Dr. EDWARD EGGLESTON. 6s.

Family Physician, The. By Eminent PHYSICIANS and SURGEONS. *New and Revised Edition.* Cloth, 21s.; Roxburgh, 25s.

Father Stafford. A Novel. By ANTHONY HOPE. 6s.

Field Naturalist's Handbook, The. By the Revs. J. G. WOOD and THEODORE WOOD. *Cheap Edition.* 2s. 6d.

Figuier's Popular Scientific Works. With Several Hundred Illustrations in each. Newly Revised and Corrected. 3s. 6d. each.
  THE HUMAN RACE.   MAMMALIA.   OCEAN WORLD.
      THE INSECT WORLD.   REPTILES AND BIRDS.
    WORLD BEFORE THE DELUGE.   THE VEGETABLE WORLD.

Flora's Feast. A Masque of Flowers. Penned and Pictured by WALTER CRANE. With 40 Pages in Colours. 5s.

Football, The Rugby Union Game. Edited by REV. F. MARSHALL. Illustrated. 7s. 6d.

Fraser, John Drummond. By PHILALETHES. A Story of Jesuit Intrigue in the Church of England. 5s.

Garden Flowers, Familiar. By SHIRLEY HIBBERD. With Coloured Plates by F. E. HULME, F.L.S. Complete in Five Series. 12s. 6d. each.

Gardening, Cassell's Popular. Illustrated. Four Vols. 5s. each.

George Saxon, The Reputation of. By MORLEY ROBERTS. 5s.

Gleanings from Popular Authors. Two Vols. With Original Illustrations. 4to, 9s. each. Two Vols. in One, 15s.

Gulliver's Travels. With 88 Engravings by MORTEN. *Cheap Edition.* Cloth, 3s. 6d.; cloth gilt, 5s.

Gun and its Development, The. By W. W. GREENER. With 500 Illustrations. 10s. 6d.

Heavens, The Story of the. By Sir ROBERT STAWELL BALL, LL.D.,
F.R.S., F.R.A.S. With Coloured Plates. *Popular Edition.* 12s. 6d.
Heroes of Britain in Peace and War. With 300 Original Illus-
trations. Two Vols., 3s. 6d. each; or One Vol., 7s. 6d.
Historic Houses of the United Kingdom. Profusely Illustrated. 10s. 6d.
History, A Foot-note to. Eight Years of Trouble in Samoa. By
ROBERT LOUIS STEVENSON. 6s.
Home Life of the Ancient Greeks, The. Translated by ALICE
ZIMMERN. Illustrated. 7s. 6d.
Horse, The Book of the. By SAMUEL SIDNEY. Thoroughly Revised
and brought up to date by JAMES SINCLAIR and W. C. A. BLEW. With
17 Full-page Collotype Plates of Celebrated Horses of the Day, and
numerous other Illustrations. Cloth, 15s.
Houghton, Lord: The Life, Letters, and Friendships of Richard
Monckton Milnes, First Lord Houghton. By T. WEMYSS
REID. In Two Vols., with Two Portraits. 32s.
Household, Cassell's Book of the. Complete in Four Vols. 5s. each.
Four Vols. in Two, half-morocco, 25s.
Hygiene and Public Health. By B. ARTHUR WHITELEGGE, M.D. 7s. 6d.
India, Cassell's History of. By JAMES GRANT. With about 400
Illustrations. Two Vols., 9s. each. One Vol., 15s.
In-door Amusements, Card Games, and Fireside Fun, Cassell's
Book of. *Cheap Edition.* 2s.
Into the Unknown: A Romance of South Africa. By LAWRENCE
FLETCHER. 4s.
Iron Pirate, The. A Plain Tale of Strange Happenings on the Sea. By
MAX PEMBERTON. Illustrated. 5s.
Island Nights' Entertainments. By R. L. STEVENSON. Illustrated. 6s.
Italy from the Fall of Napoleon I. in 1815 to 1890. By J. W. PROBYN.
New and Cheaper Edition. 3s. 6d.
Joy and Health. By MARTELLIUS. 3s. 6d. *Édition de Luxe,* 7s. 6d.
Kennel Guide, The Practical. By Dr. GORDON STABLES. 1s.
King's Hussar, A. By HERBERT COMPTON. 6s.
"La Bella," and Others. Being Certain Stories Recollected by Egerton
Castle, Author of "Consequences." 6s.
Ladies' Physician, The. By a London Physician. 6s.
Lady's Dressing-room, The. Translated from the French of BARONESS
STAFFE by LADY COLIN CAMPBELL. 3s. 6d.
Leona. By Mrs. MOLESWORTH. 6s.
Letters, the Highway of, and its Echoes of Famous Footsteps.
By THOMAS ARCHER. Illustrated. 10s. 6d.
Letts's Diaries and other Time-saving Publications published
exclusively by CASSELL & COMPANY. (*A list free on application.*)
'Lisbeth. By LESLIE KEITH. Three Volumes. 31s. 6d.
List, ye Landsmen! A Romance of Incident. By W. CLARK RUSSELL.
Cheap Edition, in One Vol., 6s.
Little Minister, The. By J. M. BARRIE. *Illustrated Edition.* 6s.
Little Squire, The. A Story of Three. By Mrs. HENRY DE LA PASTURE.
3s. 6d.
Locomotive Engine, The Biography of a. By HENRY FRITH. 5s.
Loftus, Lord Augustus, The Diplomatic Reminiscences of. First
and Second Series. Two Vols., each with Portrait, 32s. each Series.
London, Greater. By EDWARD WALFORD. Two Vols. With about
400 Illustrations. 9s. each.
London, Old and New. Six Vols., each containing about 200
Illustrations and Maps. Cloth, 9s. each.
London Street Arabs. By Mrs. H. M. STANLEY. Illustrated, 5s.
Medicine Lady, The. By L. T. MEADE. In One Vol., 6s.
Medicine, Manuals for Students of. (*A List forwarded post free.*)

Modern Europe, A History of. By C. A. FYFFE, M.A. Complete in Three Vols., with full-page Illustrations, 7s. 6d. each.

Mount Desolation. An Australian Romance. By W. CARLTON DAWE. 5s.

Music, Illustrated History of. By EMIL NAUMANN. Edited by the Rev. Sir F. A. GORE OUSELEY, Bart. Illustrated. Two Vols. 31s. 6d.

Musical and Dramatic Copyright, The Law of. By EDWARD CUTLER, THOMAS EUSTACE SMITH, and FREDERIC E. WEATHERLY, Barristers-at-Law. 3s. 6d.

Napier, Life and Letters of the Rt. Hon. Sir Joseph, Bart., LL.D., &c. By A. C. EWALD, F.S.A. *New and Revised Edition.* 7s. 6d.

National Library, Cassell's. In Volumes. Paper covers, 3d.; cloth, 6d. (*A Complete List of the Volumes post free on application.*)

Natural History, Cassell's Concise. By E. PERCEVAL WRIGHT, M.A., M.D., F.L.S. With several Hundred Illustrations. 7s. 6d.

Natural History, Cassell's New. Edited by Prof. P. MARTIN DUNCAN, M.B., F.R.S., F.G.S. Complete in Six Vols. With about 2,000 Illustrations. Cloth, 9s. each.

Nature's Wonder Workers. By KATE R. LOVELL. Illustrated. 3s. 6d.

New England Boyhood, A. By EDWARD E. HALE. 3s. 6d.

Nursing for the Home and for the Hospital, A Handbook of. By CATHERINE J. WOOD. *Cheap Edition.* 1s. 6d.; cloth, 2s.

Nursing of Sick Children, A Handbook for the. By CATHERINE J. WOOD. 2s. 6d.

O'Driscoll's Weird, and other Stories. By A. WERNER. 5s.

Odyssey, The Modern; or, Ulysses up to Date. Cloth gilt, 10s. 6d.

Ohio, The New. A Story of East and West. By EDWARD E. HALE. 6s.

Oil Painting, A Manual of. By the Hon. JOHN COLLIER. 2s. 6d.

Our Own Country. Six Vols. With 1,200 Illustrations. 7s. 6d. each.

Out of the Jaws of Death. By FRANK BARRETT. In One Vol., 6s.

Painting, The English School of. *Cheap Edition.* 3s. 6d.

Painting, Practical Guides to. With Coloured Plates:—

MARINE PAINTING. 5s.	TREE PAINTING. 5s.
ANIMAL PAINTING. 5s.	WATER-COLOUR PAINTING. 5s.
CHINA PAINTING. 5s.	NEUTRAL TINT. 5s.
FIGURE PAINTING. 7s. 6d.	SEPIA, in Two Vols., 3s. each; or in One Vol., 5s.
ELEMENTARY FLOWER PAINTING. 3s.	FLOWERS, AND HOW TO PAINT THEM. 5s.

Paris, Old and New. A Narrative of its History, its People, and its Places. By H. SUTHERLAND EDWARDS. Profusely Illustrated. Vol. I., 9s.; or gilt edges, 10s. 6d.

Peoples of the World, The. In Six Vols. By Dr. ROBERT BROWN. Illustrated. 7s. 6d. each.

Perfect Gentleman, The. By the Rev. A. SMYTHE-PALMER, D.D. 3s. 6d.

Photography for Amateurs. By T. C. HEPWORTH. *Enlarged and Revised Edition.* Illustrated. 1s.; or cloth, 1s. 6d.

Phrase and Fable, Dictionary of. By the Rev. Dr. BREWER. *Cheap Edition, Enlarged,* cloth, 3s. 6d.; or with leather back, 4s. 6d.

Picturesque America. Complete in Four Vols., with 48 Exquisite Steel Plates and about 800 Original Wood Engravings. £2 2s. each.

Picturesque Canada. With 600 Original Illustrations. Two Vols. £6 6s. the Set.

Picturesque Europe. Complete in Five Vols. Each containing 13 Exquisite Steel Plates, from Original Drawings, and nearly 200 Original Illustrations. Cloth, £21; half-morocco, £31 10s.; morocco gilt, £52 10s. POPULAR EDITION. In Five Vols., 18s. each.

Picturesque Mediterranean, The. With Magnificent Original Illustrations by the leading Artists of the Day. Complete in Two Vols. £2 2s. each.

Pigeon Keeper, The Practical. By LEWIS WRIGHT. Illustrated. 3s. 6d.

Pigeons, The Book of. By ROBERT FULTON. Edited and Arranged by L. WRIGHT. With 50 Coloured Plates, 31s. 6d.; half-morocco, £2 2s.

Pity and of Death, The Book of. By PIERRE LOTI. Translated by T. P. O'CONNOR, M.P. 5s.
Planet, The Story of Our. By T. G. BONNEY, D.Sc., LL.D., F.R.S., F.S.A., F.G.S. With Six Coloured Plates and Maps and about 100 Illustrations. 31s. 6d.
Playthings and Parodies. Short Stories by BARRY PAIN. 5s.
Poems, Aubrey de Vere's. A Selection. Edited by J. DENNIS. 3s. 6d.
Poetry, The Nature and Elements of. By E. C. STEDMAN. 6s.
Poets, Cassell's Miniature Library of the. Price 1s. each Vol.
Portrait Gallery, The Cabinet. First, Second, Third, and Fourth Series, each containing 36 Cabinet Photographs of Eminent Men and Women. With Biographical Sketches. 15s. each.
Poultry Keeper, The Practical. By L. WRIGHT. Illustrated. 3s. 6d.
Poultry, The Book of. By LEWIS WRIGHT. *Popular Edition.* 10s. 6d.
Poultry, The Illustrated Book of. By LEWIS WRIGHT. With Fifty Coloured Plates. *New and Revised Edition.* Cloth, 31s. 6d.
Prison Princess, A. A Romance of Millbank Penitentiary. By Major ARTHUR GRIFFITHS. 6s.
Q's Works, Uniform Edition of. 5s. each.

Dead Man's Rock.	The Astonishing History of Troy Town.
The Splendid Spur.	"I Saw Three Ships," and other Winter's Tales
The Blue Pavilions.	Noughts and Crosses.

Queen Summer ; or, The Tourney of the Lily and the Rose. With Forty Pages of Designs in Colours by WALTER CRANE. 6s.
Queen Victoria, The Life and Times of. By ROBERT WILSON. Complete in Two Vols. With numerous Illustrations. 9s. each.
Quickening of Caliban, The. A Modern Story of Evolution. By J. COMPTON RICKETT. 5s.
Rabbit-Keeper, The Practical. By CUNICULUS. Illustrated. 3s. 6d.
Raffles Haw, The Doings of. By A. CONAN DOYLE. *New Edition.* 5s.
Railways, Our. Their Development, Enterprise, Incident, and Romance. By JOHN PENDLETON. Illustrated. 2 Vols., demy 8vo, 24s.
Railway Guides, Official Illustrated. With Illustrations, Maps, &c. Price 1s. each ; or in cloth, 2s. each.

GREAT EASTERN RAILWAY.	GREAT WESTERN RAILWAY.
GREAT NORTHERN RAILWAY.	LONDON AND SOUTH-WESTERN
LONDON, BRIGHTON AND SOUTH COAST RAILWAY.	RAILWAY.
LONDON AND NORTH-WESTERN RAILWAY.	MIDLAND RAILWAY.
	SOUTH-EASTERN RAILWAY.

Rovings of a Restless Boy, The. By KATHARINE B. FOOT. Illustrated. 5s.
Railway Library, Cassell's. Crown 8vo, boards, 2s. each.

METZEROTT, SHOEMAKER. By KATHARINE P. WOODS.	JACK GORDON, KNIGHT ERRANT, GOTHAM, 1883. By BARCLAY NORTH.
DAVID TODD. By DAVID MACLURE	THE DIAMOND BUTTON. By BARCLAY NORTH.
THE ADMIRABLE LADY BIDDY FANE. By FRANK BARRETT.	ANOTHER'S CRIME. By JULIAN HAWTHORNE.
COMMODORE JUNK. By G. MANVILLE FENN.	THE YOKE OF THE THORAH. By SIDNEY LUSKA.
ST. CUTHBERT'S TOWER. By FLORENCE WARDEN.	WHO IS JOHN NOMAN? By CHARLES HENRY BECKETT.
THE MAN WITH A THUMB. By BARCLAY NORTH.	THE TRAGEDY OF BRINKWATER. By MARTHA L. MOODEY.
BY RIGHT NOT LAW. By R. SHERARD.	AN AMERICAN PENMAN. By JULIAN HAWTHORNE.
WITHIN SOUND OF THE WEIR. By THOMAS ST. E. HAKE.	SECTION 558; or, THE FATAL LETTER. By JULIAN HAWTHORNE.
UNDER A STRANGE MASK. By FRANK BARRETT.	THE BROWN STONE BOY. By W. H. BISHOP.
THE COOMBSBERROW MYSTERY. By JAMES COLWALL.	A TRAGIC MYSTERY. By JULIAN HAWTHORNE.
A QUEER RACE. By W. WESTALL.	THE GREAT BANK ROBBERY. By JULIAN HAWTHORNE.
CAPTAIN TRAFALGAR. By WESTALL and LAURIE.	
THE PHANTOM CITY. By W. WESTALL.	

Rivers of Great Britain: Descriptive, Historical, Pictorial.
THE ROYAL RIVER: The Thames, from Source to Sea. *Popular Edition*, 16s.
RIVERS OF THE EAST COAST. With highly finished Engravings. *Popular Edition*, 16s.

Robinson Crusoe, Cassell's New Fine-Art Edition of. With upwards of 100 Original Illustrations. 7s. 6d.

Romance, The World of. Illustrated. Cloth, 9s.

Russo-Turkish War, Cassell's History of. With about 500 Illustrations. Two Vols. 9s. each.

Salisbury Parliament, A Diary of the. By H. W. LUCY. Illustrated by HARRY FURNISS. 21s.

Saturday Journal, Cassell's. Yearly Volume, cloth, 7s. 6d.

Scarabæus. The Story of an African Beetle. By the MARQUISE CLARA LANZA and JAMES CLARENCE HARVEY. *Cheap Edition.* 3s. 6d.

Science for All. Edited by Dr. ROBERT BROWN. *Revised Edition.* Illustrated. Five Vols. 9s. each.

Shadow of a Song, The. A Novel. By CECIL HARLEY. 5s.

Shaftesbury, The Seventh Earl of, K.G., The Life and Work of. By EDWIN HODDER. *Cheap Edition.* 3s. 6d.

Shakespeare, The Plays of. Edited by Professor HENRY MORLEY. Complete in Thirteen Vols., cloth, 21s. ; half-morocco, cloth sides, 42s.

Shakespeare, Cassell's Quarto Edition. Containing about 600 Illustrations by H. C. SELOUS. Complete in Three Vols., cloth gilt, £3 3s.

Shakespeare, Miniature. Illustrated. In Twelve Vols., in box, 12s.; or in Red Paste Grain (box to match), with spring catch, 21s.

Shakspere, The International. *Édition de Luxe.*
"King Henry VIII." Illustrated by SIR JAMES LINTON, P.R.I. (*Price on application.*)
"Othello." Illustrated by FRANK DICKSEE, R.A. £3 10s.
"King Henry IV." Illustrated by EDUARD GRÜTZNER. £3 10s.
"As You Like It." Illustrated by ÉMILE BAVARD. £3 10s.
"Romeo and Juliet." Illustrated by F. DICKSEE, R.A. Is now out of print, and scarce.

Shakspere, The Leopold. With 400 Illustrations. *Cheap Edition.* 3s. 6d. Cloth gilt, gilt edges, 5s.; Roxburgh, 7s. 6d.

Shakspere, The Royal. With Steel Plates and Wood Engravings. Three Vols. 15s. each.

Sketches, The Art of Making and Using. From the French of G. FRAIPONT. By CLARA BELL. With 50 Illustrations. 2s. 6d.

Smuggling Days and Smuggling Ways. By Commander the Hon. HENRY N. SHORE, R.N. With numerous Illustrations. 7s. 6d.

Snare of the Fowler, The. By Mrs. ALEXANDER. In One Vol., 6s.

Social Welfare, Subjects of. By Rt. Hon. LORD PLAYFAIR, K.C.B. 7s. 6d.

Social England. A Record of the Progress of the people in Religion, Laws, Learning, Arts, Science, Literature, and Manners, from the Earliest Times to the Present Day. By various writers. Edited by H. D. TRAILL, D.C.L. Vol. I.—From the Earliest Times to the Accession of Edward the First. 15s.

Sports and Pastimes, Cassell's Complete Book of. *Cheap Edition.* With more than 900 Illustrations. Medium 8vo, 992 pages, cloth, 3s. 6d.

Squire, The. By Mrs. PARR. In One Vol., 6s.

Star-Land. By Sir R. S. BALL, LL.D., &c. Illustrated. 6s.

Storehouse of General Information, Cassell's. With Wood Engravings, Maps, and Coloured Plates. In Vols., 5s. each.

Story of Francis Cludde, The. By STANLEY J. WEYMAN. 6s.

Story Poems. For Young and Old. Edited by E. DAVENPORT. 3s. 6d.

Successful Life, The. By AN ELDER BROTHER. 3s. 6d.

Sun. The. By Sir ROBERT STAWELL BALL, LL.D., F.R.S., F.R.A.S. Illustrated with Eight Coloured Plates. 21s.

Sunshine Series, Cassell's. Monthly Volumes. 1s. each.

The Temptation of Dulce Carruthers. By C. E. C. WEIGALL.
Lady Lorriner's Scheme and The Story of a Glamour. By EDITH E. CUTHELL.
Womanlike. By FLORENCE M. KING.

On Stronger Wings. By EDITH LISTER.
You'll Love Me Yet. By FRANCES HASWELL; and That Little Woman. By IDA LEMON.

Sybil Knox: a Story of To-day. By EDWARD E. HALE. 6s.

Thackeray, Character Sketches from. Six New and Original Drawings by FREDERICK BARNARD, reproduced in Photogravure. 21s.

Thackeray in America, With. By EYRE CROWE, A.R.A. Illustrated. 10s. 6d.

The "Short Story" Library.

Otto the Knight, &c. By OCTAVE THANET. 5s.
Fourteen to One, &c. By ELIZABETH STUART PHELPS. 5s.

Eleven Possible Cases. By Various Authors. 6s.
Felicia. By Miss FANNY MURFREE. 5s.
The Poet's Audience, and Delilah. By CLARA SAVILE CLARKE. 5s.

The "Treasure Island" Series. *Cheap Illustrated Editions.* Cloth, 3s. 6d. each.

"Kidnapped." By R.L. STEVENSON.
Treasure Island. By ROBERT LOUIS STEVENSON.
The Master of Ballantrae. By ROBERT LOUIS STEVENSON.

The Black Arrow. By ROBERT LOUIS STEVENSON.
King Solomon's Mines. By H. RIDER HAGGARD.

Tiny Luttrell. By E. W. HORNUNG. Cloth gilt, Two Vols. 21s.

Trees, Familiar. By G. S. BOULGER, F.L.S. Two Series. With 40 full-page Coloured Plates by W. H. J. BOOT. 12s. 6d. each.

"Unicode": the Universal Telegraphic Phrase Book. *Desk or Pocket Edition.* 2s. 6d.

United States, Cassell's History of the. By EDMUND OLLIER. With 600 Illustrations. Three Vols. 9s. each.

Universal History, Cassell's Illustrated. Four Vols. 9s. each.

Wild Birds, Familiar. By W. SWAYSLAND. Four Series. With 40 Coloured Plates in each. 12s. 6d. each.

Wild Flowers, Familiar. By F. E. HULME, F.L.S., F.S.A. Five Series. With 40 Coloured Plates in each. 12s. 6d. each.

Won at the Last Hole. A Golfing Romance. By M. A. STOBART. Illustrated. 1s. 6d.

Wood, Rev. J. G., Life of the. By the Rev. THEODORE WOOD. Extra crown 8vo, cloth. *Cheap Edition.* 5s.

Work. The Illustrated Journal for Mechanics. *New and Enlarged Series.* Vols. V. and VI., 4s. each.

World of Wit and Humour, The. With 400 Illustrations. 7s. 6d.

World of Wonders. Two Vols. With 400 Illustrations. 7s. 6d. each.

Wrecker, The. By R. L. STEVENSON and L. OSBOURNE. Illustrated. 6s.

Yule Tide. Cassell's Christmas Annual. 1s.

ILLUSTRATED MAGAZINES.

The Quiver. ENLARGED SERIES. Monthly, 6d.
Cassell's Family Magazine. Monthly, 7d.
"Little Folks" Magazine. Monthly, 6d.
The Magazine of Art. Monthly, 1s.
"Chums." Illustrated Paper for Boys. Weekly, 1d. ; Monthly, 6d.
Cassell's Saturday Journal. Weekly, 1d. ; Monthly, 6d.
Work. Weekly, 1d. ; Monthly, 6d.

CASSELL'S COMPLETE CATALOGUE, containing particulars of upwards of One Thousand Volumes, will be sent post free on application.

CASSELL & COMPANY, LIMITED, *Ludgate Hill, London.*

Bibles and Religious Works.

Bible Biographies. Illustrated. 2s. 6d. each.
  The Story of Moses and Joshua. By the Rev. J. TELFORD.
  The Story of the Judges. By the Rev. J. WYCLIFFE GEDGE.
  The Story of Samuel and Saul. By the Rev. D. C. TOVEY.
  The Story of David. By the Rev. J. WILD.
  The Story of Joseph. Its Lessons for To-Day. By the Rev. GEORGE BAINTON.

  The Story of Jesus. In Verse. By J. R. MACDUFF, D.D.

Bible, Cassell's Illustrated Family. With 900 Illustrations. Leather, gilt edges, £2 10s.

Bible Educator, The. Edited by the Very Rev. Dean PLUMPTRE, D.D., With Illustrations, Maps, &c. Four Vols., cloth, 6s. each.

Bible Student in the British Museum, The. By the Rev. J. G. KITCHIN, M.A. *New and Revised Edition.* 1s. 4d.

Biblewomen and Nurses. Yearly Volume. Illustrated. 3s.

Bunyan's Pilgrim's Progress. Illustrated throughout. Cloth, 3s. 6d.; cloth gilt, gilt edges, 5s.

Child's Bible, The. With 200 Illustrations. *150th Thousand.* 7s. 6d.

Child's Life of Christ, The. With 200 Illustrations. 7s. 6d.

"Come, ye Children." Illustrated. By Rev. BENJAMIN WAUGH. 5s.

Conquests of the Cross. Illustrated. In 3 Vols. 9s. each.

Doré Bible. With 238 Illustrations by GUSTAVE DORÉ. Small folio, best morocco, gilt edges, £15. *Popular Edition.* With 200 Illustrations. 15s.

Early Days of Christianity, The. By the Ven. Archdeacon FARRAR, D.D., F.R.S. LIBRARY EDITION. Two Vols., 24s.; morocco, £2 2s. POPULAR EDITION. Complete in One Volume, cloth, 6s.; cloth, gilt edges, 7s. 6d.; Persian morocco, 10s. 6d.; tree-calf, 15s.

Family Prayer-Book, The. Edited by Rev. Canon GARBETT, M.A., and Rev. S. MARTIN. Extra crown 4to, cloth, 5s.; morocco, 18s.

Gleanings after Harvest. Studies and Sketches by the Rev. JOHN R. VERNON, M.A. Illustrated. 6s.

"Graven in the Rock." By the Rev. Dr. SAMUEL KINNS, F.R.A.S., Author of "Moses and Geology." Illustrated. 12s. 6d.

"Heart Chords." A Series of Works by Eminent Divines. Bound in cloth, red edges, One Shilling each.

MY BIBLE. By the Right Rev. W. BOYD CARPENTER, Bishop of Ripon.
MY FATHER. By the Right Rev. ASHTON OXENDEN, late Bishop of Montreal.
MY WORK FOR GOD. By the Right Rev. Bishop COTTERILL.
MY OBJECT IN LIFE. By the Ven. Archdeacon FARRAR, D.D.
MY ASPIRATIONS. By the Rev. G. MATHESON, D.D.
MY EMOTIONAL LIFE. By the Rev. Preb. CHADWICK, D.D.
MY BODY. By the Rev. Prof. W. G. BLAIKIE, D.D.
MY GROWTH IN DIVINE LIFE. By the Rev. Preb. REYNOLDS, M.A.
MY SOUL. By the Rev. P. B. POWER, M.A.
MY HEREAFTER. By the Very Rev. Dean BICKERSTETH.
MY WALK WITH GOD. By the Very Rev. Dean MONTGOMERY.
MY AIDS TO THE DIVINE LIFE. By the Very Rev. Dean BOYLE.
MY SOURCES OF STRENGTH. By the Rev. E. E. JENKINS, M.A., Secretary of Wesleyan Missionary Society.

Helps to Belief. A Series of Helpful Manuals on the Religious Difficulties of the Day. Edited by the Rev. TEIGNMOUTH SHORE, M.A., Canon of Worcester. Cloth, 1s. each.

CREATION. By Dr. H. Goodwin, the late Lord Bishop of Carlisle.
THE DIVINITY OF OUR LORD. By the Lord Bishop of Derry.
THE MORALITY OF THE OLD TESTAMENT. By the Rev. Newman Smyth, D.D.
MIRACLES. By the Rev. Brownlow Maitland, M.A.
PRAYER. By the Rev. T. Teignmouth Shore, M.A.
THE ATONEMENT. By William Connor Magee, D.D., Late Archbishop of York.

Holy Land and the Bible, The. By the Rev. C. GEIKIE, D.D., LL.D. (Edin.). Two Vols., 24s. *Illustrated Edition*, One Vol., 21s.

Lectures on Christianity and Socialism. By the Right Rev. ALFRED BARRY, D.D. Cloth, 3s. 6d.

Life of Christ, The. By the Ven. Archdeacon FARRAR, D.D., F.R.S. LIBRARY EDITION. Two Vols. Cloth, 24s.; morocco, 42s. CHEAP ILLUSTRATED EDITION. Cloth, 7s. 6d.; cloth, full gilt, gilt edges, 10s. 6d. POPULAR EDITION, in One Vol., 8vo, cloth, 6s.; cloth, gilt edges, 7s. 6d.; Persian morocco, gilt edges, 10s. 6d.; tree-calf, 15s.

Moses and Geology; or, The Harmony of the Bible with Science. By the Rev. SAMUEL KINNS, Ph.D., F.R.A.S. Illustrated. *New Edition* on Larger and Superior Paper. 8s. 6d.

New Light on the Bible and the Holy Land. By B. T. A. EVETTS, M.A. Illustrated. 21s.

New Testament Commentary for English Readers, The. Edited by the Rt. Rev. C. J. ELLICOTT, D.D., Lord Bishop of Gloucester and Bristol. In Three Volumes. 21s. each. Vol. I.—The Four Gospels. Vol. II.—The Acts, Romans, Corinthians, Galatians. Vol. III.—The remaining Books of the New Testament.

New Testament Commentary. Edited by Bishop ELLICOTT. Handy Volume Edition. St. Matthew, 3s. 6d. St. Mark, 3s. St. Luke, 3s. 6d. St. John, 3s. 6d. The Acts of the Apostles, 3s. 6d. Romans, 2s. 6d. Corinthians I. and II., 3s. Galatians, Ephesians, and Philippians, 3s. Colossians, Thessalonians, and Timothy, 3s. Titus, Philemon, Hebrews, and James, 3s. Peter, Jude, and John, 3s. The Revelation, 3s. An Introduction to the New Testament, 3s. 6d.

Old Testament Commentary for English Readers, The. Edited by the Right Rev. C. J. ELLICOTT, D.D., Lord Bishop of Gloucester and Bristol. Complete in Five Vols. 21s. each. Vol. I.—Genesis to Numbers. Vol. II.—Deuteronomy to Samuel II. Vol. III.—Kings I. to Esther. Vol. IV.—Job to Isaiah. Vol. V.—Jeremiah to Malachi.

Old Testament Commentary. Edited by Bishop ELLICOTT. Handy Volume Edition. Genesis, 3s. 6d. Exodus, 3s. Leviticus, 3s. Numbers, 2s. 6d. Deuteronomy, 2s. 6d.

Old and New Testaments, Plain Introductions to the Books of the. Containing Contributions by many Eminent Divines. In Two Volumes, 3s. 6d. each.

Protestantism, The History of. By the Rev. J. A. WYLIE, LL.D. Containing upwards of 600 Original Illustrations. Three Vols. 9s. each.

Quiver Yearly Volume, The. With about 600 Original Illustrations. 7s. 6d.

Religion, The Dictionary of. By the Rev. W. BENHAM, B.D. *Cheap Edition.* 10s. 6d.

St. George for England; and other Sermons preached to Children. By the Rev. T. TEIGNMOUTH SHORE, M.A., Canon of Worcester. 5s.

St. Paul, The Life and Work of. By the Ven. Archdeacon FARRAR, D.D., F.R.S., Chaplain-in-Ordinary to the Queen. LIBRARY EDITION. Two Vols., cloth, 24s.; calf, 42s. ILLUSTRATED EDITION, complete in One Volume, with about 300 Illustrations, £1 1s.; morocco, £2 2s. POPULAR EDITION. One Volume, 8vo, cloth, 6s.; cloth, gilt edges, 7s. 6d.; Persian morocco, 10s. 6d.; tree-calf, 15s.

Shall We Know One Another in Heaven? By the Rt. Rev. J. C. RYLE, D.D., Bishop of Liverpool. *Cheap Edition.* Paper covers, 6d.

Signa Christi. By the Rev. JAMES AITCHISON. 5s.

"Sunday," Its Origin, History, and Present Obligation. By the Ven. Archdeacon HESSEY, D.C.L. *Fifth Edition.* 7s. 6d.

Twilight of Life, The. Words of Counsel and Comfort for the Aged. By the Rev. JOHN ELLERTON, M.A. 1s. 6d.

Educational Works and Students' Manuals.

Agricultural Text-Books, Cassell's. (The "Downton" Series.) Edited by JOHN WRIGHTSON, Professor of Agriculture. Fully Illustrated, 2s. 6d. each.—Farm Crops. By Prof. WRIGHTSON.—Soils and Manures. By J. M. H. MUNRO, D.Sc. (London), F.I.C., F.C.S. —Live Stock. By Prof. WRIGHTSON.

Alphabet, Cassell's Pictorial. 3s. 6d.

Arithmetics, The Modern School. By GEORGE RICKS, B.Sc. Lond. With Test Cards. (*List on application.*)

Atlas, Cassell's Popular. Containing 24 Coloured Maps. 2s. 6d.

Book-Keeping. By THEODORE JONES. For Schools, 2s. ; cloth, 3s. For the Million, 2s. ; cloth, 3s. Books for Jones's System, 2s.

British Empire Map of the World. New Map for Schools and Institutes. By G. R. PARKIN and J. G. BARTHOLOMEW, F.R.G.S. Mounted on cloth, varnished, and with Rollers, or folded. 25s

Chemistry, The Public School. By J. H. ANDERSON, M.A. 2s. 6d.

Cookery for Schools. By LIZZIE HERITAGE. 6d.

Drawing Copies, Cassell's Modern School Freehand. First Grade, 1s. ; Second Grade, 2s.

Drawing Copies, Cassell's " New Standard." *Complete in Fourteen Books.* 2d., 3d., and 4d. each.

Energy and Motion. By WILLIAM PAICE, M.A. Illustrated. 1s. 6d.

Euclid, Cassell's. Edited by Prof. WALLACE, M.A. 1s.

Euclid, The First Four Books of. *New Edition.* In paper, 6d. ; cloth, 9d.

Experimental Geometry. By PAUL BERT. Illustrated. 1s. 6d.

French, Cassell's Lessons in. *New and Revised Edition.* Parts I. and II., each 2s. 6d. ; complete, 4s. 6d. Key, 1s. 6d.

French-English and English-French Dictionary. *Entirely New and Enlarged Edition.* 1,150 pages, 8vo, cloth, 3s. 6d.

French Reader, Cassell's Public School. By G. S. CONRAD. 2s. 6d.

Gaudeamus. Songs for Colleges and Schools. Edited by JOHN FARMER. 5s. Words only, paper covers, 6d. ; cloth, 9d.

German Dictionary, Cassell's New (German-English, English-German). *Cheap Edition.* Cloth, 3s. 6d.

Hand-and-Eye Training. By G. RICKS, B.Sc. 2 Vols., with 16 Coloured Plates in each Vol. Cr. 4to, 6s. each. Cards for Class Use, 5 sets, 1s. each.

Historical Cartoons, Cassell's Coloured. Size 45 in. × 35 in., 2s. each. Mounted on canvas and varnished, with rollers, 5s. each.

Historical Course for Schools, Cassell's. Illustrated throughout. I.—Stories from English History, 1s. II.—The Simple Outline of English History, 1s. 3d. III.—The Class History of England, 2s. 6d.

Italian Grammar, The Elements of, with Exercises. Cloth, 3s. 6d.

Latin Dictionary, Cassell's New. (Latin-English and English-Latin.) Revised by J. R. V. MARCHANT, M.A., and J. F. CHARLES, B.A. Cloth, 3s. 6d.

Latin Primer, The First. By Prof. POSTGATE. 1s.

Latin Primer, The New. By Prof. J. P. POSTGATE. Crown 8vo, 2s. 6d.

Latin Prose for Lower Forms. By M. A. BAYFIELD, M.A. 2s. 6d.

Laundry Work (How to Teach It). By Mrs. E. LORD. 6d.

Laws of Every-Day Life. By H. O. ARNOLD-FORSTER, M.P. 1s. 6d. *Special Edition* on Green Paper for Persons with Weak Eyesight. 2s.

Lessons in Our Laws; or, Talks at Broadacre Farm. By H. F. LESTER. Illustrated. Parts I. and II., 1s. 6d. each.

Little Folks' History of England. Illustrated. 1s. 6d.

Making of the Home, The. By Mrs. SAMUEL A. BARNETT. 1s. 6d.

Marlborough Books:—Arithmetic Examples, 3s. French Exercises, 3s. 6d. French Grammar, 2s. 6d. German Grammar, 3s. 6d.

Mechanics and Machine Design, Numerical Examples in Practical. By R. G. BLAINE, M.E. *New Edition, Revised and Enlarged.* With 79 Illustrations. Cloth, 2s. 6d.

Mechanics for Young Beginners, A First Book of. By the Rev. J. G. EASTON, M.A. 4s. 6d.

Natural History Coloured Wall Sheets, Cassell's New. 18 Subjects. Size 39 by 31 in. Mounted on rollers and varnished. 3s. each.

Object Lessons from Nature. By Prof. L. C. MIALL, F.L.S. Fully Illustrated. *New and Enlarged Edition.* Two Vols., 1s. 6d. each.

Physiology for Schools. By A. T. SCHOFIELD, M.D., M.R.C.S., &c. Illustrated. Cloth, 1s. 9d.; Three Parts, paper covers, 5d. each; or cloth limp, 6d. each.

Poetry Readers, Cassell's New. Illustrated. 12 Books, 1d. each; or complete in one Vol., cloth, 1s. 6d.

Popular Educator, Cassell's NEW. With Revised Text, New Maps, New Coloured Plates, New Type, &c. In 8 Vols., 5s. each; or in Four Vols., half-morocco, 50s. the set.

Readers, Cassell's "Higher Class." (*List on application.*)

Readers, Cassell's Readable. Illustrated. (*List on application.*)

Readers for Infant Schools, Coloured. Three Books. 4d. each.

Reader, The Citizen. By H. O. ARNOLD-FORSTER, M.P. Illustrated. 1s. 6d. Also a *Scottish Edition,* cloth, 1s. 6d.

Reader, The Temperance. By Rev. J. DENNIS HIRD. Crown 8vo, 1s. 6d.

Readers, The "Modern School" Geographical. (*List on application.*)

Readers, The "Modern School." Illustrated. (*List on application.*)

Reckoning, Howard's Anglo-American Art of. By C. FRUSHER HOWARD. Paper covers, 1s.; cloth, 2s. *New Edition,* 5s.

Round the Empire. By G. R. PARKIN. Fully Illustrated. 1s. 6d.

Science Applied to Work. By J. A. BOWER. 1s.

Science of Everyday Life. By J. A. BOWER. Illustrated. 1s.

Shade from Models, Common Objects, and Casts of Ornament, How to. By W. E. SPARKES. With 25 Plates by the Author. 3s.

Shakspere's Plays for School Use. 9 Books. Illustrated. 6d. each.

Spelling, A Complete Manual of. By J. D. MORELL, LL.D. 1s.

Technical Manuals, Cassell's. Illustrated throughout:—
Handrailing and Staircasing, 3s. 6d.—Bricklayers, Drawing for, 3s.—Building Construction, 2s.—Cabinet-Makers, Drawing for, 3s.—Carpenters and Joiners, Drawing for, 3s. 6d.—Gothic Stonework, 3s.—Linear Drawing and Practical Geometry, 2s. Linear Drawing and Projection. The Two Vols. in One, 3s. 6d.—Machinists and Engineers, Drawing for, 4s. 6d.—Metal-Plate Workers, Drawing for, 3s.—Model Drawing, 3s.—Orthographical and Isometrical Projection, 2s.—Practical Perspective, 3s.—Stonemasons, Drawing for, 3s.—Applied Mechanics, by Sir R. S. Ball, LL.D., 2s.—Systematic Drawing and Shading, 2s.

Technical Educator, Cassell's NEW. An entirely New Cyclopædia of Technical Education, with Coloured Plates and Engravings. Four Volumes, 5s. each.

Technology, Manuals of. Edited by Prof. AYRTON, F.R.S., and RICHARD WORMELL, D.Sc., M.A. Illustrated throughout:—
The Dyeing of Textile Fabrics, by Prof. Hummel, 5s.—Watch and Clock Making, by D. Glasgow, Vice-President of the British Horological Institute, 4s. 6d.—Steel and Iron, by Prof. W. H. Greenwood, F.C.S., M.I.C.E., &c., 5s.—Spinning Woollen and Worsted, by W. S. B. McLaren, M.P., 4s. 6d.—Design in Textile Fabrics, by T. R. Ashenhurst, 4s. 6d.—Practical Mechanics, by Prof. Perry, M.E., 3s. 6d.—Cutting Tools Worked by Hand and Machine, by Prof. Smith, 3s. 6d.

Things New and Old; or, Stories from English History. By H. O. ARNOLD-FORSTER, M.P. Fully Illustrated, and strongly bound in Cloth. Standards I. & II., 9d. each; Standard III., 1s.; Standard IV., 1s. 3d.; Standards V., VI., & VII., 1s. 6d. each.

This World of Ours. By H. O. ARNOLD-FORSTER, M.P. Illustrated. 3s. 6d.

Books for Young People.

"Little Folks" Half-Yearly Volume. Containing 432 4to pages, with about 200 Illustrations, and Pictures in Colour. Boards, 3s. 6d. ; cloth, 5s.

Bo-Peep. A Book for the Little Ones. With Original Stories and Verses. Illustrated throughout. Yearly Volume. Boards, 2s. 6d. ; cloth, 3s. 6d.

Beyond the Blue Mountains. By L. T. MEADE. 5s.

The Peep of Day. *Cassell's Illustrated Edition.* 2s. 6d.

Maggie Steele's Diary. By E. A. DILLWYN. 2s. 6d.

A Sunday Story-Book. By MAGGIE BROWNE, SAM BROWNE and AUNT ETHEL. Illustrated. 3s. 6d.

A Bundle of Tales. By MAGGIE BROWNE (Author of "Wanted—a King," &c.), SAM BROWNE, and AUNT ETHEL. 3s. 6d.

Pleasant Work for Busy Fingers. By MAGGIE BROWNE. Illustrated. 5s.

Born a King. By FRANCES and MARY ARNOLD-FORSTER. (The Life of Alfonso XIII., the Boy King of Spain.) Illustrated. 1s.

Cassell's Pictorial Scrap Book. Six Vols. 3s. 6d. each.

Schoolroom and Home Theatricals. By ARTHUR WAUGH. Illustrated. 2s. 6d.

Magic at Home. By Prof. HOFFMAN. Illustrated. Cloth gilt, 5s.

Little Mother Bunch. By Mrs. MOLESWORTH. Illustrated. Cloth, 3s. 6d.

Pictures of School Life and Boyhood. Selected from the best Authors. Edited by PERCY FITZGERALD, M.A. 2s. 6d.

Heroes of Every-day Life. By LAURA LANE. With about 20 Full-page Illustrations. Cloth. 2s. 6d.

Bob Lovell's Career. By EDWARD S. ELLIS. 5s.

Books for Young People. *Cheap Edition.* Illustrated. Cloth gilt, 3s. 6d. each.

The Champion of Odin; or, Viking Life in the Days of Old. By J. Fred. Hodgetts.	Bound by a Spell; or, The Hunted Witch of the Forest. By the Hon. Mrs. Greene.
Under Bayard's Banner. By Henry Frith.	

Books for Young People. Illustrated. 3s. 6d. each.

•Bashful Fifteen. By L. T. Meade.	•Polly: A New-Fashioned Girl. By L. T. Meade.
•The White House at Inch Gow. By Mrs. Pitt.	"Follow My Leader." By Talbot Baines Reed.
•A Sweet Girl Graduate. By L. T. Meade.	•The Cost of a Mistake. By Sarah Pitt.
The King's Command: A Story for Girls. By Maggie Symington.	•A World of Girls: The Story of a School. By L. T. Meade.
Lost in Samoa. A Tale of Adventure in the Navigator Islands. By Edward S. Ellis.	Lost among White Africans. By David Ker.
Tad; or, "Getting Even" with Him. By Edward S. Ellis.	For Fortune and Glory: A Story of the Soudan War. By Lewis Hough.
•The Palace Beautiful. By L. T. Meade.	

Also procurable in superior binding, 5s. each.

Crown 8vo Library. *Cheap Editions.* Gilt edges, 2s. 6d. each.

Rambles Round London. By C. L. Matéaux. Illustrated.	Wild Adventures in Wild Places. By Dr. Gordon Stables, R.N. Illustrated.
Around and About Old England. By C. L. Matéaux. Illustrated.	Modern Explorers. By Thomas Frost. Illustrated. *New and Cheaper Edition.*
Paws and Claws. By one of the Authors of "Poems written for a Child." Illustrated.	Early Explorers. By Thomas Frost.
Decisive Events in History. By Thomas Archer. With Original Illustrations.	Home Chat with our Young Folks. Illustrated throughout.
The True Robinson Crusoes. Cloth gilt.	Jungle, Peak, and Plain. Illustrated throughout.
Peeps Abroad for Folks at Home. Illustrated throughout.	The England of Shakespeare. By E. Goadby. With Full-page Illustrations.

The "Cross and Crown" Series. Illustrated. 2s. 6d. each.

Freedom's Sword: A Story of the Days of Wallace and Bruce. By Annie S. Swan.

Strong to Suffer: A Story of the Jews. By E. Wynne.

Heroes of the Indian Empire; or, Stories of Valour and Victory. By Ernest Foster.

In Letters of Flame: A Story of the Waldenses. By C. L. Matéaux.

Through Trial to Triumph. By Madeline B. Hunt.

By Fire and Sword: A Story of the Huguenots. By Thomas Archer.

Adam Hepburn's Vow: A Tale of Kirk and Covenant. By Annie S. Swan.

No. XIII.; or, The Story of the Lost Vestal. A Tale of Early Christian Days. By Emma Marshall.

"Golden Mottoes" Series, The. Each Book containing 208 pages, with Four full-page Original Illustrations. Crown 8vo, cloth gilt, 2s. each.

"Nil Desperandum." By the Rev. F. Langbridge, M.A.

"Bear and Forbear." By Sarah Pitt.

"Foremost if I Can." By Helen Atteridge.

"Honour is my Guide." By Jeanie Hering (Mrs. Adams-Acton).

"Aim at a Sure End." By Emily Searchfield.

"He Conquers who Endures." By the Author of "May Cunningham's Trial," &c.

Cassell's Picture Story Books. Each containing about Sixty Pages of Pictures and Stories, &c. 6d. each.

Little Talks.
Bright Stars.
Nursery Toys.
Pet's Posy.
Tiny Tales.

Daisy's Story Book.
Dot's Story Book.
A Nest of Stories.
Good-Night Stories.
Chats for Small Chatterers.

Auntie's Stories.
Birdie's Story Book.
Little Chimes.
A Sheaf of Tales.
Dewdrop Stories.

Cassell's Sixpenny Story Books. All Illustrated, and containing Interesting Stories by well-known writers.

The Smuggler's Cave.
Little Lizzie.
Little Bird, Life and Adventures of.
Luke Barnicott.

The Boat Club.
Little Pickles.
The Elchester College Boys.
My First Cruise.
The Little Peacemaker.

The Delft Jug.

Cassell's Shilling Story Books. All Illustrated, and containing Interesting Stories.

Bunty and the Boys.
The Heir of Elmdale.
The Mystery at Shoncliff School.
Claimed at Last, and Roy's Reward.
Thorns and Tangles.
The Cuckoo in the Robin's Nest.
John's Mistake.
The History of Five Little Pitchers.
Diamonds in the Sand.

Surly Bob.
The Giant's Cradle.
Shag and Doll.
Aunt Lucia's Locket.
The Magic Mirror.
The Cost of Revenge.
Clever Frank.
Among the Redskins.
The Ferryman of Brill.
Harry Maxwell.
A Banished Monarch.
Seventeen Cats.

Illustrated Books for the Little Ones. Containing interesting Stories. All Illustrated. 1s. each; cloth gilt, 1s. 6d.

Tales Told for Sunday.
Sunday Stories for Small People.
Stories and Pictures for Sunday.
Bible Pictures for Boys and Girls.
Firelight Stories.
Sunlight and Shade.
Rub-a-Dub Tales.
Fine Feathers and Fluffy Fur.
Scrambles and Scrapes.
Tittle Tattle Tales.
Up and Down the Garden.

All Sorts of Adventures.
Our Sunday Stories.
Our Holiday Hours.
Indoors and Out.
Some Farm Friends.
Wandering Ways.
Dumb Friends.
Those Golden Sands.
Little Mothers and their Children.
Our Pretty Pets.
Our Schoolday Hours.
Creatures Tame.
Creatures Wild.

"Wanted—a King" Series. *Cheap Edition.* Illustrated. 2s. 6d. each.
Great Grandmamma. By Georgina M. Synge.
Robin's Ride. By Ellinor Davenport Adams.
Wanted—a King; or, How Merle set the Nursery Rhymes to Rights.
    By Maggie Browne. With Original Designs by Harry Furniss.
Fairy Tales in Other Lands. By Julia Goddard.

The World's Workers. A Series of New and Original Volumes.
    With Portraits printed on a tint as Frontispiece. 1s. each.

John Cassell. By G. Holden Pike.
Charles Haddon Spurgeon. By
    G. HOLDEN PIKE.
Dr. Arnold of Rugby. By Rose
    E. Selfe.
The Earl of Shaftesbury. By
    Henry Frith.
Sarah Robinson, Agnes Wes-
    ton, and Mrs. Meredith. By
    E. M. Tomkinson.
Thomas A. Edison and Samuel
    F. B. Morse. By Dr. Denslow
    and J. Marsh Parker.
Mrs. Somerville and Mary Car-
    penter. By Phyllis Browne.
General Gordon. By the Rev.
    S. A. Swaine.
Charles Dickens. By his Eldest
    Daughter.
Sir Titus Salt and George
    Moore. By J. Burnley.

Florence Nightingale, Catherine
    Marsh, Frances Ridley Haver-
    gal, Mrs. Ranyard ("L. N. R.").
    By Lizzie Alldridge.
Dr. Guthrie, Father Mathew,
    Elihu Burritt, George Livesey.
    By John W. Kirton, LL.D.
Sir Henry Havelock and Colin
    Campbell Lord Clyde. By E. C.
    Phillips.
Abraham Lincoln. By Ernest Foster.
George Müller and Andrew Reed.
    By E. R. Pitman.
Richard Cobden. By R. Gowing.
Benjamin Franklin. By E. M.
    Tomkinson.
Handel. By Eliza Clarke.   [Swaine.
Turner the Artist. By the Rev. S. A.
George and Robert Stephenson.
    By C. L. Matéaux.
David Livingstone. By Robert Smiles.

** *The above Works (excluding* RICHARD COBDEN *and* CHARLES HADDON
    SPURGEON) *can also be had Three in One Vol., cloth, gilt edges.* 3s.

Library of Wonders. Illustrated Gift-books for Boys. Paper, 1s.;
    cloth, 1s. 6d.

Wonderful Balloon Ascents
Wonderful Adventures.
Wonderful Escapes.

Wonders of Animal Instinct.
Wonders of Bodily Strength
    and Skill.

Cassell's Eighteenpenny Story Books. Illustrated.

Wee Willie Winkie.
Ups and Downs of a Donkey's
    Life.
Three Wee Ulster Lassies.
Up the Ladder.
Dick's Hero; and other Stories.
The Chip Boy.
Raggles, Baggles, and the
    Emperor.
Roses from Thorns.

Faith's Father.
By Land and Sea.
The Young Berringtons.
Jeff and Leff.
Tom Morris's Error.
Worth more than Gold.
"Through Flood—Through Fire;"
    and other Stories.
The Girl with the Golden Locks.
Stories of the Olden Time.

Gift Books for Young People. By Popular Authors. With Four
    Original Illustrations in each. Cloth gilt, 1s. 6d. each.

The Boy Hunters of Kentucky.
    By Edward S. Ellis.
Red Feather: a Tale of the
    American Frontier. By
    Edward S. Ellis.
Seeking a City.
Rhoda's Reward; or, "If
    Wishes were Horses."
Jack Marston's Anchor.
Frank's Life-Battle; or, The
    Three Friends.
Fritters. By Sarah Pitt.
The Two Hardcastles. By Made-
    line Bonavia Hunt.

Major Monk's Motto. By the Rev.
    F. Langbridge.
Trixy. By Maggie Symington.
Rags and Rainbows: A Story of
    Thanksgiving.
Uncle William's Charges; or, The
    Broken Trust.
Pretty Pink's Purpose; or, The
    Little Street Merchants.
Tim Thomson's Trial. By George
    Weatherly.
Ursula's Stumbling-Block. By Julia
    Goddard.
Ruth's Life-Work. By the Rev.
    Joseph Johnson.

Cassell's Two-Shilling Story Books. Illustrated.

Stories of the Tower.
Mr. Burke's Nieces.
May Cunningham's Trial.
The Top of the Ladder: How to
    Reach it.
Little Flotsam.
Madge and Her Friends.
The Children of the Court.
Maid Marjory.
Peggy, and other Tales.

The Four Cats of the Tippertons.
Marion's Two Homes.
Little Folks' Sunday Book.
Two Fourpenny Bits.
Poor Nelly.
Tom Heriot.
Through Peril to Fortune.
Aunt Tabitha's Waifs.
In Mischief Again.

Cheap Editions of Popular Volumes for Young People. Bound in cloth, gilt edges, 2s. 6d. each.

In Quest of Gold; or, Under the Whanga Falls.
On Board the *Esmeralda*; or, Martin Leigh's Log.
The Romance of Invention: Vignettes from the Annals of Industry and Science.

For Queen and King.
Esther West.
Three Homes.
Working to Win.
Perils Afloat and Brigands Ashore.

The "Deerfoot" Series. By EDWARD S. ELLIS. With Four full-page Illustrations in each Book. Cloth, bevelled boards, 2s. 6d. each.

The Hunters of the Ozark. | The Camp in the Mountains.
The Last War Trail.

The "Log Cabin" Series. By EDWARD S. ELLIS. With Four Full-page Illustrations in each. Crown 8vo, cloth, 2s. 6d. each.

The Lost Trail. | Camp-Fire and Wigwam.
Footprints in the Forest.

The "Great River" Series. By EDWARD S. ELLIS. Illustrated. Crown 8vo, cloth, bevelled boards, 2s. 6d. each.

Down the Mississippi. | Lost in the Wilds.
Up the Tapajos; or, Adventures in Brazil.

The "Boy Pioneer" Series. By EDWARD S. ELLIS. With Four Full-page Illustrations in each Book. Crown 8vo, cloth, 2s. 6d. each.

Ned in the Woods. A Tale of Early Days in the West.
Ned in the Block House. A Story of Pioneer Life in Kentucky.

Ned on the River. A Tale of Indian River Warfare.

The "World in Pictures." Illustrated throughout. 2s. 6d. each.

A Ramble Round France.
All the Russias.
Chats about Germany.
The Land of the Pyramids (Egypt).

The Eastern Wonderland (Japan).
Glimpses of South America.
Round Africa.
The Land of Temples (India).
The Isles of the Pacific.
Peeps into China.

Half-Crown Story Books.

Margaret's Enemy.
Fen's Perplexities.
Notable Shipwrecks.
At the South Pole.

Soldier and Patriot (George Washington).
The Young Man in the Battle of Life. By the Rev. Dr. Landels.

Books for the Little Ones.

Rhymes for the Young Folk. By William Allingham. Beautifully Illustrated. 3s. 6d.

The History Scrap Book: With nearly 1,000 Engravings. Cloth, 7s. 6d.

My Diary. With 12 Coloured Plates and 366 Woodcuts. 1s.
The Sunday Scrap Book. With Several Hundred Illustrations. Paper boards, 3s. 6d.; cloth, gilt edges, 5s.
The Old Fairy Tales. With Original Illustrations. Boards, 1s.; cloth, 1s. 6d.

Albums for Children. 3s. 6d. each.

The Album for Home, School, and Play. Containing Stories by Popular Authors. Illustrated.
My Own Album of Animals. With Full-page Illustrations.

Picture Album of All Sorts. With Full-page Illustrations.
The Chit-Chat Album. Illustrated throughout.

Cassell & Company's Complete Catalogue *will be sent post free on application to*

CASSELL & COMPANY, LIMITED, *Ludgate Hill, London.*

www.ingramcontent.com/pod-product-compliance
Lightning Source LLC
Chambersburg PA
CBHW021115270326
41929CB00009B/885